AF650111

YOUTH & INDIA'S

SUSTAINABLE DEVELOPMENT GOALS

YOUTH & INDIA'S

SUSTAINABLE DEVELOPMENT GOALS

Editor
Saigita Chitturu

Vitasta
LET KNOWLEDGE SPREAD

Published by
Renu Kaul Verma
Vitasta Publishing Pvt Ltd
2/15, Ansari Road, Daryaganj
New Delhi - 110 002
info@vitastapublishing.com

ISBN 978-81-948200-8-6
© Saigita Chitturu
First Edition 2021

MRP ₹750

All Rights Reserved.
No part of this publication may be reproduced, stored in a retrieval system, or transmitted in any form, or by any means—electronic, mechanical, photocopying, recording or otherwise—without the prior permission of the publisher. Opinions expressed in this book are the authors' own. The publisher is in no way responsible for these.

Editor: Papri Sri Raman
Cover by Somesh Kumar Mishra
Layout by Ram Kumar
Printed by Chaman Enterprises, New Delhi

Dedication

This book is dedicated to my father MV Gopalkrishna

Contents

Foreword

Indeed, it is well recognised that India is the youngest country in the world with well over 40 per cent of the population comprising youth. It is said that by 2022, the average age of India's population will be 29 years. How is the country preparing to channelise the energy and spirit of this young population? The 'demographic dividend', as it is often referred to, may well remain a heart-warming thought if youth in the country are not empowered to become catalysts of change and leaders who will shape the social and economic thinking in the next two decades. It cannot be said that the policy-makers of the country have been unaware of this or have ignored acting upon it, as it is the Government of India itself which has initiated two of the largest youth programmes which the world has seen. These are the National Service Scheme (NSS) and the Nehru Yuva Kendra Scheme (NYKS) through which thousands of young people in the country have been introduced to ideas of social change, civic participation and recognition of their fundamental rights and duties.

However, with globalisation and the shrinking of the world to a global village, social, economic and environmental issues are no longer confined to one's national boundaries. Nor are health issues, as the Corona virus pandemic has shown in recent months. For the past two decades, it has been seen that it is imperative for countries to recognise regional concerns rather than only national concerns. And these regional concerns have soon been transformed into global concerns. Of course, the most obvious issue to exemplify this statement is climate change. Add the pandemic to it now.

At the international level, the Millenium Development Goals (MDGs) have been replaced by Sustainable Development Goals. These UN initiatives are intended to provide time-bound and quantitative global goals to guide and influence national and international strategies for development. However, the implementation of the SDGs will require political commitment, affirmative policies, sufficient resources and infrastructure and a population which is aware and motivated to work on the same. No longer can we depend only upon the public systems to deliver on their own. The handshake of public institutions and civil society is the only way forward. And if we have said that our population has the benefit of youth in large numbers, who better to be in the vanguard of being prominent actors in the realisation of the SDGs?

Towards this end, this book is an important contributor to envisaging the role that youth can play in the realisation of SDGs in India. The contents focus upon achieving youth participation in SDGs 4 and 5 and present efforts from government and civil society which have been able to engage youth in advancing the goals for greater equity and equality in health, mental health, education, skilling and gender inclusion. The contributors to the book include academicians, practitioners of social work and government bureaucrats.

I am grateful to Dr Saigita Chitturu, Faculty, Centre for Lifelong Learning, TISS, Mumbai for having undertaken this academic task of getting all the thinking on the subject together and completing it successfully. In the editing of this book, she has drawn upon her almost two decades' of experience in academia and experience in networking with State and central government departments who administer youth programmes in India.

I commend this book to readers who are interested in working with the youth and believe in the power of the young generation to change the world we live in.

—**Nasreen Rustomfram**
Professor and Chairperson,
Centre for Lifelong Learning
Tata Institute of Social Sciences

Preface

If you are planning for a year, sow rice; if you are planning for a decade, plant trees; if you are planning for a lifetime, educate people.

—Chinese proverb

The youth represent the most dynamic and vibrant segment of the population. India is one of the youngest nations in the world, with about 65 per cent of the population under 35 years of age. The youth in the age group of 15-29 years comprise 27.5 per cent of the population. India was expected to become the 4th largest economy by 2025, contributing about 5.5 per cent-6 per cent to the world GDP. While the US, China and Japan coming before India face the risk of an ageing workforce, India is expected to have a very favourable demographic profile. It is estimated that by the year 2020, the population of India would have a median age of 29 years only as against 38 years for US, 42 years for China and 48 years for Japan. This 'demographic dividend' offers a great opportunity. In order to capture this demographic dividend, it is essential that the economy has the ability to support the increase in the labour force and the youth have the appropriate education, skills, health awareness and other enablers to productively contribute to the economy. [1]

---

1 https://yas.nic.in/sites/default/files/Annual%20Report%20%28English%29%20 2018-19.pdf accessed on 13th June, 2020

Since 2018, India's working-age population (people between 15 and 64 years of age) has grown larger than the dependant population – children aged 14 or below as well as people above 65 years of age. This bulge in the working-age population is going to last till 2055, or 37 years from its beginning.

Many Asian economies – Japan, China, South Korea – were able to use this 'demographic dividend', defined by the United Nations Population Funds.[2]

Equally important is to note that definitions of youth have changed continuously in response to fluctuating political, economic and socio-cultural realities. Globally, there has been no standardised definition of youth-hood as a stage of human development. It has been highly debated in terms of age and characteristics and has been defined differently in different cultures and societies. In other definitions, the age span of 15-25 years is often referred to as Youth, and the age range of 25-35 years is considered Young Adulthood (UN World Plan of Action for Youth; Commonwealth).

The Indian National Youth Policy of 1983 defines those in the age range of 13-35 years as 'youth', and the National Youth Policy document of 2003 as those of 13-35 years, while the National Youth Policy of 2014 includes those in the age group of 15-30 years, excluding 7 years of people from the 1983 grouping. This age range has different social roles and requirements, and, the age group is divided into two broad sub-groups of 13-19 years [adolescents] and 20-35 years (youth).

The legal definitions of children, adolescents and youth vary according to the roles expected, and the services to

---

[2] https://economictimes.indiatimes.com/news/economy/indicators/india-enters-37-year-period-of-demographic- dividend/articleshow/70324782.cms?utm_source=contentofinterest&utm_medium=text&utm_campaign=cppst

be provided. The UN Convention for the Rights of the Child defines a child as any one up to the age of 18 years, which overlaps with the definition of youth. The ICDS (the Integrated Child Development Services in India) considers its beneficiaries (adolescent girls) as those between 11 and 18 years; the Reproductive and Child Health programme in India defines Adolescents as being between 10-19 years. The legal age for voting in the Central and State elections in India is 18 years, while the permissible ages for marriage are 18 years and 21 years for girls and boys respectively.

Demographic Bomb

Young people in India have great potential and its demographic dividend is greater than most other countries. India is at present in a position that has great possibilities for economic and social progress. However, what will define the nature of progress, positive or negative, depends on the country's current ability to attend the needs and aspirations of these young people. It is a time when the state and civil society will have to work with youth, empower and engage with them in different forms, especially in academic deliberations. To facilitate this process, it is also felt important for youths as well as adults to engage in continuous dialogue with each other. There is no other easy way of exchanging knowledge without communicating with each other. Realising the importance of the potential for the growth of the country and to be in constant touch with this energy, uncoupled in the nation's youthful population, is critical.[3] India has 18 per cent of the world population and a workforce of more than 520 million. Historically, the

---

[3] https://yas.nic.in/sites/default/files/Annual%20Report%20%28English%29%20 2018-19.pdf accessed on 13th June, 2020

demography has contributed about 15 per cent of the overall growth in advanced economies. India has one of the greatest opportunities to change its economic fortunes. To reap the benefits of this demography, we need to make a dramatic shift in our present economy in the coming decades, as every economy will be data-driven. The biggest asset will be data and human capital.[4]

Further, youth are also considered to be 'a significant stakeholder, a catalyst, a change maker' in the United Nations' newly adopted 2030 Agenda for Sustainable Development as an important actor of the agenda. As in the whole developing world, youth in India can play an important catalytic role in accelerating the process of National Development. Owing to its size and aspirations, its influence and dynamism is a powerful factor in setting trends in political, social, economic, educational, cultural and development fields. Their boundless energy and innate idealism could introduce into the various development activities a direction which could bring out the social transformation needed to make it suited for their future.

Percent of Youth Population, Statewise Census Data, 2011

Involvement of youth in the developmental process is relevant particularly because of the resolve of the country to progress in the direction of building up an egalitarian society, not only in economic and technological development but also by improvements in the quality of the common man's life. It is believed that young people need to be in the forefront to discuss, formulate designs and device action plans to promote change than merely act as recipients of knowledge and values. This, in

4 https://asiatimes.com/2019/04/india-17th-general-election-a-choice-between-demographic-dividend-and-democratic-disaster/ accessed on 13th June, 2020

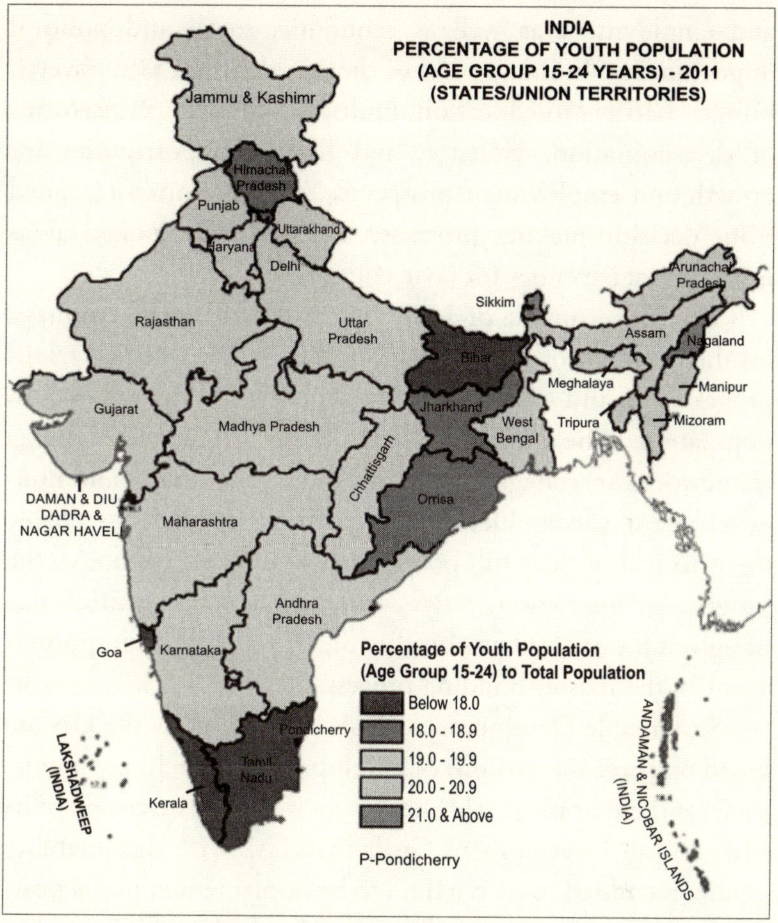

turn, calls for an urgent need to train them, to empower them to act as a catalyst in educating all and transforming India in all aspects.

According to the *Youth in India Report of 2017*, the life experiences and perspectives of young people in the 21st century differ greatly from country to country. About 87 per cent of young women and men living in developing countries face challenges brought about by limited and unequal access to resources, healthcare, education, training, and employment as well as economic, social and political opportunities. In many parts of the world, youth face poverty, hunger, barriers to education, multiple and intersecting forms of discrimination, violence, and limited opportunities for growth and employment prospects. Youth are often excluded from decision-making processes and generally looked at as untraditional avenues for civic engagement.

The Government of India has now laid much emphasis on this segment of the population, thereby instituting various programmes and schemes for the benefit of the nation's youth population. The National Youth Policy 2014 laid down a framework for strategic interventions by government and non-government stakeholders, to empower the youth to enable them to realise their full potential as also to contribute to the progress of the nation. *Draft National Youth Policy, 2020* also has given lot of emphasis on the role of youth as an important agent in the nation-building process.

Sustainable Development Goals (SDGs) set by the UN are based on three dimensions of development, namely, economic, social and environmental. They are viewed as an extension of its Millennium Development Goals (MDGs), with sustainability parameter added to each MDG to be implemented in the post-2015, along with a set of all-new goals which were ignored in the MDGs. These are a new, universal set of goals, targets and indicators that the United Nations (UN) member states are expected to use to frame their agendas and political policies over the next ten years, that is till 2030.

The SDGs are a set of 17 specific goals, offering a special focus on important areas related to sustainable development that require urgent and extensive attention now and in the near future. The SDG framework undertakes to provide systematic solutions to the obstacles identified in the case of the MDGs, like inequality, sustainability, institutional resourcefulness, implementation efficacy, environmental deterioration etc (UN 2014a).

Understanding Skills

Skills are considered to be the ability, competency and efficiency of an individual to apply one's knowledge and experience to a situation. They are of two kinds; soft and hard. Soft Skills are known to be a combination of people skills or interpersonal skills and social skills. These are needed to interact with others effectively and efficiently, also, they are needed to establish or maintain a good human relationship. These are subjective and are context dependant hence cannot be quantified or measured. While some soft skills are acquired through formal training, a large number of them typically develop through personal experiences and self-reflection. Some examples of soft skills are: communication, critical thinking, working in a team, time management, creative thinking, crisis management, conflict management, assertive skills, conflict resolution etc. Hard Skills are said to be technical or administrative skills which are easily measured, tested and quantifiable. This includes technical as well as vocational skills like carpentry work, mobile repairing, computer skills, data analytics etc. These are acquired through formal training. It is important to note that there is an increasing importance of both hard and soft skills in the workplace.

Lifelong learning is a complex process to understand. However, it refers simply to the idea of upgrading knowledge, skills and attitude by time and context. It involves both soft as well as hard skills. It is a process which improves skills set through formal, informal and non-formal ways. Lifelong learning skills are needed for an individual's intellectual, physical, and emotional success, regardless of occupation or life role. It works well for somebody who is motivated and wants to grow in life. Life Skills are those skills which are required in day to day life. These are simple, basic, yet very important skills to lead one's life successfully by adapting oneself to the surrounding. It includes all soft skills. It involves behaving positively in adverse situations. Many life skills have been listed by different authors; however, WHO has defined ten core life skills which are the standard ones. Life skills along with soft skills are needed for an integrated happy life. They are necessary for adolescents and young children to fight health-related issues – such as alcohol, tobacco, and other drug use; nutrition; pregnancy prevention; and preventing HIV/AIDS and other sexually transmitted infections (STIs).

Challenges and Responses to Covid-19 Pandemic

The lives of people along with their world of work are being profoundly affected by the global Covid-19 pandemic. Along with health of millions of people which is at risk, their long-term livelihoods and wellbeing are also at stake.

It is a global health, social and economic crisis. It is a major accelerator that has led to a mega shift in digital teaching and learning approach. The world has seen a paradigm shift in the working and learning styles of people at large, especially young professionals. The Covid-19 pandemic and global lockdown has presented before people unprecedented challenges for skills development systems.

In this context, we have an opportunity to explore the concept of 'learning and training anywhere, anytime', an idea central to the concept of lifelong learning. This, in turn, requires examination of a range of issues such as how technically prepared we are to support new ways of working in the face of disruptors like a pandemic, and how quickly we can organise digital education and training and mobilise teachers and trainers to maintain services to learners.

We also need to explore innovative and creative learning methodologies for apprentices and workers who primarily acquire or upgrade skills at the workplace

Lockdown has had an immediate devastating impact on the world economy, which varied dramatically across sectors and regions. Many sectors have nearly stopped operating; others are facing activity peaks with shortages of skilled workers. Some have altered their production, either to provide much-needed masks, for instance, or to produce health equipment. Besides the loss of activity, workers have to face a new organisation of work, eg sanitary constraints at the workplace, or telework.

The impact of confinement is bound to be most severe for vulnerable workers, especially poor, informal-sector workers in low-income countries with daily earnings and no savings, raising concerns for their survival. Women, who are overrepresented among wage labourers, own-account workers and unpaid family workers, stand to lose the most.

Young people face a particularly difficult entry into the labour market, which risks having long-term consequences on their careers and earnings. Some innovations in this space include simulated environments and live recordings including for work-based learning. Numerous challenges for initial and continuous skills development processes have become more visible.

The loss of several weeks or months of learning and training is likely to affect the outcomes and motivation of students, especially from a disadvantaged background, and may result in dropping out of educational institutions, changes in career plans and need for short skilling programmes. Workers participating in skills development programmes (apprentices, interns, adults in continuous development training including literacy etc) as well are affected by these disruptions. Currently, online work or online-based learning depends on the digital skills of both trainers and learners but equality is an issue.

What is urgently needed is to address the crisis and its impact. To develop and share innovative experiences exploring the effectiveness of strategies tackling the immediate and longer-term effects of the Covid-19 crisis. Identifying what are the key building blocks of a resilient and labour-market relevant system. Training or teaching children, adolescents and youth the significance of life skills to deal with the adverse situation successfully. Encouraging and promoting lifelong learning to overcome the educational crisis which the world is facing currently. It is quite evident that during the pandemic situation, as well as when people rejoin the workforce, post the lockdown, they will need to diversify their skill sets and be prepared for future unforeseen times too.

Young people in current times are growing up in a transforming world. Along with the Covid pandemic, technology, migration, climate change, poverty etc are reshaping society, forcing people across the globe to adapt to unexpected changes in their lives and work. Being confined to homes has been very constricting, especially for children and young people. Developing psychosocial competency to deal effectively with the demands and challenges of everyday life has been gaining importance.

To keep up, children, adolescents and young people must be able to seize opportunities and confront challenges. They need skills to become lifelong learners, secure safe and productive work, make informed decisions and positively engage in their communities. Maintaining a state of mental well-being and to demonstrate this in adaptive and positive behaviour while interacting with others, society etc has boosted the morale of people.

Coping skills to overcome trauma and build resilience needs to be taught. Not just this, but investment and coordination to strengthen education systems for future children, especially the most marginalised so that they acquire life skills that will help them fulfil their potential, their families and their communities is needed to be worked upon. People having mastery over skills like problem-solving, negotiation, managing emotions, empathy and communication etc are the ones who have handled their problems and others with ease.

Life skills in adverse conditions of life enable individuals to translate knowledge, attitudes and values into actual abilities– i.e. 'what to do and how to do it'. According to the Social Learning Theory developed by Bandura, learning is considered to be an active acquisition, processing and structuring of experiences. While new technologies and digital media are facilitating imagination and inventiveness in young people, one also sees young volunteers working in the communities selflessly as corona warriors, providing cooked meals, organising ration, supporting migrants financially etc. Through these activities, they are demonstrating skills of empathy with people, solving problems of health, food and shelter, communicating and negotiating with governments while coping with their own changed lifestyle. While doing so, they are equally polishing all the necessary skills needed for life.

The positive aspect of the Corona outbreak and the lockdown also cannot be overlooked. People, especially young people, have picked up many skills simply by being at home. Right from cooking skills to managing with what is available; from organising skills to valuing the mundane jobs at home, respecting the homemaker more than ever before, improved communication skills with family and friends and overall change in the mindset regarding gender biases are some of the common scenes seen around us.

At a larger level, the feeling of connectedness, socialisation has grown. People all around the world are finding new ways to address the need for interconnectedness. It has offered a new perspective on everything we have taken for granted for so long – our freedoms, leisure, connections, work, family and friends. These are the lessons one would retain for future decades too. The pandemic outbreak has kind of prepared people emotionally and mentally to take on future challenges in life with ease. *Skills, whether, soft or hard, learnt and developed during this outbreak will prove to be an asset for future life and in the attainment of the Sustainable Development Goals.*

Introduction

Saigita Chitturu

THE TATA INSTITUTE Of Social Sciences has been engaged with the concerns of youth in various ways, in terms of research, training and action. Several Centres of the Institute are engaged with the youth or youth issues, though the focus is largely on the issues or a vulnerable population. *The Centre for Lifelong Learning has been exclusively engaged with the issues of the youth population as one of its core activities.* The Centre has been providing certified training to those who are working with youth/youth workers in various capacities. Several training programmes, researches, conferences, seminars, panel discussion etc related to youth issues have been undertaken as significant tasks of the Centre.

Every year, this Centre has been organising the National Youth Day to commemorate the birth anniversary of Swami Vivekanand who is known as an icon for the youth in India. Conferences, Seminars and Panel Discussions to celebrate youth power have been organised in the past years. Discussion on subjects related to Youth Policy and Sustainable Development Goals also have been the area of interest to the Centre.

This book is an outcome of one such major conference held at the Tata Institute of Social Sciences on Sustainable Development Goal, 2030 and the Role of Youth and Youth-based Organisations in Achieving these Goals.

The first chapter on *State and Non-state Sector's Role towards Youth: Challenge to be Met,* written by Veerendra Mishra, believes in the power of youth. He says that SD Goals can be achieved only if youth are in a position to actively participate in achieving them. However, it is still to be ascertained if the capacity of the youth of India, whom we claim to be the country's demographic dividend, is properly built. Are we just content with the number game, basking in the glory that the average age of India's population is going to be 29 years by 2022? Are we in any way concerned with the quality of this enviable numbers? The dividend that we are talking about can become a baggage or burden, if the energy and aspirations of our youth are not channelised constructively. The article attempts to critically analyse some aspects of the role of state and non-state sectors in shaping the youth. The volunteering role of NSS and NYKS, which are two of the biggest organisations in the world, with the former working in educational institutions and the latter in villages, has also been analysed.

The second chapter written by Mathew Mattam on *Fostering 1st Generation Micro-entrepreneurs in India: Opportunities and Challenges,* talks of how youth as the creative innovators, can positively contribute to the sustainable development through active participation. This section of the population needs to be mobilised, motivated, skilled and supported to bring rapid progress in any developing country. Youth Aid Foundation is providing exposure to budding entrepreneurs to a new experience to generate new thinking, promote the spirit of entrepreneurship culture and promote entrepreneurs who have been successful locally and regionally.

The third chapter highlights the role of teachers and quality education in the lives of young people. Shamim Suryavanshi, in her chapter on *Teachers and Society in Mumbai and Hong Kong, Comparative Perspectives for Quality Education of Youth in India* talks about how teachers play a pivotal role in developing young adults as change agents. This paper puts forth comparative perspectives on pre-service teacher education (PSTE) by highlighting the lives and training of secondary school teachers in Mumbai and Hong Kong in terms of the respective societies, teacher education background, structure and institutional context of teacher education as well as role, working conditions and perceptions of PSTE by the in-service teachers. The paper enables policy-makers and academics in India to not just increase the supply of qualified teachers and to seek international cooperation for teacher training and targets of Sustainable Development Goals 2030, but also ensures quality in teacher education.

The fourth chapter is on *Gender Equality and Youth Development: With regard to SDG 5* by Vibhuti Patel. It talks about SDG and Gender. She says that SDGs explicitly acknowledge that gender – what a given society believes about the appropriate roles and activities of men and women and the behaviours that result from these beliefs – can have a major impact on development, helping to promote it in some cases while seriously retarding it in others. SDG 5 (out of 17) is calling for an end to disparities between boys and girls at all levels of education. It is important for the Indian youth to be aware and pro-active about concerns of girls and women in the context of the fast changing socio-economic and cultural scenario in the country.

The fifth chapter by Trupti Panchal and Nolina Sarah Minj on *Violence against Young Women and Girls in India: Need for Strategic Action through State-based Social Services,* highlights the issue of violence against women and girls (VAWG) which is one of the most oppressive forms of gender inequality in India, and is a fundamental barrier to the equal participation of women and men in social, economic, and political spheres. It impedes gender equality and the attainment of a range of development outcomes. It is a complex and multifaceted problem that cannot be effectively addressed from a single vantage point. It is crucial that the youth too are actively engaged and their voices heard in the development of strategies, policies and initiatives to prevent and end violence against women and girls. For this to occur, it is important that the youth today (of all genders) move closer to a violence-free and gender-equal world, thereby unleashing their full potential. Accordingly, this paper attempts to build an argument for state policy on the CJS to be more accessible to young women and girls facing violence through social and state support.

The sixth chapter titled, *From Recipients to Change Agents, Participation in Enhancing Health & Sanitation in Marginalised Urban Geographies* written by Rama Shyam, Anuja Jayraman, Vinita Ajgaonkar and Neeta Karandikar from SNEHA is focussed on health issues of youth and is an endeavour to review and explore the intersectionalities that affect the Water, Sanitation and Hygiene (WASH) framework within the context of improving the health of young people in vulnerable urban geographies and reflecting on their role in contributing to this improvement. The paper posits that it is important to strengthen provisions and services that will allow young people to enhance their capabilities based on the freedom to determine their development.

The seventh chapter titled, *Beyond Skilling: an Alternative Praxis of Livelihood for Urban Poor Youth* written by Alicia Tauro and Sachin Nachnekar is based on Youth for Unity and Voluntary Action's years of work with youth and youth collectives. It presents an alternative praxis of youth development through livelihood. Based on YUVA's experience, some of the strategies for youth development and youth work are decentralised skilling, life skills training, collectivisation of youth and experiential learning. In this paper, these alternatives are explored through the work of YUVA.

The eighth chapter titled, *Creating Level Playing Field: Participatory Action Research for Gender Equality and Youth Development* by Anita Patil-Deshmukh, Sunil Gangawane and Payal Tiwari speaks about PUKAR's work with Youth.

With a focus on the marginalised during the coproduction of knowledge, PUKAR specifically works with youth intersecting across caste, class, gender and ethnicity. Borrowing from Freire, feminist pedagogies and other engaged perspectives. PUKAR helps create critical thinkers who conduct community based participatory action research on their respective communities and lived realities, theorising their personal experiences and challenging the politics of knowledge. The youth use their research as a tool for social change and to challenge unequal power relations. PUKAR's programme creates critical thinkers and leaders who are sensitive to issues of their community and of the society. Its in-depth course work focuses on being aware of one's own self, location and the impact of larger power structures on their social realities.

The above two chapters represent best practices of civil society organisations working with and for the youth.

The last chapter on *Creating Spaces for Lifelong Learning Skills in Youth-An Intervention to Generate Sustainable Workforce of the Future*, written by Saigita Chitturu, reviews the current status of youth development and the core skills necessary to engage youth meaningfully in their work life. Drawing from the experience of working with National Youth Volunteers of NYKS and NSS, India's most popular youth-based programmes, the paper discusses the ongoing need of training and academic intervention to facilitate a smooth transition of young people into the world of work.

The book is a meaningful combination of perspectives on Indian youth through the lens of the Civil Society Organisations, Academia and the state. It also highlights the need for India to align every youth work to the targeted SDG goals by the country.

Thus, the book has critically examined the role of youth in achieving the goals of SDGs by creating an avenue for knowledge sharing on current trends and best practices by different stakeholders in achieving the larger goal. Also, it has specifically looked at some of the thematic issues of the Sustainable Development Goals framework like Gender, Violence, Education, Skilling and Entrepreneurship, Health and Lifelong Learning Skills, showcasing youth power and supporting India's agenda of Sustainable Development. It has provided space for NGOs, Academicians, Practitioners, Youth Volunteers, Researchers and government officials to embark together from one platform for the development task.

In nutshell, the book provides perspectives, role and contribution of youth and the civil society organisations in the path of achieving the goals of sustainable development.

Changing Narrative

State and Non-state Sector's Role in SDG & Youth

Veerendra Mishra

The best way to find yourself is to lose you in the service of others

— **Mahatma Gandhi**

Introduction

SUSTAINABLE DEVELOPMENT GOALS can be achieved only if Youth are in position to actively participate in achieving them. However, it is still to be ascertained if the capacity of youth of India, whom we call our demographic dividend, is properly built up. Is it enough to be content with the number game, basking under the thought that the average of India's population is is less than 30 years at the time of writing, with life expectancy of about 70 years? Or are we in any way concerned about the *quality* of this enviable number? The dividend that is talked about can very easily become a baggage or burden if the energy and aspirations of youth is not channelised constructively. It is pertinent to critically analyse some aspects of the role of state and non-state sectors in shaping this youthful population.

Indians do not miss a chance to announce that it is a powerful nation and a prospective superpower. And, why not? The country has proved its resilient power by absorbing shock of recent global recession by maintaining steady economic growth. The country is inching forward towards gaining the status of its claim of superpower. One of the factors contributing to its confidence for sure-shot enviable growth, even challenging the failing economy globally, is its demographic dividend. Average age of India's population is 29 years (*FE Online* 2017).

It has to be understood that whenever there is mention about India's population, it is not about millions, but the reference is to more than 1.32 billion people (Stastia 2018). Putting together the population of 28 countries of the European Union, the total population is 508 million (Europa.eu website). The population of African countries all combined together is 1.2 billion (Worldometers 2018). So, the population of India is more than all countries put together in many continents. Hence, when it is said that the average age of India's population is 29 years, that means we are talking about the average age of about 1.32 billion people. Even in real numbers, the number of youth in India would be for all practical reasons more than youth population of most of the continents.

Interestingly, the Youth Policy of India, which was promulgated in 2014 by Ministry of Youth Affairs and Sports, considers youth to be a person in the age bracket of 15 to 29 years. Therefore, by definition itself, the average age of a person in India will fall within the definition of youth. So, India is a country of youth! And historically a young country.

Now, the pertinent question to be asked is if this factor of contributory demographic number, which is talked about as an *advantage*, having the so called potential to cruise the country to the status of superpower, automatically gets translated into *dividend*? Is this mindboggling figure of youth population in India a dividend by default (by virtue of numbers) or does it have to be made a dividend by design? This number has to be cautiously and scientifically analysed to understand the dividend rhetoric.

There is a popular adage, 'Youth of today is the future of tomorrow'. Interestingly, for India, there is no time to wait for tomorrow, as it is going to be too late if time is wasted in hope of tomorrow to unfold itself. *Focus has to be on today*, as the young population has already taken over space and time and is anxious to make its presence felt in the prevailing national scenario. Tomorrow, this youth who are today promisingly moving around to take up the challenge of painting the broad Indian canvas with bright colours will move into the age bracket, which will then require support system for healthy living.

Between forty to fifty years from now this youth will become senior citizens, and a major section of the Indian population will be old. And in any country's life, forty years is hardly considered to be a long period. Hence, it is high time that the youth are engaged constructively without losing time. How, when and in what way can they participate and contribute has to be specifically defined and the youth need to be guided to their roles. If they are left directionless and left to vent out their aspirations and frustrations without hope for meaningful existence and role, the social situation in India can get anarchic.

United Nations mandated Sustainable Development Goals in 2015 and the protocol came into effect in January 2016, with the aim of holistic growth and to alleviate the gaps in societal development worldwide by 2030. Undoubtedly, the role of youth becomes instrumental in fulfilling the UN mandate, especially for a youthful nation. However, a strong contingent of youth, by themselves, cannot be expected to march towards achieving Sustainable Development Goals and deliver the deliverables, unless they are properly guided and mentored.

Youth have already started to take charge in all fields of work in the country. Their role will be pivotal, but only if they are well informed and engaged with the global vision for the future. Over the next ten years, from 2020-2030, youth will not only directly experience the outcome of SDGs and plans, but will also be the key driver for their successful implementation–that is why it is important to reap the democratic dividend. Five years of the designated time frame of 15 years, that is one-third of this time, is already over.

Today the situation has changed, and posed a new type of challenge with the outbreak of the pandemic of disproportional virulence. Covid-19 has brought the world to an edge of economic crisis. Achieving of the SDGs has strong financial implication. The coffers of most of the aid-providing international institutions are drying up as the contributing countries are struggling to chip in their share. It is an unprecedented economic recession which looms large throughout the globe, and the reason for the recession is not failure in policies but a natural threat. The world is engaged in a very abnormal crisis. India's youth are in the centre of it, the nation's existence is dependent on how the youth, 40 per cent of its population, respond to the crisis.

Many of the goals of SDG can be realised only when youth fruitfully participate. This requires two things: one to build capacity of youth to prepare them and second, to motivate them to contribute. It has dual benefits: it benefits the community at large and eventually translates into nation-building and secondly, it benefits the participant (that is the youth) in honing their personality and preparing them for facing future challenges with confidence and élan.

The role of state and non-state sectors is important in making feasible the fulfilment of the requirement for fruitful participation of youth. The concerted effort of both is important, so that a strong support system is built and put in place to help youth realise their true potential. Ecology has to be created where youth of the country contribute their share in nation-building fruitfully. State support is designed through policies and establishment of institutions to engage youth constructively.

The non-state sector's role is very important, not only as an extended hand of the state but also in creating an environment of close monitoring through process of social audit. However, besides these, the non-state sector plays a vital role of collaboration with youth in real-time action.

Sustainable Development Goals

United Nations defines Sustainable Development Goals as, '… *the blueprint to achieve a better and more sustainable future for all. They address the global challenges we face, including those related to poverty, inequality, climate, environmental degradation, prosperity, and peace and justice*'. The 17 Sustainable Development Goals can be classified into two categories:

One,[1] which are concerned about social evils, not in pure sense but have cause and effect relation to direct discrimination in society, like poverty, hunger, gender inequality, unclean water and sanitation inequalities, poor education, bad health and no

[1] https://www.un.org/sustainabledevelopment/sustainable-development-goals/

wellbeing, unavailability of work and economic growth, and lack of peace, justice and strong institutions.

The second type of goals is related to conscious growth, considering factors that would ensure sustainability of earth's atmosphere, like climate action, life below water, life on land, sustainable cities and communities, responsible production and consumption, industry, affordable and clean energy, and innovation and infrastructure.

The role of youth in realising the first category of sustainable development goals, which has been classified above, is very vital. In all societies, there are two categories of youth:

One, that section of youth who face the brunt of discrimination due to the absence of the factors enshrined in the first category of SDGs (missing components of these goals) and another section, those youth who enjoy the accomplishment of SDG as the privileged and Haves of the society, by virtue of birth in certain class and caste.

The first lot of SD goals cannot be accomplished immediately, hence youth, irrespective of which socio-economic section they hail from, have to be prepared to bridge the gap and contribute meaningfully without vitiating the atmosphere through discriminatory approach of Haves and Have Nots. This category of SDGs being more related to social issues, in achieving these goals, the role of the non-state sector and community, which is now full of youth, is more important. Proper policy support, with effective and efficient implementation through collaborative partnership of non-state players and youth would help in achieving the goals soon.

The role of youth in the second category of SDGs is also equally relevant and important. However, the role of the state is more important, as they frame policies, plan action and implement plans through state agencies. The rules and regulations are set by the state and it decides the course of action. Youth can play an effective contributory role by timely voicing their concerns during formulation of policies and become partner in implementation and timely course correction through feedback.

As the role of youth in all SDGs is vast, it is difficult to discuss all of it in one article, hence largely: the discussion in this essay is focused on Goal 8 of the Sustainable Development Goals. Goal 8 mandates that every state (nation, country) should be committed to promote sustained, inclusive and sustainable economic growth, full and productive employment and decent work for all.

The United Nations has observed that there is need to increase employment opportunities for young people worldwide.

At the time of setting all the goals[2] in 2014, it also observed that youth were three times more likely to be unemployed than adults in 2017. Another strong observation was that gender inequality in earnings is still pervasive. Three years on, the statistics has not changed much; rather, with a pandemic lockdown sweeping the world, like in the rest of the world, in India too, the youth are less likely to retain their jobs. It is unlikely that in the organised sector employment opportunities will increase in coming few years. With economy shrinking the employability opportunities will squeeze, posing greater threat to the youth of being left out.

---

2 The Sustainable Development Goals Report 2018 reviews progress in the third year of implementation of the 2030 Agenda for Sustainable Development. This overview presents highlights of progress and remaining gaps for all 17 Sustainable Development Goals (SDGs), based on the latest available data, and examines some of the interconnections across Goals and targets retrieved https://unstats.un.org/sdgs/report/2018/overview/

Demographic Dividend Rhetoric

Demographically, India definitely stands to advantage before any other country. However, *the demographic dividend rhetoric is certainly causing a lot of confusion. Unfortunately, for results, a lot is being banked upon quantity rather than on quality.*

It is presumed that this magical number of close to 500 million youth in a country is a panacea to all ills, a huge workforce at hand, ready to take up challenges. *This myth needs to be busted* because if this number is not handled properly, and the quantity is not moulded qualitatively, the same dividend can become a baggage or burden. An unguided missile can be devastating.

Demographic dividend rhetoric is fuelled just by the number game. It is on the presumption that numbers automatically translate into constructive action. The huge figures reflecting on the screen, whenever the strength of youth in India is typed, give immense pleasure to those who are delusionally fond of big numbers. But, to a practical person, it calls for great concern. The worry lies in mismanagement of resources. Certainly, if human resource, which by virtue of age is highly energetic and ambitious, is not engaged in meaningful ways, then it spells doom.

The Information Trap

In a highly automated and digital world, the movement of information is very fast. Any information shared is often exaggerated and biased. The youth, in loop of this information-sharing network through social media connectivity, is influenced a lot by what information is being served to them.

They are living in the world of simulation, where image is etched in their minds through media, *which is not the actual reality.* It may be a piece of reality picked and simulated as per convenience of either an individual on the other end of technology or by a state or a non-state player, an organisation or institution or religious or political grouping and circulated. French social theorist Jean Baudrillard (1994) has explained the concept of Simulacra and Simulation vividly in his book and depicted how a postmodernist is moving away from reality. He elucidates how simulacrum has become the *hyper-real*, as it is not a copy of the real, but has become the truth in its own right. He further goes on to say that simulacrum 'bears no relation to any reality whatsoever'.

In the *Encyclopedia of Case Study Research (2010)*, simulacrum (plural: simulacra) has been defined as a concept that describes the phenomenon whereby what is presented, in particular through the media but also through more pervasive culturally significant spectacles, can no longer be assumed to refer to any real or actual state. Philosopher Fredric Jameson (cited in Brian 1987), while explaining simulacrum in art, has offered photorealism as an example of artistic simulacrum. In photorealism, a painting created is copy of a photograph that is itself a copy of the real.

Youth's aspirations and frustration gets impractically high because of a very competitive and comparative life they live because of exposure to such simulated information, which keeps challenging their *locus standi* vis a vis others depicted in the virtual world. The challenge to meet the ignited desire to achieve what may not be real can redirect the youth into undesirable domains, which could be perilous to the overall growth of a society.

Proper strategy and planning is required to channelise the energy of the aspiring youth in constructive ways. The role of both, state and non-state players is vital. Immediate action is desired to drive this numbers into meaningful engagement.

However, mere aspiration does not culminate into desired output. If there is no proper system and structure in place to groom youth to participate meaningfully – then the sense of underutilisation or a non-contributive force, shrouded in obscurity, will frustrate them.

Youth in themselves cannot be construed as a homogenous group for just being in a defined age bracket (15-29 years in India). They are susceptible to be divided on the grounds of caste, economic class, ethnicity, gender, disability, sexual orientation and other such social divides. Synergising the energy and potential of these diverse groups is a big challenge for a quasi-developed country like India.

Some of the challenges faced by youth of India are briefly analysed, so that the 'demographic dividend' is understood in its right perspective.

Education and Employability

Educational institutions are mushrooming in India without enough capacity to hone the potential of youth. In fact, the poor quality institutions vitiate the scenario as they distribute certificates without building mandated and desired capacity of employable youth. A passed out student from any such educational institution, irrespective of his true potential, claims his due in the market by displaying his certificate.

Young people, with some education, do not appreciate being engaged in low-productivity, low-income work in the informal sector (Ghost 2004). If he or she fails to acquire the desired job, s/he gets frustrated for being unemployed or underemployed; and many choose to be unemployed rather than underemployed; at the same time many choose to take up any job rather than one for which they are somewhat qualified.

Also, sometimes, a deserving candidate has to bear the brunt of nepotism and favouritism in the presence of a huge labour force and competing for the same job. As a result, often, a qualified and deserving candidate is left to struggle in the market. However, Visalia (1998) has observed that many of the unemployed have fairly poor performance at the examinations and do not have the desired aptitude or the capacity in commensuration to their aspiration for a particular type of work. Unemployment and underemployment can cause havoc in the society, if the youth do not get opportunity to engage constructively. This is exactly what faces India at the moment.

The mismatch between what is *produced* through educational institutions in India and the potential of (institutionally groomed) *produced* youth needs to be analysed to understand the misnomer of demographic dividend. The terms *production* and *produce* are used deliberately, to highlight the educational industry in operation in the country. According to data presented in *India Today* (2017), in 2016 there were around 10,361 engineering colleges approved by AICTE (All India Council for Technical Education) with intake capacity of 37 lakh students.

It was then found (by government as well as other quality assessment bodies) that in many of these 'recognised' institutions, the quality of education was compromised. As many as 800 of these engineering institutions were then closed by the State governments and central government authorities. That still leaves 9000+ colleges in operation. There is no doubt that many hundreds of these institutions must have warded off penalty by acting 'smartly', whatever that necessitated.

Since 2003, India has been adding almost 1,000 colleges per year with addition of 7,206 colleges between 2007 and 2009. According to Manuel (2016), the number of colleges in this country has crossed the 36,000 figure. All these colleges are affiliated to some university or the other. According to the UGC website, as of February 2017, there are 789 universities, 37,204 colleges and 11,443 stand-alone institutions in India. These figures are enough indication to suggest how easy it is to get degree certificate in the country now.

With educational institutions cropping up everywhere without enough paraphernalia to run courses, such institutions are bound to give below par education, not only in engineering but in arts and science as well. Nevertheless, the certificate they carry is from some university, which has good serious institutes as well. Due to absence of differentiation on the basis of certificate and for creating environment of equal claim in labour market on the basis of degree, the actual potential of an individual is often compromised.

According to the employability-focused study conducted by Aspiring Minds, on 150,000 engineering students who graduated in 2013, only 7 per cent engineering graduates were employable. The study also found that 93 per cent MBA graduates were unemployable (Chakrabarty 2018). As per The Pearson Voice of Teacher Survey (2015), teachers consider 64 per cent of students at the higher-education level to be unemployable.

The 2018 study done by RN Nadar on the Indian Education system[3] revealed that the Indian Education System has failed to create the required employability according to the

---

[3] The 2018 study done by RN Nadar (then Vice-Principle Guru Nanak College of Arts, Science & Commerce) on the Indian Education system widely criticised its failure to create required employability in its students according to the industry requirements and its inability to contribute to inclusive growth in the nation as a whole. http://iosrjournals.org/iosr-jbm/papers/Conf.ADMIFMS1808-2018/Volume-1/13.%2086-91.pdf

industry's expectations and needs and has failed to contribute to inclusive national growth as a whole.

An analysis of labour bureau data done by Woetzel, Madgavkar and Gupta (2017) projects that over a period of four years – from 2012 to 2016 – on an average, 4.75 million people are added to the labour force in India every year. As per Dewan (Dewan, 2018), between 2001 and 2005, on an average, roughly 12 million people entered the labour force every year, but now the number has come down to 4.75 million. Entering the labour force means that *one is either employed or unemployed but actively looking for work.*

As per World Development Indicators (2016) of the World Bank, India had a total workforce of 503.8 million in 2015. According to their report, in India between 2011-2016, on an average per year there was addition of 6.6 million people to the labour force. Thus, using both the Labour Bureau's estimate of addition of around 4.75 million people and the World Bank's estimate of 6.6 million people being added to the workforce every year, it can be estimated that roughly 5-7 million people have been entering the Indian workforce on an annual basis. This figure is apt to be dramatically revised by 2021, as it is roughly estimated that only 20 per cent of the workable population will hold jobs by the end of 2020.[4]

---

[4] An unemployment tracker survey is released by the Centre for the Monitoring of Indian Economy (CMIE), the only data source of its kind that reports unemployment on a daily, monthly and quarterly basis

Mahesh Vyas, the CEO and Director of CMIE, reported in April 2020: 'An unemployment rate of 23.4 per cent during this week; an LPR [labour participation rate] of 36 per cent and an employment rate of 27.7 per cent.' Now, over 20 per cent joblessness is bad news for any country. The real eye-popping figure, however, is that just 27.7 per cent of the working-age population is employed

This was reported in https://theprint.in/opinion/india-lost-more-jobs-due-to-coronavirus-lockdown-than-us-did-during-depression/397693/

Here it is relevant to look into the country's estimated growth in job creation to meet the demand of its labour market. According to the 2017 report of McKinsey Global Institute by Woetzel et al (2017), a global private sector think-tank set up as the business and economics research arm of McKinsey & Company, the Indian economy generated only 7 million jobs during 2013-2016.

The Government of India's Labour Bureau (2016) has suggested that from 2013 to 2016, India's labour market had meager job growth in the range of 150,000 to 400,000 jobs each year. The government's Chief Economic Advisor Arvind Subramanian observed in the second edition of 2016-2017 Economic Survey, 'The lack of reliable estimates on employment in recent years has impeded its measurement and thereby the Government faces challenges in adopting appropriate policy interventions.' This was three years ago. The situation has only deteriorated.

When the Labour force is talked about, it has to be understood that not necessarily all in the 29-years age group enter either the education or employment market.

There is a concept called NEET (Not in Education, Employment, or Training) which means a young person who is no longer in the education system and who is not working or being trained for work. According to 2017 India report of the OECD[5] Economic Surveys, in 2015, 30.8 per cent of youth aged 15 to 29 years were NEET youth. So, obviously, they are not reflected in any of the labour force data. However, the contribution of this NEET Youth too is equally important in nation-building and achieving of Sustainable

---

[5] Organisation for Economic Co-operation and Development, an intergovernmental organisation

Development Goals. The number of NEET youth is only growing in the country. We have to also acknowledge that that a huge young population is out of the school system despite the Sarva Sikhsha Abhiyan, Right to Education and growth in number of schools in the country. In 2017, the United Nations Educational, Scientific and Cultural Organisation (UNESCO)'s representative Shigeru Aoyagi said that, 'almost a fifth of the country's population – 266 million adults – are still unable to read and some 12 million children are yet to get enrolled in schools'. Making education accessible to all as well as improving the quality of education available is one of the 17 sustainable development goals but as per the UNESCO estimates we are far from achieving the goal as 35 per cent of the world's illiterate population is in India. The data has not changed significantly for the last three years.[6]

So, now, if the linkage between education and employment is analysed, then the situation faced is very challenging. As already described in preceding paragraphs, the labour force may not necessarily project the right picture. Different reports reflect different scenario. The educational system does not promote employability, as it is not equipping students with skills and competencies required in the global knowledge economy. There is evidence of growing unemployment and underemployment and paradoxically, it coexists in India with mounting skill shortages (Agarwal 2007).

Recently, some studies have indicated that the nature of jobs available in the market in coming decades will change drastically. With the more advanced Artificial Intelligence (AI) and automation of most of the activities, the demand for

---

6 https://www.livemint.com/Politics/Xy9Yn0MsHBLiurzxfVR7aK/266-million-adults-cant-read-12-million-children-out-of-sc.html

professions will change. Researchers from the Oxford University, Frey and Osborne (2016) think that artificial intelligence will put at high risk 47 per cent of jobs in US over the next 20 years. The fallout will be seen in other countries, as well. The negative impact can be seen in all kinds of employment – including jobs in logistics and transport, mining, construction, police force, and food preparation.

The study also found that 'high value' roles such as lawyers and doctors would also be undermined by artificial intelligence (as Hurlburt in 2017 noted). But, surprisingly, none have been able to predict the forthcoming changes or what will be the scenario. It is merely speculated that the current traditional professions will not exist; meaning that current professionals may become redundant or less in demand, but what job will be available is hard to define.

Add to these futuristic studies, the current situation of a pandemic lockdown. The crisis is demonstrating that only essential services are important, all other work is irrelevant; as such, every job is being looked at with eyes of requirement only. For one primary school class, where five teachers were needed for five sections of class 1, now one teacher will be enough for five sections of Class 1. As distance education becomes the norm and zoom classes usual, tele-teaching can render half of the teaching community itself unemployed. Student capability assessment and employability may also fall by the wayside.

The Challenge in India

The biggest challenge faced is creating of opportunities for 'gainful employment' for India's fast multiplying youth force as 'labour force' or part of NEET. Also, it is important to understand that when the subject of 'gainful employment' is discussed, then the idea is not about merely creating job opportunities, i.e. number of jobs, but it is also about the quality of work, which promises job content that includes creation of fulfilling jobs in commensurate with the potential of the job seekers, with promise of better pay and chance of high productivity.

In India, policies have been developed to encourage entrepreneurship by enhancing Skill and promoting Start Ups. But, the existing infrastructure is not enough to cater to the existing demand.

Mental Health Issues

The sense of deprivation for different kinds of youth, those who are capable and those who claim to be capable, may ultimately lead to mental health problems. *The biggest challenge that youth of India is going to face is the issue of mental health.* WHO Report (2001) defined mental health as: a state of well-being in which the individual realises his or her own abilities, can cope with the normal stresses of life, can work productively and fruitfully, and is able to make a contribution to his or her community. According to Medilexicon's medical dictionary, mental health is: 'Emotional, behavioural, and social maturity or normality; the absence of a mental or behavioural disorder; a state of psychological well-being in which one has achieved a satisfactory integration of one's instinctual drives acceptable to both oneself and one's social milieu; an appropriate balance of love, work, and leisure pursuits.'

An online survey conducted by ICICI Lombard in 2017 states that 65 per cent of youth between the age group of 22-25 displayed early signs of depression. Though it has to be clarified that the manifestation of mental health issues is not just depression. According to Mayo Clinic (2015) 'Mental illness refers to a wide range of mental health conditions – disorders that affect your mood, thinking and behaviour. Examples of mental illness include depression, anxiety disorders, schizophrenia, eating disorders and addictive behaviours.' As per World Health Organisation, suicide was the second leading cause of death among 15–29-year-olds globally in 2016, and there are many more people who attempt suicide every year. Due to prevalence of stigma with regard to mental disorder, people thinking of committing suicide or attempting suicide fail to seek help.

The definition of Mental Health and the symptoms given indicates that mental health reflects a person's state of mind. The quality of contribution of youth is certainly compromised if their state of mind is not healthy. In fact, if there were illness it would jeopardise the initiatives and efforts of state and non-state sectors in engaging youth in nation building. As a matter of fact, it becomes very important to understand what is being done to ensure that youth of India have a healthy state of mind.

Now, the question arises as to how to work on maintaining a 'healthy state of mind'. Medication is no solution. Sylvano Arieti (1975) suggested that to enhance creativity, 'Instead of resorting to toxic procedures, we must consider, and possibly recommend, special attitudes, habits, and environmental conditions'. Similarly, to prevent occurrence of Mental Health issues, rather than prescribing medicinal interventions, *the solution lies in creating a preventive atmosphere,* which enables overall fulfilling development of youth.

While discussing education and employment, intentionally a perspective was discussed where better pay structure was emphasised as a precondition for job satisfaction. However, in reality, better pay is not necessarily the only condition or necessary condition for job contentment. For different people, different motivating factors work.

When productivity is discussed as one of the factors for job enrichment, productivity has to be defined. Productivity can be in terms of output in measurable terms at work place and also it can be the contribution and impact in community development when engaged. Dolan (2006) and Brennan (2006) in their independent writings have recognised the need for theory, research, and applied programmes that contribute to both community and youth resiliency.

In India, a review was done focusing on the health behaviours and problems affecting young people in the age group of 10-30 years. The review examined some policy initiatives and interventions and identifies issues that need to be addressed for health and safety of young people in India. The researchers claimed 10-30 per cent of young people suffer from health-impacting behaviours and conditions, which calls for urgent attention of policy makers and public health professionals (Singh and Gopalkrishna 2014).[7]

The policies, however, are influenced by how the youth are *perceived* in the country. The developmental and sociological perceptions of youth can affect the policy related to young people (Raj 2015).[8] There are two kinds of perceptions about youth. One as 'Resource' and another as 'Problem' and based on these perceptions the policies are designed. Roger (2008) opines that if youth is considered to be a social resource, the development, the growth and the promotion of this resource becomes the major aim of the national youth policy. However, Woong (2008) finds that the image of youth as 'problems' is still dominant in the public discourse, professional work, and social science.[9]

---

7 https://www.ncbi.nlm.nih.gov/pmc/articles/PMC4216492/

8 https://www.researchgate.net/publication/281707329_CONTEMPORARY_YOUTH_IN_INDIA_PROSPECTS_PROBLEMS_AND_PERSPECTIVES

9 https://core.ac.uk/display/101020184

Youth certainly seem to be facing challenges. With extremely fast pace of globalisation and networking, it is needed to develop sociological analyses, theories and concepts to address the challenges faced due to these changes.

Here no theory is being propounded to address the challenges faced by youth, but certainly emphasis is being laid on a concept as a promising solution to the challenges.

Concept of Volunteerism

As per the definition given in Collins dictionary, volunteerism is 'the *principle* of *donating* time and energy for the *benefit* of other people in the *community* as a social *responsibility* rather than for any *financial reward*'. The importance of volunteerism was realised a long time ago in history and recently it has grown in popularity as an important activity, which is beneficial to community and volunteers, both.

Many States have taken conscious and planned action to encourage volunteerism, as a solution to the problems faced by the community and also to prepare good responsible citizens.

In the USA, consecutive governments have appreciated and acknowledged the importance of volunteerism and as a policy decision, have decided to engage citizens through voluntary activities. Ronald Reagan emphasised voluntary activities through his so-called 'new federalism', reiterating on the responsibility of service to the community as a personal task for each individual (Baynoli and McKee 1991). That initiative was followed by Bush's concept of 'thousand points of light'. Volunteerism represents an arena in which individuals may address their needs, pursue their hopes and aspirations, as well as augment efforts to keep the government responsive and effective. (Zech 1982).

Then came President Clinton. *'On April 27th...[we] will convene the first President's Summit on Citizen Service. Our goal is to mobilize America's citizen power in a united effort to solve our common problems, especially those that threaten our young people.'*—President Clinton, 24 January 1997.

Three former presidents were invited to participate along with numerous wealthy entertainment celebrities and generals. The theme of the conference was that the answer to the country's pervasive social problems was in private voluntary involvement and not public sector programmes. The 'summit declaration of commitment', accepted as an outcome of the conference, declared that the main commitment is 'Volunteer solution'. President Clinton called it 'an era of big citizenship', which would encourage individuals to engage in unpaid labour (Petras 1997). This statement was made expecting that the big challenges faced by the big government can be solved only by citizens' contribution through volunteerism.

In India

In India, historically, volunteerism has been encouraged since time immemorial. However, the concept was lost over time and now it is being revived in a different format, quite naturally. The importance of volunteerism in social construction of a community member and in building right kind of citizens was well established in the Indian scriptures and religiously practiced in earlier times. The four stages in human lifecycle, as per Indian ancient scriptures were described as four Ashramas – brahmacharya, grihastha, vanaprashtha and sanyas ashramas. In broader terms, the role of every person in each ashrama, stages in life, was described. It was based on the basic premise that every community member had some responsibility towards community and to prepare them to take that responsibility and accountability sincerely, it was necessary for them to go through a grooming process.

Children were groomed in Brahmacharya ashrama into becoming matured adults, where they were supposed to take decisions in the community. Children were taken out of their comfort zone, from under family umbrellas, and put in a Gurukul to live a life of austerity; to live in a group of non-blood related members, where they volunteered services. They were supposed to go to the community and interact with all sections of the society, as non-entity. This helped them to understand 'community' from close quarters and learn in detail the needs and gaps. This ensured that by developing strong foundation in Brahmacharya ashrama, the child and person in early period of youthhood would be prepared to lead a successful and fulfilling Grihastha role.

Unless a person is connected closely with the community, he or she cannot be grounded, cannot empathise and cannot be a responsible citizen. Grihastha ashrama was for later stage of youth and until middle age. Like Brahmacharya ashrama, even a person in Vanaprashtha ashrama was expected to volunteer, with a paramount motive to serve selflessly for the growth of the community.

The continuous invasions in the country and attack on traditional lifestyle to accommodate the invaders way of thinking gradually diluted the ashrama system. Later, the colonial rule, which realised that the educational system of the Gurukul was cause of traditional cohesion and solidarity, strategically planned to denigrate it by introducing western education. The English system was glorified, which gradually pulled away the starry-eyed youth from traditional educational system, where primarily community was in focus than the individual growth. The traditional system was based on the idea of knowledge and, duty and responsibility after education. The new introduced educational system focussed on individualism and was based more on academic knowledge. Hence the concept of volunteerism which was inbuilt in the societal norms got lost.

However, some social reform movements found expression in social work and in their teaching institutions set up to train young people in social work. Ramkrishna Mission, Arya Samaj of Dayanand Saraswati and many other social reformers, who believed in the rich Indian scriptures, continued grooming contingent of youth with the fervour to volunteer. The underlying aim remained the same: to selflessly work in the community by starting with the analysis of the need of the community and focusing on a welfare approach.

Youth Schemes in India

At a very early stage after Independence, the Government of India realised the importance of voluntary contribution of youth. The draft First Five year Plan, adopted by the Government of India in 1952, just within five years of independence, stressed on the need for social and labour service for students for one year. Consequently, various educational institutions put into operation various labour and social service camps, campus work projects, village apprenticeship scheme etc.

In 1958, the then Prime Minister, Pandit Jawaharlal Nehru, mooted the idea of having social service as a prerequisite for graduation, and to push his point he wrote a letter to all the Chief Ministers. He instructed the Ministry of Education to formulate a suitable scheme for introduction of national service into the academic institutions. The efforts finally took shape in Mahatma Gandhi's Birth Centenary Year, 1969, with launching of a formal organisation called 'National Service Scheme' (NSS). The aim of the NSS is to arouse Social Consciousness of the youth with an overall objective of 'Personality Development of Students through Community Service'.

Later, 'Nehru Yuva Kendra Sangathan' (NYKS) was established in 1972. The core objective of NYKS is to organise non-student rural youth, orient and train them for inculcating national values and channelise their energy and participation in various developmental initiatives at grassroots level.

Both organisations attempt to capture geographically, politically, socially, culturally, and economically diverse youth in India and mentor them to synergise their energy for nation building through community service.

NSS currently engages more than 4.1 million students in more than 32,000 educational institutions, whereas NYKS engages around 3.5 million rural youth through various youth clubs in villages and semi-urban settings. Through these two organisations, the government tries to touch base with both categories of youth, urban youth in educational institutions (NSS) and the collegiate rural youth (NYKS). This is less than 8 million of India's 500 million young people.

Despite having a strong base of government-aided volunteerism in India, the desired impact seems to have eluded the policy makers. While the state claims to be making serious efforts to mobilise the youth and mentor them, many gaps have remained, which has thwarted the government's and society's fulfilling engagement with the youth. On paper, the NSS and NYKS look very successful schemes, which claim to engage around 8 million youth of country. But, as discussed earlier, how fulfilling has been this engagement and how much has this engagement over years translated into building a strong community, still remains unanswered.

It remains unanswered for two reasons: one because there has been no scientific evaluation ever done. The studies conducted have been piecemeal, limited and not sociologically planned. Second, whatever efforts are reflected in annual reports over the years has not sustained and hence can be said to have *limited impact*. Even the number of youth registered with these two organisations is very little when compared to the youth population of the country. And, all those registered do not necessarily have the same level of commitment and passion. Low registration and lack in commitment and passion can be a result of negative belief in volunteerism.

According to Law and Shek (2011), there can be two main reasons for negative beliefs in volunteerism, which are: Conceptual bias and Instrumental bias. This biasness has been derived from the social norm theory and social exchange theory (Batson 1995). Social norm theory explains sociologically, the societal and cultural beliefs about helping. Social exchange theory, in turn, explains psychologically about focus on 'give and take' in helping. This defines if volunteerism is self-centered or other-centered.

Conceptual biasness discusses the general impression of a volunteer – that volunteering is a waste of time and meaningless.

On the other hand, Instrumental bias reflects on the psychological nature of the bias– that a volunteer carries a perception that efforts to help is not genuine and do not bring favourable consequences. It is presumed that due to lack of genuineness, the participation of volunteers is more pretentious than motivated participation and guided by selfish intentions like obtaining a certificate or career progression rather than contributing to community development.

The assumption of unfavourable consequences comes from the belief that volunteerism has adverse impact on academic performance or eats into important time, impeding career progression.

A study was conducted on school students in Boston, USA, to assess if service (voluntary or mandated) by high school student had the capacity to turn youth into active and engaged citizens who are capable of assessing and solving problems (Metz and Youniss 2003). The study reflected strongly on the socialisation process. The study found that students who participated were motivated to continue volunteerism even after high school, and believed in civic engagement. The same study included a batch of students, not participating in voluntary services. It found that the students who did not volunteer were not motivated. Similarly, students not having any family background of volunteerism were also not motivated. However, students who volunteered even with no prior voluntary background were motivated to volunteer even after graduating from high school. This proved that the experiences gained through services are a motivating factor for future volunteering.

The above study explains that disinterest in volunteerism among the young people is more a matter of perception than as an outcome of experiencing reality. The existing biasness, as explained earlier is because of the fact that volunteering has been more a perfunctory than mindful and fruitful engagement; if at all one has participated in volunteerism.

The narrative of volunteerism has to be changed. Especially in India, with a huge youth population. Every engagement of youth through volunteerism should be meaningful engagement. When 'meaningful' is the term used, then it means that the volunteers participating in any activity should know the purpose, structure and content of participation, and the desired outcome and impact of their contribution. India has more than 300 million people worth of unharnessed energy and willpower that can change the face of the country, if society wills it. Even in times of unprecedented crisis, the strength of India's volunteerism remains untapped, untested and unrecorded.

ME+MP= BIO (Fruitful Engagement)

Meaningful Engagement (ME) coupled with Mindful Participation (MP) is the key to desired result. Mindful participation means that the volunteer is aware of his participation, is living that moment of participation, realising the aspired change inside and outside through contribution. Mindful participation would ensure a volunteer's conscious involvement and engagement.

To ensure Meaningful engagement, it is important for the planners of voluntary activities to understand the letter and spirit of volunteerism themselves, so that they are able to orient the volunteers accordingly. Hence, it is the responsibility of the planners and organisers to ensure that volunteers have meaningful engagement. If any activity undertaken is initiated within this framework, then both, the volunteer and the community stand to gain. Because, in such an ideal situation, there is a sense of belongingness to whatever the volunteer decides to do and does, and such activity, being inclusive in nature, all stakeholders start owning the work. This model of work has inherent BIO qualities i.e. sense of belongingness (B), sense of inclusiveness (I) and sense of ownership (O).

The outcome and impact of volunteerism certainly is two pronged: one way, it is beneficial for the volunteer through exposure to a value system of community service, which is based on the fundamentals of learning and sharing, an evolved stage of giving and taking. This inward-looking process helps the volunteers to assess themselves and, acknowledge and appreciate the contribution of the ecosystem they live in.

Second, after self-realisation and enhancement in understanding of the surroundings, the volunteer acts as change agent to help others understand the process so they become more sensitive to environment and ecosystem they live in. Volunteerism brings the volunteers close to reality and exposes them to the existing truths in the society. So, naturally, the one who volunteers is aware of the surroundings or ecosystem, as they work in close proximity with the community.

However, these learnings are possible only if the volunteer is seriously, mindfully engaged and is not present for lip service. Eventually, through mindful participation and meaningful engagement, there is improvement in the cognitive and non-cognitive skills of the youth.

Volunteer Skill Sets

Non-cognitive skills are defined as the 'patterns of thought, feelings and behaviours' (Borghans, Duckworth, Heckman and Ter Weel 2008) that are socially determined and can be developed throughout the lifetime to produce value. Non-cognitive skills comprise personal traits, attitudes and motivation (Zhou, 2016). They are reflected in a person's behavior and attitude. Non-cognitive skills are also called as 'socio-emotional skills' or 'soft skills' because they are related to an individual's personality, temperament and attitudes, which influence a person's motivation, integrity and interpersonal interaction. Soft skills are now virtually required in all jobs for a person to work well with other people and function effectively in a work environment.

Pierre, Puerta, Valerio and Rajadel (2014) puts cognitive skills as those skills, which involve the 'ability to understand complex ideas, to adapt effectively to the environment, to learn from experience, to engage in various forms of reasoning, to overcome obstacles by taking thought'. Cognitive skills are the core skills that brain uses to think, read, learn, remember, reason, and pay attention. Working together, they take incoming information and move it into the bank of knowledge you use every day at work, and in life.

If the development of non-cognitive skills is focused, the youth will be prepared to adopt and adapt to the changing socio-economic scenario.

The mental health issues of the youth, which is of profound concern for every nation, will be reduced. If they learn the skill to cope with the changing market pressure, they will be capable of readjusting their skill to make themselves meaningful in all situations. Volunteerism makes individuals better prepared to acknowledge and address social problems and with their right, constructive inputs the policies framed by states can be made more robust, vibrant, realistic and achievable.

Volunteerism is an integral part of positive youth development. Youth can achieve social, emotional, cognitive, behavioural and moral competence through service (Catalano, Berglund, Ryan, Lonczak, & Hawkins 2004). Critical thinking should be promoted amongst the volunteers, as that will encourage them to question any misgivings and at the same time, inculcate in them a sense of responsibility. By volunteering, the adaptive capacities of the youth are enhanced, which improves their resilient capacity.

Through volunteerism, youth develop practical skills, which help them acclimatise into society by developing the coping skills needed for resiliency. Of late, youth have played, and continue to play, a progressively more important role in the development of their communities (Huber, Frommeyer,

Weisenbach & Sazama 2003). Career development theorists have long stressed the importance of providing students with realistic exploratory opportunities that lead to an increasingly comprehensive understanding of self and the world of work (Hoppock 1976, Ginzberg, Ginsberg, Axelrad& Herma 1951). Volunteerism can play a big role in providing students with invaluable opportunities to explore the contemporary work place (Beale 1984).

Conclusion

It is important to understand that volunteerism in not 'giving' but 'learning and sharing'. This has been the essence of Brahmacharya ashrama, which is missing in today's concept of volunteerism in India. Every volunteer, nowadays, steps into the world of volunteerism with a strong sense of arrogance – with a delusion that he is there to help someone who is less privileged than him. This creates a mental block and obstructs the learning process. They presume that they 'know all'.

Nowadays, due to too much emphasis on quantifiable benefits of volunteerism, volunteers are missing out on lot of non-cognitive benefits accrued automatically by conscious volunteering, i.e. through mindful participation, as it existed in the ancient concept of volunteerism in India. Due to misguided arrogance, there is lack of sense of inclusiveness, belongingness and ownership, which are mandatory components for volunteerism to effectively impact one's attitude. Hence, their contribution remains *merely an activity rather than becoming meaningful engagement* and half-hearted volunteerism fails to play desired role in shaping the personality of volunteer, which hold them in good stead in later years.

The social condition of the 19th century led to socio-religious reform movements. Some of such reform movements were the Brahmo Samaj, the Arya Samaj, Ramakrishna Mission, Satyasodhak Samaj, Prarthana Samaj, The Theosophical Society and Poona Sarvajanik Sabha.

In spite of the fact that charity and renunciation were placed on a high pedestal in Indian culture, no cadre of workers mainly committed to social service was created until Swami Vivekananda emerged on the Indian scene. He found that the bulk of the Indian masses were deprived of even the basic amenities of life. Poverty, disease and ignorance were widely prevalent. He could see that spiritual development can be brought about only after basic requirements for human existence are adequately met. This led him and his colleagues to give birth to a new order of renunciate social workers and it was named as the Ramakrishna Mission.

Raja Ram Mohan Roy was another great Indian of the 19th century. He was the morning star of Indian renaissance that sowed the seeds of religious and social reforms. He used his power and influence towards the abolition of *sati* and he was in favour of widow remarriage and female education. Education per se was also championed by Ishwar Chandra Vidyasagar of Bengal. Savitribai and Jyotirao Phule too were engaged in spread of education.

The unique leadership of Mahatma Gandhi during the freedom struggle was instrumental largely in creating greater awareness about the role of voluntary or selfless service. He laid great emphasis on the role of voluntary social workers in nation-building. A significant aspect of Gandhi's leadership has not been fully understood by many.

Another expression of the social reform movement in NGOs was in field programmes focusing on relief, rehabilitation, welfare and charity. Today, a strong Indian civil society with myriad Non-Government Organisations – large, medium and small – which grew from 1.2 million in 2002 (PRIA 2002) to 3.1 million (*Indian Express,* 7 June 2020), and is perhaps the largest such community in the world (Shukla A, 2010). These NGOs complement the government's macro social safety net using volunteers in many ways to tackle many of India's crying needs in human and social infrastructure. Currently there are many social work schools across the country where volunteerism is part of the curriculum.

The youth of today are living in a multi-cultural society, and they can capitalise on this opportunity if they involve themselves positively and constructively. It is going to bring greater cultural enrichment and with multitude exposure, their coping capacity will be enhanced. They also get prepared to take advantage of the globalisation and networking opportunities available. With shrinking labour markets and growing labour force, parochial attitudes and outlooks will no longer help, and travelling to gain experience is an expensive affair not only monetarily but also emotionally. A multi-cultural society provides the ideal chance to learn and share in a neighbourhood setting.

With growing challenges faced due to gaps in education and employability and consequent mental health issues, India's youth today have to be provided by the state with some alternate opportunities to contribute and share their learning.

Volunteerism has been found to be a good outlet for youth, which provides them a sense of involvement and provides opportunity for them to engage in fields of their choice. When they mindfully participate and meaningfully engage, it acts as an 'alternative fruitful employment' and being an area of interest ensures job contentment and intrinsic gratification. As it provides opportunity to be close to reality, they become mature contributors at workplaces. Their cognitive and non-cognitive skills improve, apparently leading to better interpersonal relations and strengthening their skill of taking decisions objectively.

Properly guided and directed, volunteerism is the only safe vehicle available to channelise positively the '*yuva shakti*' that India is gifted with. This will slowly and gradually help the youth of India to overcome the frustration creeping in due to under-employment and unemployment, and provide opportunity to fruitfully engage them, even if it is not monetarily fulfilling. Social recognition is a huge motivator for human beings as they are social animals by nature. Being close to community helps to get a reality check and hence the simulated environment – which falsely ignites desires for the unachievable – is contained. Motivated youth hold all the promises to achieve the goals set by SDGs.

Non-state sectors will have to work on creating constructive ambience where the potential of youth is tapped properly. They have to work on engaging youth, bridging the challenges faced through diversity. State Youth Policies should be based on comprehensive knowledge and a well-researched understanding of young people's experiences, needs and expectations.

The state should cautiously plan in the field of work for the youth, and create better opportunities to capitalise on the increased knowledge and understanding of youth gained through volunteering work. Youth contribution can be harnessed to provide them with greater involvement in nation-building and to raise social consciousness.

The next chapter talks about how youth, as creative innovators, can positively contribute to the idea of Sustainable Development by engaging actively in the processes of existence growth and how Youth Aid Foundation, as an organisation, provides space for young people to develop their entrepreneurship skills.

Fostering First Generation Micro-entrepreneurs

Opportunities and Challenges

Mathew Mattam

The best way to predict the future is to create it

— Abraham Lincoln

Introduction

A COUNTRY'S POTENTIAL for growth is determined by the size of its youth population. The energy and passion of the youth, if utilised properly, can bring about a huge positive change to society and progress to the nation. Youth as the creative innovators can positively contribute to sustainable national as well as personal and social development through active participation. This section of the population needs to be mobilised, motivated, skilled and supported to bring rapid progress in any developing country. Entrepreneurship is considered as one of the solutions to not just the socio-psychological problems but also in addressing the issues of rising crime and delinquency that arises from joblessness.

Today's youth population can be divided into 4 distinct categories. Those who belong to top 10 per cent and economically well off families, next 40 per cent belong to the middle class population while the third category comprises of 20 per cent, who belong to the lower middle class and the bottom 30 per cent belong to economically weaker or poor background.

This paper talks about the bottom 30 who belong to the economically weaker or economically poor background, who very often do not have the support, skills or knowledge to be part of the entrepreneurial ecosystem. They have an aspiration but do not know how to take the first step towards initiating a business plan and implementing it. For this, we need to understand what entrepreneurship is.

Definitions of Entrepreneur

In general terms, according to Nelson (as cited in Gurnani, 2016), 'an entrepreneur is a person who is able to look at the environment, identify opportunities to improve the environmental resources and implement action to maximise those opportunities'. It is important to bear in mind the entrepreneurial skills that will be needed to improve the quality of life for individuals, families and communities and to sustain a healthy economy and environment for anyone to become an entrepreneur.

Definition of Micro-business or Enterprise

A **micro-enterprise** (or **micro-business**) is generally defined as a small business employing less than nine people, having a balance sheet less than Rs 25 lakh (MSME). The term micro-enterprise and **micro-business** have the same meaning, though traditionally when referring to a small business financed by micro-credit, the term micro-enterprise is often used.

Similarly, when referring to a small, usually legal business that is not financed by microcredit, the term micro-business is often used.

Internationally, most micro-enterprises are family businesses employing one or two persons. Most micro-enterprise owners are primarily interested in earning a living to support themselves and their families.

Where does India Stand in Entrepreneurship Index?

Governments and local communities across the world have recognised that key to building prosperity and stimulate regional growth is fostering entrepreneurship among their people especially youth. Youth entrepreneurship has become a topic of interest for research scholars and also a subject of major concern for the government. While youth entrepreneurship is an under-explored field, the main factor for its growing importance is the increased number of unemployed young people. Furthermore, entrepreneurship is seen as a channel for the talents of many highly educated young people to explore their potential and cash their business acumen[1]

A study by Mckinsey & Company-Nasscom (as cited in Hariharaputhiran, 2011) stated that India needed at least 8,000 new businesses to achieve its target of building a US$87 billion IT sector alone. 'In the next 10 years, 110-130 million Indian citizens will be searching for jobs, including 80-100 million looking for their first jobs' this report had predicted. That was based on studies a decade ago.

The share of workers in the unorganised sector (enterprises with fewer than 10 workers, including own-account workers)

---

[1] Baporikar Neeta. (2015).Youth entrepreneurship in Indian scenario. 10.4018/978-1-4666-8468-3.ch0055. accessed on 1st July, 2020

fell from 86.3 per cent in 2004-05 to 84.3 per cent in 2009-10, and further to 82.2 per cent in 2011-12. (As cited in The Puzzles and Contradictions of the Indian Labour Market: What Will the Future of Work Look Like? Sher Singh Verick ILO and IZA.) At the same time, the share of informal workers in the organised sector (i.e. workers without access to social security in larger enterprises) increased significantly through the greater utilisation of contract and other forms of casual labour. As per Economic Survey (2018-19), 93 per cent of the Indian workforce belongs to the unorganised sector.

In new circumstances, in 2020-2021, the forecast dramatically changes. Only 47 per cent of Indian school graduates by 2030 will have the basic skills to be employable, said the UNICEF report titled GBC-Education 2030 Skills Scorecard (www.gbc-education.org). However, the number will be an improvement from the present 19 per cent. With almost half of its population of 1.8 billion below the age of 24, led by India, Pakistan and Bangladesh, South Asia will have the largest youth labour force in the world until 2040. This offers the region the potential to drive vibrant and productive economies. If strong investments in skills development are made, the region is poised to maintain strong economic growth as well as an expansion of opportunities in the education and skills sectors in the coming decades.

Centre for Monitoring Indian Economy in May 2020 said 27 million youth in the age group of 20-30 years lost their jobs in April 2020 following a nationwide lockdown to prevent the spread of Covid-19. Data from CMIE's Consumer Pyramids Household Survey shows youngsters in the age group 20-24 years accounted for 11 per cent of those who lost jobs while they constituted 8.5 per cent to the total employed persons in the country in 2019-20. According to CMIE, another 14 million jobs were lost in the age-group 25-29 years.

These three characteristics of the labour market will shape the future of work in India, which, due to having the largest youth population in the world, will also be a major determinant of the future of work globally. In this respect, the nature of work in India in the coming decades will depend on whether and how women work, whether more formal jobs are created and which sector will be the main generator of jobs for youth. If the world is to achieve the targets under Goal 8 of the Sustainable Development Goals by 2030, it will depend on India's success in creating more inclusive growth and decent work, overcoming the challenges inherent in these three employment dimensions.

Amongst a ranking of 137 countries, India has been ranked at 78th spot on the Global Entrepreneurship Index of 2019. India performs very low in Global Entrepreneurship Index and also performs badly in the areas of Global Youth Development Index too.

If we equate the current situation and the large-scale of unemployment present in the country today, micro-entrepreneurship seems to be the only way out.

Need for Micro-entrepreneurship in India

Entrepreneurs improve economies and people's lives by creating jobs, developing new solutions to problems, creating technologies that improve efficiency and exchanging ideas locally and globally. However, India scores 25.1 out of 100 in Global Entrepreneurship Index. The Global Entrepreneurship Index is a composite indicator of the health of the entrepreneurship ecosystem in a given country (GEI, 2018). The Global Entrepreneurship Index measures both the quality of the entrepreneurship and the extent and depth of the supporting entrepreneurs and ecosystem (GEI, 2018). The GEDI methodology collects data on the entrepreneurial attitudes, abilities and aspirations of the local population and then weighs these against the prevailing social and economic 'infrastructure' – this includes aspects such as broadband connectivity and the transport links to external markets. This process creates 14 'pillars' which GEDI uses to measure the health of the regional ecosystem.

According to the Global Entrepreneurship Development Institute (GEDI), there is a strong positive association between entrepreneurship, economic growth and innovation. The Covid-19 lockdown has further reduced opportunities for job seekers. The changing economy will lead to a cut in the number of jobs and also reduction in salaries. The lockdown has also impacted the continuity of micro-businesses with a majority of them shut completely and loss of income for over two months. As these businesses have small or no cash reserves and small profit margins for managing sudden losses, the major challenge faced is the lack of working capital to revive their businesses. Existing businesses are also exploring ways to adapt and survive the lockdown.

Due to Right to Education, more young people are getting into the formal education system. Soon, these young people are going to seek employment and also opportunities for self-employment. The job losses due to lockdown will have long-term repercussions as there will be a larger population in their 20s seeking employment for fewer jobs.

An encouraging environment that provides talented and entrepreneurial-minded people the freedom to innovate, whilst at the same time supporting them with the resources to quickly bring their innovations to market is lacking. Job cuts in India have further reduced opportunities for employment for the youth and there is a rising need of self-employment and entrepreneurship development, especially amongst the youth.

Disasters have been pivotal in building survival mechanisms in communities by exploring new opportunities and adapting to the changing environment. There is an opportunity in this crisis, for the post pandemic future environment will be different with an integration of both online and offline business opportunities especially for the youth. Entrepreneurs will have an important role to play in creating innovations and helping communities get through the economic crisis. One of the ways is to promote entrepreneurship among the 1st generation micro-business from the marginalised population in the country. If we use this productive demographic dividend, it is possible that India can achieve the UN's Sustainable Development Goals.

Who is a 1st Generation Micro-entrepreneur?

The first generation micro-entrepreneur is the last mile. S/he belongs to the bottom of the economic ladder, s/he is not highly educated, not well trained and most of them live in rural areas and urban poor communities. They lack acumen in business and are not able to move freely to access information as well as in getting financial support from any other source. Most of them are women and young people who want to get into the eco-system of building a sustainable livelihood, but are not able to get into it due to various reasons.

One of the major problems that first generation micro-entrepreneurs face is that they are not able to distinguish between business management and household management. They are not able to develop business as a business.

Most of these micro-entrepreneurs are not able to invest any fund as capital, neither do they have acumen in the technical issues, nor have access to any innovative solutions for the problems that dog their particular dreams.

The entrepreneur can be a solo person or a group of people starting a shop or a service to provide services or requirements in the community. Such entrepreneurs see starting a business or enterprise as an 'opportunity to increase their income' by expanding their services as well as skills. It is not right to deduce that entrepreneurs have no scope in lower income communities. Lack of higher education may be a deterrent for large and medium sized businesses but are capable of starting small entrepreneurial activities with their will power, hard work and a good business idea.

The Global Entrepreneurship Index study 2018 has found that the highest self-employment rates are seen in low income countries such as Zambia and Nigeria. This is because 'low-income economies lack the human capital and infrastructures needed to create high-quality jobs' (GEI, 2018), this study says. While such data provides a rationale and instils motivation to work for bettering this field, one needs to also consider that such magnanimous changes can take place only when there is space for subjective creativity and freedom.

Creating a Conducive Environment

The International Labour Organisation (ILO) has released a report that finds the number of young people around the world not in employment, education or training (NEET) (SDG target 8.6.1) has been increasing since 2017. The report states that this SDG target 'will be missed', underscoring the need to increase 'efforts to generate decent jobs for the next generation of workers'.The report titled, 'Global Employment Trends for Youth 2020: Technology and the Future of Jobs', highlights that the number of young people classified as NEET has risen from 259 million in 2016 to 267 million in 2019, and is expected to continue increasing to approximately 273 million in 2021. Young women are twice as likely as young men to face precarious employment situations, and two-thirds of those classified as NEET are young women.

In India too, we find that most people from low income category set up small businesses and work hard to come up in the entrepreneurial ladder. With wage employment becoming difficult, there is an increase in the number of youth aspiring to become entrepreneurs. Along with access to funding, ability to take risks are major obstacles for young entrepreneurs. Creating awareness and training young people about innovation and entrepreneurship is another critical step. Allowing them time and space for innovation, discussing the progress, encouraging and supporting them, thereby creating a culture where people learn from mistakes and do not forget to celebrate successes, will be an important process. The public and private sector each have an important role to play in creating ecosystems to encourage and support entrepreneurship development.

Policies to Support Entrepreneurs

The National Policy for Skill Development and Entrepreneurship 2015:

The primary objective of this policy is to meet the challenge of skilling at scale with speed, standard (quality) and sustainability. It aims to provide an umbrella framework to all skilling activities being carried out within the country, to align them to common standards and link skilling with demand centres in India.

In addition to laying down the objectives and expected outcomes, the policy also identifies the overall institutional framework which will act as a vehicle to reach the expected outcomes. Skills development is the shared responsibility of the key stakeholders, viz. Governments, the entire spectrum of the corporate sector, community-based organisations, those outstanding, highly qualified and dedicated individuals who have been working in the skilling and entrepreneurship space for many years, industry and trade organisations and other stakeholders. The policy links skills development to improved employability and productivity in paving the way forward for inclusive growth in the country. The skill strategy is complemented by specific efforts to promote entrepreneurship in order to create ample opportunities for the skilled workforce.

Pradhan Mantri MUDRA Yojana (PMMY)

Pradhan Mantri MUDRA Yojana (PMMY) is a scheme for providing loans up to Rs 10 lakh to the non-corporate, non-farm small/micro enterprises. MUDRA is an NBFC supporting development of micro enterprise sector in the country. MUDRA provides refinance support to Banks / MFIs / NBFCs for lending to micro units having loan requirement up to Rs 10 lakh. MUDRA provides refinance support to micro business under the Scheme of Pradhan Mantri MUDRA Yojana with three products to signify the stage of growth/development and funding needs of the beneficiary micro unit/entrepreneur and also provide a reference point for the next phase of graduation/ growth:

- Shishu: covering loans up to Rs 50,000.
- Kishor: covering loans above Rs 50,000 and up to Rs 5 lakh.
- Tarun : covering loans above Rs 5 lakh and up to Rs 10 lakh.

Atal Innovation Mission (AIM) including Self-Employment and Talent Utilisation (SETU)

This is the Government of India's endeavour to promote a culture of innovation and entrepreneurship. Its objective is to serve as a platform for promotion of world-class Innovation Hubs, Grand Challenges, Start-up businesses and other self-employment activities, particularly in technology-driven areas.

The Atal Innovation Mission has two core functions:

- Entrepreneurship Promotion through Self-Employment and Talent Utilisation, wherein innovators are supported and mentored to become successful entrepreneurs
- Innovation Promotion: to provide a platform where innovative ideas are generated

Role of Organisations in Entrepreneurship Development

To promote first generation rural and urban poor micro-entrepreneurs, there is a need to equip them with skills required to generate and incubate ideas, learn to make business plans, help them to do a market study and explore specific business opportunities and finally, to provide counselling to link with banks and start-up eco-systems in the country and abroad.

The process of awareness has to continue but there have been certain stories that make us believe that our goals are achievable and hence act as a source of inspiration.

Case Study I

Aniket is from an urban slum in Pune city, a youth who wanted to give a better life to his mother and family. He says: 'I am Aniket. I live with my family, father is having health problems as he is paralysed and mother is an Angandwadi sevika and she works hard. I took on the responsibility of my wife, father and mother trying to give them a better life. I had started working part time to get a fixed salary but that was not my dream to earn money. It was very difficult to work in a night job, but I am doing it as I have no other options left. I believe life always gives an opportunity and I have now.'

Aniket attended the entrepreneurship development programme, learnt various strategies of business, financial literacy, market survey and business scoping. This provided a platform to think about various business ideas and he decided to set up a Food Stall infront of an IT park. With mentoring support, he had a business plan, he applied for Mudra loan in SBI which was rejected and he dropped the idea due to lack of working capital. His mentor did not let him give up his idea and instead, helped him get a loan, and the necessary Udyog Aadhar and Shop Act license for his business venture 'Bun Maska', a snack centre he manages in the mornings and does a part-time job in the evenings. Aniket earns a monthly profit of Rs 8,000 and has the corporate employees as his regular customers!

Each entrepreneur needs to be nurtured and mentored so that s/he can make his or her presence felt in the entrepreneurship eco-system and contribute to inclusive socio-economic growth. The young entrepreneur needs hand-holding support in his or her journey to take the risk of starting a micro-business and to ensure that legalities and statutory obligations are adhered to and helps him/her move towards systematic planning, implementing and managing resources and team.

The negative role of the nation's largest bank in disbursing a national scheme for the poor is also to be noted.

Case Study II

Husenbi Shaikh dreamt of coming out from poverty, 'I am from a socio-economic backward class, I was a housewife, one person's income was not sufficient to manage a big family. Every time there would be a need to work on different options to get money but a time came when we wouldn't have money to support all family members. I always had a dream to have a clothes business. I started with buying sarees and selling it to my community for a small margin, I lacked the skills and knowledge to sell, pricing and budgeting', she says.

She joined the entrepreneurship development programme which helped develop her skills to convert her idea into a business opportunity which helped to uplift her current economic level. Handholding support helped her in making her business plan, develop marketing strategies, financial literacy and book keeping. She contacted her customers and advertised her tailoring skills which helped increase her business turnover. She also got the Udyog Aadhar registration and the shop act license and runs a saree shop, the 'Ekra Saree Center' where women frequently visit to buy sarees for festivals.

Areas of intervention include:

- Support to develop idea into business plan
- Learn from entrepreneur mentors
- Build networks
- Explore funding opportunities
- Access to legal assistance
- Meet up with successful entrepreneurs
- Mentoring by experts

Case Study III

Indutai identified a business that she would like to start during an entrepreneur incubation meeting. She decided to sell Papad as there was demand and then she added dry fish. She developed her business plan and the entrepreneurship development programme helped her understand the concept of self-employment, the legal documents and formalities required to start the business, the need of Bank account and the documentation and knowledge about Income and Loss statements.

'Indu Papad & Dry Fish' started catering to the needs in her community at the initial stage with a start-up capital of Rs 5,000. With the mentorship support she developed a marketing strategy and expanded her business by setting up a stall outside the community and simultaneously selling her products door to door and is earning a monthly income of Rs 20,000. She is saving now Rs 1000 per month in the bank for further expansions and she now needs funds for purchasing a Papad-making machine.

Challenges Faced

- The major challenge is to create awareness amongst potential entrepreneurs on the opportunities in store for them, especially for scale and expansion, so that they adhere to statutory and legal compliances. This requires mentorship and helping the entrepreneurs to understand best practices so that she/he climbs the entrepreneurial ladder.
- To convince family members to agree to setting up businesses over job is a very tough task for many of these entrepreneurs. The local educational institutions lag behind in promoting entrepreneurship.
- Colleges very often conduct idea competitions and even provide prizes but when it comes to providing the handholding support to those who have won prizes, the educational institutions do not even support those who have excellent business ideas.

- The main hurdle is how these budding entrepreneurs can get financial assistance for start-up capital. It is very often observed that these micro-entrepreneurs do not need huge funding. Their demand range from Rs 10,000 to Rs 100,000 which depends on the type of business one wants to do. For them, getting an initial seed funding support becomes a huge challenge, despite existing government promotional programmes like MUDRA schemes etc.

Conclusion

India as a nation is entrepreneurial and entrepreneurs play an important role in the economic growth and development of the economy. Entreprise in the informal sector is the backbone of the Indian economy, providing services and goods to the formal sector. The informal sector provides 81 per cent of all jobs in the country, says the 68th National Sample Survey. With India being the world's youngest country, there is an imperative need to focus on entrepreneurship development, especially amongst the bottom of the pyramid and grassroots population.

The organisations need to engage with youth in early education, provide mentorship support to translate ideas to business opportunities. They also need to take steps to help them towards entrepreneurial growth to mainstream the budding entrepreneurs and link with banks and start-up eco-systems in the country and abroad. The public and private sector must work towards creating an enabling environment towards entrepreneurship development, contributing to the United Nation›s Sustainable Development Goal No 8, i.e., to generate employment and economic growth and SDG No.10 to reduce inequalities by reaching out to people, who are mostly outside of development initiatives.

Education is a key to seeking good employment. However, there is a huge challenge in getting equal access to quality educational opportunities, thereby affecting knowledge and skill development of youth in India today. In alignment to this issue is the next chapter which highlights on issues of quality education in India.

Teachers and Society in Mumbai and Hong Kong

Comparative Perspectives for Quality Education

Shamim Suryavanshi

The destiny of India is now being shaped in her classrooms. This, we believe, is no more rhetoric. In a world based on science and technology, it is education that determines the level of prosperity, welfare and security of the people.

— **The Kothari Commission on Education (1964, p2.)**

Introduction

THE GOALS AND targets set out by the United Nations' 2030 Agenda for Sustainable Development (United Nations, 2015) are based on a vision of a world wherein, amongst other things, every country enjoys sustained, inclusive and sustainable economic growth and decent work for all. These countries are expected to be a part of the world in which consumption and production patterns and use of all-natural resources are sustainable.

Democracy, good governance and the rule of law and an enabling environment for sustainable development are expected to be cornerstones of societies. Sustained and inclusive economic growth, social development, environmental protection and the eradication of poverty and hunger are expected to be key focus of nations. The United Nation (UN) envisages a future where countries will be part of a world in which development and the application of technology are climate sensitive, respect biodiversity and are resilient. Nations are expected to be part of a world in which humanity lives in harmony with nature and in which wildlife and other living species are protected.

As a member state, India is already committed itself to this supremely ambitious and transformational vision of SDG 2030. In fact, as home to one-sixth of the world's population India is bound to play a leading role in determining the global success of the SDGs; especially with its astounding wealth of young population.

By 2021, the average age in India will be 29 years and it is set to become the world's youngest country with 64 per cent of its population in the working age group. With these kinds of statistics, the Indian youth (20-35 years) definitely has the potential to play a critical role in achieving the SDG 2030 agenda and thereby transforming India.

While much has already been written about it, a group which has equal and if not more potential are those in the youth sub-group of 13-19 years (GOI, 2017). This age group should be currently in secondary and higher secondary schools in the country. These are the young adults who will join the workforce around 2030 after having completed their formal education in the next few years. With every fifth person in India in the age group 10-19 (Henry, 2018), they are a force to reckon with. Investing in quality education of this segment of the population will further consolidate the nation's competitive advantage – its demographic dividend.

SDG 2030 and Education of Youth

Leaving no one behind, as envisaged by SDG 2030, requires improving human capital to make informed decisions in all walks of life; including those related to breaking out from the vicious cycle of intergenerational poverty. Investing in human development requires a heavy focus on education.

According to the UN's 'Quality Education: Why it Matters' document 2018, education enables upward socioeconomic mobility and is a key to escaping poverty. Education is also essential to achieving many other Sustainable Development Goals. It is believed that when people are able to get quality education they can break from the cycle of poverty. Education helps to reduce inequalities and to reach gender equality. One extra year of education, according to the same document, is associated with a reduction of the Gini coefficient by 1.4 percentage points. Education empowers people everywhere to live more healthy and sustainable lives. Education is also crucial to fostering tolerance between people and contributes to more peaceful societies. Education, thus, is considered central to the realisation of the 2030 Agenda for Sustainable Development.

Within the comprehensive 2030 UN and country Agenda for Sustainable Development, education is essentially articulated as a stand-alone goal SDG 4:

> *Ensure inclusive and equitable quality education and promote lifelong learning opportunities for all. Further, it is broken into seven outcome targets and three means of implementation*
>
> SDG 2030

Significantly, education in the 2030 Agenda for Sustainable Development is not restricted to SDG 4. It is mentioned in targets of the five other goals namely – Health and Well-being, Gender Equality, Decent Work and Economic Growth, Responsible Consumption & Production and Climate Change Mitigation. It is actually linked to almost all of the other SDGs in one way or another.

Interestingly, while the Millennium Development Goals focused on increasing student enrolment, the SDGs place particular emphasis on improving the quality of education and learning outcomes. The shift in the approach towards school education from input to outcome-based interventions has put the education sector on a new pedestal. While SDG 4 focuses on equity, inclusion and quality of education, it also aims to build and upgrade education facilities that are sensitive to the needs of children and persons with disabilities.

As a global education agenda, SDG 4 differs from both the education-related Millennium Development Goal (MDGs) and from Education for All (EFA).

While MDG was focused on children and access to primary education, EFA had a broader agenda aimed at 'meeting the basic learning needs of children, youth and adults'. As we know, the EFA commitment to ensure the right to basic education for all was not achieved by the deadline set for 2015. SDG 4 therefore pursues this unfinished education agenda, but also goes beyond, committing all countries to ensure *equal opportunity in access to quality learning opportunities* at all levels of education in a lifelong perspective.

Similarly, from the narrower MDG focus on access to, and completion of, primary education, EFA was concerned with access to quality basic education for all children, youth and adults. This included early childhood care and education, primary and secondary education, as well as youth and adult literacy and life skills. SDG 4 continues the EFA focus on quality basic education for all and broadens the agenda further to include concern for equitable access to post-basic education and training for youth and adults through equitable access to appropriate learning opportunities. What is also new to SDG 4 is the focus on the relevance of learning outcomes both for the world of work, as well as for citizenship in a global and interconnected world.

India and SDG of Educating its Youth

In the SDG India, Index and Dashboard 2019-20 developed by the National Institution for Transforming India, Government of India (GOI, 2019) it is acknowledged that India, with the world's 17 per cent of the population, holds the key to global SDG achievement. It further states that after having gained considerable success in enhancing the enrolment rates, the emphasis has moved towards improving the quality of education and outcomes. To this effect, the Government of India has intervened through its various Centrally Sponsored Schemes such as *Samagra, Sarva Shiksha Abhiyan* (SSA), *Rashtriya Madhyamik Shiksha Abhiyan* (RMSA) and Teacher's Education (TE), all aiming primarily at the following areas:

1. Free, equitable and quality primary and secondary education
2. Access to quality early childhood development, care and pre-primary education
3. Accessible, Affordable and Quality Higher Education
4. Skill Development and Economic Growth (Enhancing the employability of youth through skill development)
5. Conducive educational facilities that are child, disabled, and gender-sensitive.

The same report further clarifies that despite various government efforts and progress achieved in the education sector in different dimensions, several challenges need to be addressed. Various learning assessments point at the regional disparity in literacy and numeracy skills among children in primary schools. Data also suggest that a sizable proportion of children still need to meet the level of learning outcomes prescribed for their respective class. Tackling these challenges requires a focus on curriculum development, greater use of technology, active community participation, and last but not the least, training of teachers and eventually to Target 4.c of SDG 4:

> *By 2030, substantially increase the supply of qualified teachers, including through international cooperation for teacher training in developing countries, especially least developed countries and small island developing states.*
>
> SDG 2030

Increasing Supply of Qualified Teachers

The Incheon Declaration and SDG 4 Education Framework for Action (UNESCO, 2015) that was adopted in May 2015 at World Economic Forum by 169 countries (including India) committed that teachers and educators are empowered, adequately recruited, well-trained, professionally qualified, motivated and supported within well-resourced, efficient and effectively governed systems. While elaborating on Target 4.c of SDG 4, the declaration emphasised that teachers are the key to achieving all of the SDG 4 targets. Target 4c, it stated, requires urgent attention, because the equity gap in education is exacerbated by the shortage and uneven distribution of professionally trained teachers, especially in disadvantaged areas.

Towards this end, NITI Aayog has developed the SDG India Index, 2019-20 (a coordinating and monitoring progress and outcome mechanism for its States towards SDG 2030 in India) and included two indicators:

> *Indicator 1.* Proportion of trained teacher, by education level (elementary, secondary) with a national target value of 100. The justification of target value is offered as its alignment with SDG Global Target 4.c and the draft National Education Policy, 2019 (DNEP, 2019) of the Government of India which also aims to ensure that all students at all levels of school education are taught by passionate, motivated, highly qualified, professionally trained, and well equipped teachers.
>
> *Indicator 2.* Percentage of schools with Pupil Teacher ratio less than/equal to 30 with national target value 100. Here again, it clarifies that the target is aligned with SDG Global Target 4.c and also with DNEP 2019 that mandates a PTR under 30:1 at every school.

Any State in India with a 100 would be called Achiever since the State would have achieved all the targets outlined by the SDGs

Challenges Beyond Qualified Teacher Shortage

Despite of all these policy measures, teacher shortage continues to plague India's school education system. The NITI Aayog's School Education Quality Index (GOI, 2019) found that a large percentage of schools across States failed to meet the Right to Education's norms for pupil-teacher ratio – only 50 per cent of upper primary schools in 22 States fulfilled the norms. As per RMSA norms, teacher recruitment is based on Pupil Teacher Ratio (PTR) and the subject-specific requirements of the State.

Each school is mandated to have a minimum of five subject teachers specifically for the core subjects: English, Language, Mathematics, Science and Social Science.

The reference year data shows that only seven States and UTs have at least 50.0 per cent of their secondary schools meeting the prescribed core subject teacher norms. Delhi and Chandigarh have the highest percentages; 91.9 and 86.9 per cent respectively. In contrast, Puducherry is meeting the core subject teacher availability norms in only 2.7 per cent of their schools.

The average value for Union Territories (UT) and Small States is 53.5 and 37.4 per cent respectively.The average for Large States is relatively lower, at 28.0 per cent. Most States and UTs have reference year values similar to their base year. In contrast, Lakshadweep recorded a significant change, with a 26.0 percentage point increase from its base year value.

While India clearly needs more teachers, but simply increasing the number of teachers or meeting set norms will not improve learning outcomes and augment the quality of human capital. There are other ground realities also that one will have to take cognisance of.

As mentioned earlier, The Incheon Declaration and SDG 4-Education Framework for Action categorically state that increasing the supply of qualified teachers alone will not guarantee quality education. Even the apex body National University of Educational Planning and Administration (NUEPA, 2016) notes, 'the question that leaps at us is whether having more teachers would solve the learning crisis' (p.1). This is a cause of concern in the present policy context, especially in context of achievement of SDG 4 in India.

In case of India, quality of education has been a struggle for a long time. The last decade ending on a sour note for the Indian economy is attributed to the third-rate education system (Aiyar, 2019) and by association its teachers. The Indian education system is under tremendous pressure to adapt to the growing demand for meaningful education for all, and the teacher, the only visible functionary in an otherwise opaque system, is facing the brunt of the attack from all sides.

Public perception of school teachers is quite negative in many parts of the country (Kumar, 2019), to the extent that some experts believe it is leading to the teaching community feeling demotivated and demoralised. Others point out that while we bemoan the quality and dedication of the teaching community, the teacher in India is but a cog in a hierarchical administration, a powerless pawn in an intricate game of electoral politics (Ramachandran, Beteille, Linden, Tobias et al., 2017). This ambivalence,they say, is not new, but what is new is the hopelessness that permeates the discourse across the country. There are three possible reasons for this state of affairs:

The first reason could be the country's long history of bringing in regulatory changes or policy frameworks that are weak on research (Menon & Mathew, 2016, Kingdom 2007, Roy, 2019).

Secondly, most studies look at what is wrong with the education system or what are the challenges of the system. The voice of the classroom teacher is rarely heard in the policy making. For far too long educationists and researchers have only analysed and pointed out what is wrong and how terrible the system is. Negative images have continuously found their way not only into the media but also into power and influence.

Thirdly, classroom practice in contemporary India is largely seen to be determined by 'what is taught' and 'how it is taught' (Batra, 2017). In this framework, the teaching-learning process is viewed narrowly as the effective delivery of the school curriculum which in turn can only be measured through learning outcomes.

This chapter attempts to broaden the discourse on teachers in India, presenting a picture of the life of actual teachers in some of the schools in India. A unique feature of this chapter is that it is based on a cross national comparative study where in entry requirements, role and working conditions of Indian teachers were put alongside that of their counterparts in another Asian society. This is significant especially in today's era of globalisation where 'strategies for developing high quality teachers vary from one nation to another' (Mohanty, 2015, p. 33) and a comparative education research can fulfil the need to study some of these strategies.

A comparative study has the potential to act as a mirror for evaluation of our own reform policies and prevalent practices (Bereday, 1964).

Comparative studies are also known to help countries understand their own history better, locate their present systems more exactly in the current global scenario, and form more clear visions of their teacher development programmes bearing the future in sight. They acknowledge the cultural complexities across and within the borders of different countries and focus on making overall sense of teaching and learning relationships; an endeavour considered worthy of pursuit in today's Indian context according to many scholars like Sarangapani (2010) and Singh (2011).

It is hoped that this chapter will help towards achieving not only SDG 4 of being able to offer quality education to youth of India but also enable them to transform India and attain the other SDG 2030 goals as well.

Units of Comparison: Mumbai and Hong Kong

By virtue of the researcher's own personal and professional background, her home city of Mumbai was an obvious choice where India was concerned. Her search to identify 'another society' to compare with her own and a chance opportunity to live for extended periods pulled her towards the People's Republic of China. Her choice was supported by studies like the one by Costa P Guntupalli et al (2006) which observed that the rate at which India and China have been growing since the early 1990s, they have been a major topic of discussion around the world. Both the societies look towards each other for lessons. And that India and China occupy a special place in the imagination of the observers in the OECD and elsewhere (Herd and Dougherty, 2007).

However, India and China being two of the largest education systems in the world, it was necessary to spend more time for further narrowing down actual units of comparison in terms of their area of location. The predominant use of Chinese in Mainland China would have been a major barrier for this research. 'For comparative studies to thrive, the linguistic barrier remains the greatest to be overcome' (Halls in Bray, 2004, p. 248). This challenge was circumnavigated as best by narrowing the unit of comparison to the English-speaking Chinese city of Hong Kong. Interestingly, these two regions have very distinct similarities and differences.

Mumbai (formerly known as Bombay) and Hong Kong (officially the Hong Kong Special Administrative Region, HKSAR) are port cities and gateways to the world for their countries. They share a common British colonial past. While Mumbai is part of the sovereign nation India, Hong Kong has a very unique form of governance called 'one country, two systems'. The two regions are similar in some ways because of their economic background as they are considered as indicators of their countries' financial strength. The two cities are also similar in terms of their unique socio-cultural composition. In Mumbai, there exists linguistic diversity apart from cultural diversities which can be attributed to the conglomeration of people coming from different parts of the nation in quest for better life and prosperity. Hong Kong too is a home to many who have migrated from mainland China in addition to the expatriates from different parts of the world. Last but not the least, both these cities are fine examples representing the aspirations of the youth of their respective societies.

Other than the above contrast, this pair is also significant as Hong Kong is also listed as one of Asia's high performing education system – a tag that Mumbai and India at large are really striving hard to earn.

The methodology designed for the execution of this research used a threefold approach: documentary, empirical and comparative. Documentary analysis was carried out to develop a thorough understanding of the context, role and working conditions of the teachers catering to youth in secondary schools in Mumbai and Hong Kong.

The empirical approach taken in this study is qualitative in nature. Even though this limits the generalisability of the findings, the propositions can definitely be effectively utilised for other cases. Semi-structured interviews were used, as they are ideal for exploring issues and for gaining an in-depth understanding of a situation. Altogether 55 respondents were interviewed in between February 2017 to September 2017. These included secondary school teachers, local school heads, researchers and other key informants in the field of Education. A comparative approach was used in the analysis of the data gathered so as to enrich the outcome and understanding of both cases.

The quotations that appear in the comparison presented below are taken directly from the interview transcripts. Pseudonyms are used as is a common practice in qualitative research since ethical issues are especially critical in qualitative research (Johnson & Christensen, 2014). Last but not the least, international comparison has the potential of being abused, exaggerated, and used without appropriate contextual information. Care has been taken in this study to as far as possible to identify the researcher's prejudices and offer in-depth contextual reference.

Educational Philosophy in Mumbai

The educational philosophy in Mumbai can be traced to ancient India's Vedic system. The Gurukul system prevalent then fostered a bond between the Guru (the teacher) and the Shishya (the student) and established a teacher-centric system in which the pupil was subjected to a rigid discipline and was under certain obligations towards his teacher. The importance of education was well recognised in India: *Swadeshe pujyate raja, vidwan sarvatra pujyate – A king is honoured only in his own country, but one who is learned is honoured throughout the world.* The ultimate aim of education in ancient India was not knowledge, as preparation for life in this world or for life beyond, but for complete realisation of self.

This philosophy of education has evolved over time. Cheney, Ruzzi & Muralidharan (2005) in their *India Education Profile* describe the Indian education system as elitist where the traditional Hindu education was tailored to the needs of Brahmin boys who were taught to read and write by a Brahmin teacher. Under British rule from the 1700s until 1947, India's education policies reinforced the pre-existing elitist tendencies, tying entrance and advancement in government service to academic education. Colonial rule contributed to the legacy of an education system geared to preserving the position of the more privileged classes.

Education in India thus began to serve as a 'gatekeeper' of caste and class, permitting an avenue of upward mobility only to those with resources.

This has further aggravated in today's context. Avijit Pathak, a professor of Sociology at Jawaharlal Nehru University in his widely popular article on social media, *A Sick Society That Manufactures Failures – the True Face of Education in India* (Pathak, 2018), lamented the fact that today young minds in India are product of an 'oppressive reality characterised by a faulty pattern of education, parental ambitions and the aggression of hyper-competitiveness resulting from the increasing gap between the number of aspirants and availability of opportunities in an over-populated and uneven society'.

Educational Philosophy in Hong Kong

Confucianism not only shapes the social, ethical and political aspect of the Chinese culture in Hong Kong (Grace, Huang, & Gove, 2012) but also has a significant influence on education. In Confucian Heritage Culture (CHC), the aim of education is not the pursuit of knowledge for knowledge's sake, but the development of the character of the learner. Thus, the locals in Hong Kong lay high emphasis on education. Right unto the present day, one can see the influence of Confucian values in the Chinese attitude to knowledge, education and achievement (Rao & Chan, 2010). The concept that all children can do well if they try hard enough is a deeply held belief.

Major changes in educational goals can be traced back to late 1970s and the 1980s. As a result of manufacturing shifting its base from Hong Kong to Shenzhen, Hong Kong began to redevelop its economic base. From a manufacturing hub, it changed into a finance center, services, tourism and so on. This, the policy makers realised, required higher education levels. The rate of access to higher education, according to one respondent was raised from 5 per cent to 18 per cent in the 80s and 90s.

In addition to old universities like the University of Hong Kong and Chinese University of Hong Kong, new universities like City University of Hong Kong, Poly University of Hong Kong and The Hong Kong Baptist University were set up. The prevailing conditions back then also led to rise of the middle class in Hong Kong. People started sending their children overseas for schooling. There was a 'brain drain'. Improving quality of education was part of the way of keeping people in Hong Kong happy and keeping the people in Hong Kong, resulting in post 1982, six years of compulsory education

Today, the educational achievement of children in Hong Kong is visible and measurable. It is clearly defined by one's test performance, school entered and degree received.

> *Schools do not follow to the letter what the curriculum development institute in the government would like them to do. They will follow where possible. The bottom line in the school's reputation is exam success!*
>
> Charles Samson
> Teacher Educator, Hong Kong

Thus, earning higher academic grades, attending high ranking schools, and receiving higher degrees are still believed to be indisputable routes to success in the Chinese society of Hong Kong.

School education in Mumbai

Historically, school education in the city of Mumbai has been delivered either through;

- government schools, which are wholly publicly funded and managed, or
- private aided schools, which are managed privately but partially funded by government, or
- private unaided schools, which are wholly privately funded and managed.

Students can choose to study in English or the State language, Marathi, or the national language, Hindi. Additionally, there are schools offering education in other Indian languages in certain locations with a sizable population from other States. The Maharashtra State Board of Secondary and Higher Secondary Education (MSBSHSE) conducts public examinations at the end of Classes 10 and 12. At the end of Classes 10, students either take up general graduation (i.e. Bachelor in Art, Bachelor in Science, Bachelor in Commerce and other newer undergraduate programmes) or enrol in professional courses (i.e. engineering, medicine etc). Twelfth grade is normally a requirement for vocational courses and to take up blue collared jobs.

The above structure and examinations is followed by the schools affiliated to the above mentioned MSBSHSE board; more popularly known as 'State' Board.

Although the above kinds of schools continue to be in a majority, the city is now witnessing a rapid change in landscape of school education. Firstly, there is a steady growth in the number of private schools in the city, and the increase has been particularly high in schools with English as the medium of instruction (EMI) (Sujatha & Rani in Bhorkar, 2017).

Secondly, there is a change in affiliation from State board to national boards. While until few years ago most of the schools in Mumbai were affiliated to the State board and there were few which were affiliated to Indian Council of Secondary Education (ICSE) or Central Board of Secondary Education (CBSE). *Today, more and more existing schools are now converting from State boards to ICSE or CBSE board (Borwankar, 2018).* The newer ones prefer to opt for these national boards rather than the State board.

Another interesting trend observed by this researcher is the rise in 'international schools'. Since early 2000s there is a slow but quite steady rise in number of schools affiliated to internationally recognised International General Certificate in Secondary Education (IGCSE) and International Baccalaureate (IB) board.

Observations shared by the respondents in this study were supported by recent media reports such as '*IB and Cambridge-affiliated schools are leaping in popularity*' (Borwankar, 2018). the report quotes the principal of a leading school in Mumbai as explaining:

> *By the end of the 1990s, parents began feeling the pressure of Indian boards, which were more focused on rote learning. Many NRIs* [Non Resident Indians] *were moving back to the country and were looking for international curriculum with local values. That's when the need for international education came in.*
>
> Principal, International School
> Mumbai (Borwaskar, 2018)

The surge of international schools has even led to the Secretary, School Education Department declaring that today boards from outside the country are so popular that even the

State wants to be able to provide similar high-quality education (Borwankar, 2018).

Thus, one can conclude that school education in Mumbai is in a flux in terms of medium of instruction, funding as well as affiliation to different boards. That apart there are subtle but significant changes within classrooms as well. While in Mumbai the birth rate has decreased in the past decade and it is considered as the main reason for decreasing enrolments in the primary section; the number of enrolment in secondary section has increased. Secondary enrolment in the State of Maharashtra which includes Mumbai has increased with a jump of 18 per cent in 2017-2018 from that in 2012-2013.

School Education in Hong Kong

Schooling in Hong Kong used to be entirely the domain of philanthropy, and it was only when the economy gathered strength in the 1960s that the government began to subsidise education. Today, there are three main types of local schools – government schools which are operated by the government; aided schools which are fully sub vented by the government but run by voluntary bodies; and private schools, some of which receive financial assistance from the government.

Government and aided schools deliver a curriculum recommended by the government. They offer free primary and secondary education. A striking feature of Hong Kong local schools is their unofficial division into three 'bands' wherein the Band 1 schools are most sought schools. Students who perform best at primary level are allotted these band one schools. The schools belonging to the other bands can upgrade depending on their students' performance at primary level.

Interestingly, most band one schools are also the ones with English as medium of instruction. This is in line with the official language policy as described on the Education Bureau (EDB) website. The government has been promoting the use of the mother tongue, Chinese, as the principal medium of instruction (MOI) for local schools. But as both Chinese and English are the official languages in Hong Kong, the government of Hong Kong invests heavily in training students to be biliterate (Chinese and English) and trilingual (Cantonese, Putonghua and English). However, there seems to be a duality where language as medium of instruction is concerned. One teacher said, 'only really few...only really few truly use English as medium of instruction. The scenario of schools with respect to medium of instruction was summarised by a teacher of Indian origin in the following words:

> *Here, dynamics are completely different... different districts have different kind of students and children can get along without using English for the rest of their lives.*
>
> Smriti Sharma
>
> Secondary School Teacher, Hong Kong

This diversity within schools was said to be 'making people crazy'. Apart from differences in cultural background, one teacher educator highlighted the presence of children with different abilities wherein in the same class 'you will have students with gifted abilities, normal students, not so normal students, students with special educational needs – may be physical or mental'. Irrespective of the kind of school they are, all local schools uniformly follow the new academic structure (NAS) that has been implemented since September 2009. All students undergo six years of secondary education (i.e. three years of junior secondary and three years of senior secondary education). On completion of Secondary six, students take one public examination – the Hong Kong Diploma of Secondary Education Examination (HKDSE), which has replaced the former Hong Kong Certificate of Education Examination and Hong Kong Advanced Level Examination.

Besides the above described local schools, there are small but steady number of international schools offering non-local curricula mainly to children of overseas families living in Hong Kong and coming to Hong Kong for work or investment. Students studying in various international schools go on to appear in examinations as prescribed by their schools.

Requirement for Secondary School Teachers in Mumbai

All the teachers interviewed for this research confirmed that a Bachelor of Education (B Ed) with a Bachelor's degree in any school subject is the minimum requirement for teaching in a secondary school in Mumbai. This is a mandatory requirement for seeking a job in a secondary school. However, respondents offered that while this was followed by all government aided schools; there could be private secondary schools in the city that have hired untrained teachers in lieu of lesser salaries.

That apart, for a person to be eligible for appointment as a teacher for class I- VIII in any of the schools referred to in Clause (n) of section 2 of the RTE Act is that he/she should pass the Teacher Eligibility Test (TET) which will be conducted by the appropriate State government in accordance with the Guidelines framed by the NCTE. The rationale for including the TET as a minimum qualification for a person to be eligible for appointment as a teacher is as under:

- It would bring national standards and benchmark of teacher quality in the recruitment process;
- It would induce teacher education institutions and

students from these institutions to further improve their performance standards;

- It would send a positive signal to all stakeholders that the government lays special emphasis on teacher quality.

Requirement for Secondary School Teachers in Hong Kong

Graduates holding the following qualifications are qualified to become teachers in Hong Kong:

- A bachelor degree in education (i.e. BEd programme); or
- An undergraduate degree in programmes other than education plus a Postgraduate Diploma in Education (PGDE).

Furthermore, any person who wishes to teach in a school in Hong Kong must be registered under the Education Ordinance as either a registered teacher or a permitted teacher. Registered teachers are persons who possess the approved teacher qualifications laid down in the Education Ordinance, whereas permitted teachers are in possession of academic qualifications only. Permitted teachers are given a permit to teach specified subject(s) in specified schools. Teacher registration is supposedly meant to ensure the professional standards of teaching.

Moreover, all English and Putonghua teachers holding a permanent post in a public-sector school or a local private primary/secondary day school offering full curriculum should meet the Language Proficiency Requirement (LPR) of the relevant language(s).

Historically, Hong Kong has had untrained teachers recruited by schools. From the 2004/05 school year, all graduates of pre-service primary and secondary teacher education programmes are required to be degree holders. That apart, in-service teachers are mandated to fulfil Continuous Professional Development (CPD) requirements as stipulated by the Education Bureau (EDB).

Profile of Secondary School Teachers in Mumbai

All teachers who were interviewed were of Indian origin including the ones who taught in schools affiliated to international boards. The teachers interviewed in this study were graduates from the one-year Bachelor of Education programme from the aided teacher education colleges affiliated to University of Mumbai. The earliest that a teacher had passed out was from the batch of the academic year 1986-1987. The most recent one was from the last cohort of the one year pre-service teacher education programme in Mumbai i.e. 2014-2015 batch. Interestingly, quite a few of these teachers had taught in more than one school during their teaching career. Data analysis indicates that 25 per cent in this sample of secondary school teachers in Mumbai had taught in more than one kind of schools affiliated to different boards mentioned in the section of school education in Mumbai. This meant that they had taught different syllabi over the course of their careers. There was at least one teacher who had taught over three boards. At the time of the interviews, most teachers aimed to teach in international schools with IGCSE board.

During the semi-structured interviews, some teachers shared that they had tutored school going children before acquiring formal teaching qualification and securing job in schools. Teaching had been only career for all but one teacher. A senior male teacher said, getting into teaching 'was more of a conscious decision' in the middle of his adult life:

11 years in advertising and market research... and then my heart dragged me into teaching.

Rajiv Rai
Secondary School Teacher, Mumbai

The interviewed teachers clarified that teaching may not be the first choice of career for most of them. Some pick up the job as a half-day profession. A teacher's job seemed to be taken up because it lets a woman manage home and work-life.

Profile of Secondary School Teachers in Hong Kong

In terms of ethnicity, five out of the 18 secondary school teachers interviewed and a total of eight out of the overall 22 school staff interviewed for this research in Hong Kong are of non-Chinese background. All of these teachers were qualified teachers with a wide variety of first teacher training programmes:

- Double degree
- Post Graduate Diploma in Education (Full time)
- Post Graduate Diploma in Education (Part time)
- Part time day release course and
- Post Graduate Certificate course

Beside these, there were teachers working in Hong Kong schools who had done their Double degree from mainland Chinese universities as well as a BA in Education from UK. All these teachers co-exist in Hong Kong schools. That apart, there are Native English Teachers (NET) who are mostly foreign nationals who are native English speakers.

One respondent brought to fore what she claimed was a 'special characteristic' of teachers in Hong Kong.

> *For outside this group nice, very friendly. They are very conservative. They don't know collaborative work. They prefer to work by themselves.*
>
> Selina Zhao
> Secondary School Teacher, Hong Kong

Another teacher described this group as 'traditional teachers', irrespective of the kind of schools they taught in.

Role of a Secondary School Teacher in Mumbai

Traditionally, a teacher in India has had to function as an agent of social change. Education system vests him/ her central role as a teacher of children. This was evident from the responses of the teachers interviewed for this research.

> *We are shouldering* [responsibilities] *which* [are] *not part of our teacher training.*
>
> Heena Soman
> Secondary School Teacher, Mumbai

Besides teaching and non-teaching duties, the teachers teaching in secondary schools mentioned that they believed guiding and mentoring their students is one of their major roles. They seemed to have assumed the responsibility of counselling their students at their own level.

Few teachers like Rajiv segregated his role as formal and informal. Teacher Rajiv explained that his formal role comprised of preparing students for IGCSE while his informal role was to sensitise them to other's feelings and being responsible towards environment. *What did emerge was that for most teachers in Mumbai, the role of the teacher was not limited to subject teacher but extended to being a guide or a mentor.* They perceived their role to be more than being mere transmitters of knowledge. They saw being a guide, mentor or counsellor as a part of their duty as a teacher.

Role of a Secondary School Teacher in Hong Kong

Amongst the secondary school teachers in Hong Kong, almost all local Chinese teachers went ahead to say that their role went beyond the teaching of subjects. They considered themselves as role models for their students. Teachers believed that no matter what subject they teach, a teacher will 'always think about the students' first. Most local Chinese teachers opined that a teacher should have 'heart to teach'. They cautioned that if the teachers treated teaching profession as a job, they will not go beyond the call of their duty, for example, wait for the students after work or prepare for their students. Another example of reaching out to students as part of her role was shared by teacher Victor Hu who said:

> *I also need to help one SEN [Special Education Needs] student from form two because he is suffering from dyslexia and I need to help him develop the habit of revising at home.*
>
> Victor Hu
> Secondary School Teacher, Hong Kong

This teaching philosophy was once again attributed as a sign of Confucius Heritage Culture. As Prof Samson, a non-Chinese teacher educator who has spent many decades in mainland China and Hong Kong, pointed out – that he found the Chinese culture very caring towards its young people. It is very caring about the future of young people. On the other hand, one teacher of Indian origin explained that discipline in

Hong Kong meant normally there is no discipline problem. Students sit quietly and listen to the teacher whether they understand or not.

This classroom scenario is slowly undergoing change. The government has begun to lay more emphasis on learner-centered approaches wherein local school teachers are also expected to conduct activity-based lessons. The threshold where a teacher in Hong Kong stands was described as:

> *I have this split personality! So, you can say 'learn through play'. But next sentence you have to say* [to your students] *is – if you don't pass in your paper you are scr*wed for your whole life.*
>
> Min Min,
> Secondary School Teacher, Hong Kong

Working Conditions of Teachers in Mumbai

The teachers interviewed for this research tried accomplishing the above perceived roles within their scheduled six-hour working day. Some lamented that apart from their teaching duties, teachers have to do other peripheral tasks which used up their day. One teacher noted how the focus of teachers at times is not on teaching but on keeping ready the paper work needed by the education department and its official requirements of submission of various documents. This apart, teachers seem to be stressed with that particular school climate where it was revealed that when a child spoke wrong English, as an English teacher, she would be 'pulled up'. Another example was:

> *If I don't give an activity* [in the class], *I don't think I can get away.*
>
> Zohra Kadri
> Secondary School Teacher, Mumbai

Working in newly started international schools also seemed to cause anxiety in teachers where teachers shared that they were 'scared' as they had no formal training in teaching in such schools. This is the case even with teachers who are very senior and have acquired their BEd degree from one of the reputed colleges of education in Mumbai. More recently-qualified teachers had similar worry. Heena who teaches in two different sections affiliated to different boards (SSC and IGCSE) in the same school shared:

> *SSC – I know my matter... IGCSE– I have to read up my matter. I have to have an activity. Everything has to be spic and span.*
>
> Heena Soman
> Secondary School Teacher, Mumbai

These teachers felt overwhelmed by the 'newer' demands on teachers in current times and reported feeling stressed due to their observation that there were more and more new recruits and 'old teachers are being pulled down'. Factors like handling students which, they said 'comes from experience', did not seem to bother these teachers. But what did worry them more was use of technology in education. Fear or inability to keep pace with technology was one factor that contributed to stress in teachers across all kinds of schools. Along with it was the worry regarding judicious use of the same.

> *Nowadays all are getting impressed with all foreign things... educom, smart class...but technology is misused.*
>
> Mini Gupta
> Secondary School Teacher, Mumbai

Despite this worry, almost all teachers unanimously wanted to update themselves with technological advances in education and made sure to recommend this aspect for strengthening teacher education in Indian universities.

Working Conditions of Teachers in Hong Kong

Most teachers preferred to meet this researcher for the semi-structured interviews on weekends or late evenings. They explained that during the day they were very busy. One teacher who met at 9 pm in the evening for the interview explained that teachers in Hong Kong are 'very very busy'. Their regular working hours are 7am to 6 pm. Teachers justified that the long working hours were in commensuration of the 'high' salary. Teachers felt they only 'worked, worked and worked'. The level of job-related stress was described as:

> *Teaching is a very demanding job... full of tension... I know of some teachers* [who] *cannot go to sleep well in night...tomorrow double lesson...six lesson...they did* [can] *not fall asleep.*
>
> Selina Zhao
> Secondary School Teacher, Hong Kong

One senior teacher said that in Hong Kong, teachers felt very very lucky to retire. The pressure that the teachers felt can be understood from the fact that most leading newspapers have education pages that deal on a daily basis with policy debates as well as disputes in schools. Principals and teachers are supposed to be facing a daily struggle to balance administrative accountability, client accountability and professional accountability. In such a scenario with:

> *Old Confucian values [are] dwindling. Students find no purpose. Teachers are in a position where they may be told 'your fault'. So, s/he thinks, 'will I be blamed'. Head master may not stand by the*

> *teacher. This was observed in all kinds of schools–government as well as private.*
>
> Chelsea Chen
> Secondary School Teacher, Hong Kong

While the above were local school teachers, teachers even in international schools had similar things to say and described their schedules to be 'fanatic'. However, the resilience of these teachers was also evident from the remark:

> *We say the term is bad. Then we laugh and say it is pretty much the same all the time.*
>
> Urvashi Goyal
> Secondary School Teacher, Hong Kong

These findings could be further substantiated by an article by Sweeting (2008) where the author cites Lo (2004) – that heavy work load and stress had led to several teachers committing suicide and alarming statistics about depression and anxiety disorders amongst teachers. According to the polls then, 'about a third of the teaching forces were seriously considering leaving the profession' (Law and Tong in Sweeting 2008, p 61).

Comparison and Implications for Quality Education in India

As we look at each of the dimensions of comparison, we can see from the Hong Kong experience,valuable lessons unfolding before us that can aid apex bodies in India that are working in the area of youth and SDG 2030.

At the outset, the juxtaposition of the educational philosophy in both – the Chinese city of Hong Kong and

Indian city of Mumbai – shows distinct similarity. Traditionally, education in both these societies was meant for complete realisation of self and development of character of the learner. In today's time, both Mumbai and Hong Kong are fast becoming part of the global rat race where academic success equals to quality education. More often than not, critics of the Indian education system forget the larger aims of education and judge it in terms of simply learning outcomes – that is the scores in the international OECD's Programme for International Student Assessment (PISA) or in the locally conducted Annual Status of Education Report (ASER).

If the young adults are to be inspired to play a role in nation building, they will need to be provided an education that is more than just their ability to read or their proficiency in solving mathematical problems. While education should definitely prepare them for the world of work, it should also engage them in community building. If education is truly-affirming, it must awaken the minds of the youth, touch their deeper level of consciousness, and give them the psychic/spiritual strength to deal with crisis such as that of Covid-19 (Pathak, 2020). The core question – what is quality education– should thus guide in all decision-making and policy making and implementation.

Next, one can note that Hong Kong has a uniform local education system; Mumbai has a blend of schools belonging to four Indian educational boards along with small but fast-growing international boards IGCSE. This unique *potpourri* of education systems along with the dynamics of public and private schools creates a complex system to navigate for the local teachers who are all basically given the same pre-service education leading to a single qualification i.e. the Bachelors in Education. Constantly upgrading the pre-service teacher education programmes is one sure way to cope up with the changing landscape of school education. However, the other more effective and sustainable solution is in-service teacher education that finds its due place as indicator 4.c.7 in SDG 2030 in UNESCO's *Unpacking Sustainable Development Goal 4, Education 2030 Guide:*

> *Percentage of teachers who received in-service training in the last 12 months by type of training*
>
> Education 2030 Guide. UNESCO, 2017.

Yet another reality the comparison highlights is: teaching has been reduced to the least preferred career choice. This is not the case just in Mumbai but was also reported to be the same in Hong Kong. In fact, globally, most societies are struggling with the same bitter reality. Here it might be worthwhile to look at multiple pathways to teacher education. It will not only increase the number of qualified teachers, but also enable mature but passionate individuals to join the field. The DNEP 2019 does propose four-year integrated programme and other separate programmes for deserving graduates but its recommendations are to be adopted as policies. At this critical juncture, societies like Hong Kong with a long tradition of different routes for teacher preparation could further aid in achieving target 4c of SDG 4.

The comparison also reveals another feature of the existing teaching force in India. Despite the prevalent negative public image, teachers in Mumbai just like their counterparts in Hong Kong, perceive their roles to be beyond subject teaching.

They assume the role of a guide and counsellor to their students. In the midst of umpteen non-academic and administrative duties they make sure to reach out to their students. This vital attribute should be acknowledged as the teachers' contribution in educating youth who would then engage in nation building. The total size of the secondary school teacher workforce in India is 0.95 million., of which 0.42 million are employed in government schools and 0.49 million in private schools, the latter being spilt almost equally between aided and unaided schools (Ramchandran, Beteille, Linden, Dey et.al. 2017*). If this huge resource is engaged and teachers are made aware of SDG 2030, their existing self-assumed roles as mentors for the young adults in their care, can expedite manifolds India's efforts in reaching its SDG 2030.*

While we look at expanding roles of the existing teachers in improving the quality of education and thereby achieving not only SDG 4 but overall goals of SDG 2030, one cannot ignore the stress that teachers as a group undergo. Continuous reforms, changes in teaching learning techniques, teaching in different boards, parental expectations has created tremendous pressure in both Mumbai and Hong Kong. In the present scenario of the pandemic, teachers across the boards in India are facing unforeseen challenge of conducting all their teaching learning online. Just as respondents to this study shared their struggle with technology, newspaper reports, Whatsapp messages, Face book posts – all are inundated with how difficult this sudden change has been for teachers and the toll that it is taking on their mental and physical well-being (*The Hindu*, 2020). If Mumbai and India does not take a cue from Hong Kong, we too soon will have teachers who will be waiting to retire. If teachers are to deliver quality education for our youth, their well-being needs to be safe guarded. Indicator

4.c.7. in SDG 2030 should serve as an important reminder for the same –

> *Teacher attrition rate by education level*
>
> Unpacking Sustainable Development Goal 4, Education 2030 Guide. UNESCO, 2017.

Conclusion

In the final analysis, the comparison brings us to realise that one cannot translate Target 4c of SDG 4 as simply increasing the number of qualified teachers. It will be critical to raise the status of teachers in society. There is ample research that says that teacher self-efficacy and self-belief are passed on to their students. Teachers who are today a centre point of all criticism, their uniqueness will have to be identified, recognised and suitably supported. Only then can they play their roles effectively in educating the Indian youth. Indian implementers will have to constantly remember that –

> *Teachers being fundamental condition for guaranteeing quality education; teachers and educators should be empowered, adequately recruited and remunerated, motivated, professionally qualified, and supported within well-resourced, efficient and effectively governed systems.*
>
> UNESCO, 2017

Crisis like Covid 19 should serve as a wake-up call, whereby a multipronged strategy is needed to be devised not just to manage the school closures but to build a resilient Indian education system in the long run (Choudhary, 2020).

The shift to online or distance learning during the pandemic should be seen first and foremost as an emergency response. *However, the crisis also provides an opportunity for the development of more flexible learning solutions that make better use of distance learning and digital solutions.*For this, along with the teachers, trainers and learners also need to be trained and supported to engage in distance and online learning. (Comyn, 2020). Rather than inundating teachers with all kinds of online resources, a thoughtful, well rounded and effective approach is the need of the hour. The aim should be to make teachers 'do work' but continue to provide education to young minds that will support their employability, productivity, health and well-being in decades to come, and ensure overall progress of India.

In the end, one can say that in a country where superstitions, social evils and unemployment enjoy a fairly dominant position in society, the place of education/ educators within the social structure is of utmost importance. India will have to find a balance as it juggles with the challenge of quantity, quality, and equity in education provision. In such a scenario, how India's school teachers are positioned and managed is critical to turning the system around. As India galvanises its youth towards attainment of SDG 2030, ensuring that the right kind of people are recruited into teaching, managed sensitively, and most importantly, are given the administrative and academic support required to meet the goal of quality education for all (Ramachandran, Beteille, Linden, Dey et.al, 2017) will be perhaps one of the key differentiators.

Only then can we be assured on the –

> *Quality and number of persons coming out of our schools and colleges on whom will depend our success in the great enterprise of national reconstruction, the principal objective of which is to raise the standard of living of our people.*
>
> Kothari Commission, 1964, p.2.

Gender Equality and Youth Development

With regard to SDG 5

Vibhuti Patel

Any serious shift towards more sustainable societies must include gender equality.

— Helen Clark

Introduction

THE SDGS EXPLICITLY acknowledge that gender – what a given society believes about the appropriate roles and activities of men and women, and the behaviours that result from these beliefs – can have a major impact on development, helping to promote it in some cases while seriously retarding it in others.

The Sustainable Development Goals (SDGs 2015-2030) are a derivative of the Millennium Development Goals (2000-2015), which spells out the following values: freedom, equity, equality, human rights, solidarity, peace, security, tolerance, respect for nature, and shared responsibility. They are a clarion call of 189 governments, on behalf of their citizens, to free our fellow men, women and children from the abject and dehumanising conditions of extreme poverty, to which more than a billion of them are currently subjected (Patel, V and Karne, M, 2007).

The SDGs are benchmarks of development progress, based on such fundamental values as freedom, equity and human rights and peace and security. SDGs can be achieved if all actors work together – heads of the nation states, civil society organisations, international financial institutions, global trade bodies and the UN system – and do their part. Poor countries have pledged to govern better and invest in their people through health care and education. Rich countries must stick to their pledge to support the poor countries through aid, debt relief, and fairer and just trade. Only if there is commitment on the part of the rich as well as poor countries to fulfil these promises, can all the SDGs be achieved and distributive justice, gender justice and social justice can be achieved.

Gender Concerns in SDGs

As per the World Economic Forum, India stands at a 114 amongst 142 countries in terms of Gender Gap Index. All goals are expected to mainstream SDG 5 that aims to achieve gender equality and empower all women and girls.[1]

All 17 SDGs and 169 Targets, are mandated a special focus on gender and challenges discrimination against women by addressing feminisation of poverty due to neo-liberal structural adjustment policies, focusing on school education, ensuring that more women become literate, guaranteeing more voice and representation in public policy and decision-making political participation, providing improved job prospects–

---

1 https://www.youthkiawaaz.com/2014/10/w-e-f-2014-gender-gap-index-report/, accessed on 20-1-2018

36 per cent Work Participation Rate for women, food and nutrition security, support to women farmers.[2]

One of the revelations of the goals of SDGs is that it falls short by not addressing issues of social reproductive work which leads to gender inequality. SDGs do not consider the account of unpaid labour/household work which is majorly performed by women and, therefore, they kind of fail to move towards the decent work agenda with gender inclusivity.

Historically, looking at the struggles of women's union and trade unions, the aim has been to widen their outlook with respect to formal and informal work conditions (Ruwanpura, 2019).

Indian Women and SDGs

SDG 5 (out of 17) is calling for an end to disparities between boys and girls at all levels of education. There is general agreement that education is vital to development and ensuring that girls as well as boys have full opportunities for schooling will help improve lives in India, especially in rural India, in countless ways.

It is important for the Indian Youth to be aware and pro-active about concerns of girls and women in the context of the fast-changing socio-economic and cultural scenario in the country. The mind-boggling challenges intertwined with survival struggles of women are as follows:

Child Sex Ratio

Boy/men outnumber girls/women in India, unlike in most other countries. As per Census 2011, Gender ratio of India is 943 females per 1000 males. In rural area, there are 949 females to 1000 men, while in urban area there are 929 females to

---

[2] http://www.un.org/sustainabledevelopment/gender-equality/, accessed on 20-1-2018

1000 males. Rural India has 21,813,264 more males and urban India has 13,872,275 more males than females. India's Sex Ratio has improved by just ten in term of numbers from 933 in 2001 to 943 in 2011. In rural and urban India, Sex ratio has improved by three and 29, respectively. In 1901, India had the highest sex ratio of 972 females per 1000 males.

As of 2020, India has more males than females in the 64-69 age group and there are 10 more males per 100 females in the 34-69 age group. Beyond the 25-29 years age group, the female to male ratio keeps improving.

According to the Civil Registration System Report 2016 released in 2019, India's sex ratio at birth fell from 908 in 2012 to 877 in 2016. Alarmed over the report, civil society activists fear that that the findings would reflect on India's child sex ratio in the 2021 census report.[3]

Among States, Kerala has the highest sex ratio of 1084 females to 1000 males and Haryana has the lowest sex ratio of 879 females per 1000 males. Among union territories, Pondicherry has highest sex ratio of 1037 and Daman and Diu has the lowest sex ratio of 618.[4]

As per Sample Registration System (SRS) survey, the number of females per 1000 males, declined to 896 in 2015-17 from 898 in 2014-16. The rural and urban divide is also showing a critical pattern when it comes to child sex ratio. The sex ratio in rural India declined in India from 902 in 2014-16 to 898 in 2015-2017. The sex ratio at birth ranges from 828 to 985 for rural areas of Haryana and Kerala, respectively.[5]

---

[3] (https://timesofindia.indiatimes.com/india/indias-child-sex-ratio-to-dip-further-in-2021-census-experts/articleshow/67836441.cms)

[4] http://statisticstimes.com/demographics/sex-ratio-of-india.php, accessed on 9th June,2020

[5] https://www.livemint.com/ accessed on 7th June 2020

Reduction of Gender Gap in Education

At an elementary level, the literacy gap among males and females has declined in all the States. But at the higher secondary level, the variation is quite high across States in gender parity index. It has happened because some States have achieved equality in male and female education levels. Many States have failed to encourage girls' education that led to high gender gap in those States. The large gap at higher secondary and senior secondary level is because all the efforts of the central government have remained concentrated to ensure access at elementary level education to all the students.

According to a study by the International Monetary Fund (IMF), the enrolment of Indian girls in higher education increased from 39 per cent to 46 per cent from 2007 to 2014, but work participation of women in India has declined from 34 per cent in 1999 to 27 per cent in 2014.[6]

Reproductive and Child Health

The MDG Report published by the Ministry of Statistics and Programme Implementation in November 2017 and the NFHS 4 All India Report released in January in 2018 on reproductive and child health, morbidity, mortality, fertility, family planning, nutrition revealed that, in 1992-93, the Under Five Mortality Rate (U5MR) at all-India level was 118.8, for Scheduled Castes it was 149.1 and for Scheduled Tribes, it was 135.2.

According to the target set under MDG 4, this should have been reduced by 2/3rd to become 40.4 (all India), 50.7 (SCs) and 56.0 (STs) respectively in the year 2015. This,

---

[6] http://www.indiaspend.com/cover-story/more-girls-studying-but-84-drop-out-after-graduation-16526, accessed on 20-1-2018

obviously, did not happen. But data from NFHS 4 shows that the U5MR, at all-India level is 49.7, for SCs 55.8 and for STs 57.2, respectively. The reduction in U5MR was maximum for SC population (93.3 points), followed by ST (78 points) and total population (69.1 points) in the time frame 1992-2015.[7]

According to a paper published in *The Lancet*, even as the under 5 mortality rate (U5 MR) in India has reduced by almost 50 per cent in the past two decades, the country is still losing at least a million children annually before they reach their fifth birthday. Of these, half a million children die within 28 days of being born (neonatal mortality) primarily due to lower respiratory tract infection, pre-term birth and diarrheal diseases. As per the global SDG target, NMR must be brought down to 12 per 1000 live births universally by 2030. India's current NMR remains around 23 per 1000 live births.[8]

Now, concerted efforts will have to be made to meet the targets of SDGs in reduction of U5MR and maternal mortality by improving overall health and nutritional standards of women and children, campaign against child marriage and effective health delivery system for girls and women.

Smart Cities must be Safe Cities

The Union Budget, 2017-18 gave priority to formation of 100 smart cities in terms of high allocation for physical infrastructure, IT based and cyber-technology-based governance. Smart

---

7 http://www.huffingtonpost.in/kumar-rajesh/the-scs-and-sts-still-have-the-highest-child-mortality-cases_a_23335275/, accessed on 20-1-2018

8 https://www.hindustantimes.com/india-news/india-losing-almost-a-million-under-5-children-annually-study/story-UpyB00QmJkopbmPzpJpDeM.html accessed on 13th June 2020

cities must be Safe cities. Town planners, policy makers and budget experts need to do gender budgeting to ensure women-friendly civic infrastructure–water, sanitation, health care, safe transport, public toilets, help lines, *skill development for crisis management* and, safety at work place.

While making budgets for social defence services, consideration must be given to safety of girls and women in schools and colleges, in terms of prevention of child sexual abuse through public education and counseling facilities, separate toilets for girls and boys in schools, legal literacy on the POCSO Act, 2012 and Prevention of Sexual Harassment Workplace Act, 2013 (Patel, 2015). Provision must be made to have special cells in the local police departments to take action against display of pornographic images, SMS messages, cyber crimes that victimise young girls at public places or in public transport – city buses, local trains, rickshaws and taxis.

There is need to integrate safety of women as a major concern in flagship centrally-sponsored infrastructure development schemes to ensure support services such as crèche, working women's hostels, schools, ICDS centers, all of which must converge to make an effective utilisation of infrastructure.

With the national government adopting constantly-changing methods to realise its promise of sustainable development, the very concept of development is undergoing dramatic change. Not only is india's youth, uneducated, untrained and unemployed, the global pandemic has added to their problems, resulting in job losses and starvation. At this juncture, it is important that one begins to question past and present policies and ask of government as well as civil society, whither progress for India's young women and men and what their future is likely to be.

With work divided in formal and informal sector, where the former has relatively more security than the latter, the concept of a 'safe city' seems only a dream. In the metropolitan cities like Mumbai, Delhi, we can see a huge gathering of the worst-affected among the people. Take the example of Dharavi in Mumbai. Majority of workers in the city are forced to live in the slums because of raging houses prices and rents, with diminishing work and lowering of the quality of life, and massive overcrowding. Looking at the pandemic condition, social distancing is practically impossible. The cities are not designed in a way which can cater the underprivileged and vulnerable section of the city. Women become more invisible as they are majorly employed in the low paid, unskilled labour force with barely any security.

Relevance of Skill Development for Crisis Effect of COVID-19 on Labour Participation of Women

In India, while all vulnerable populations have and will suffer a gender lens is warranted as women are ranked lowest in the hierarchy of caste, class, or religious stratification. Gender inequality in labour force participation, wages, and the burden of care, household work and sharing of resources needs to be substantially altered due to the crisis. The periodic labour force survey (PLFS), 2018-19, shows that 53 per cent of women's workforce is in self-employment. This can be further disaggregated into three subcategories – own account enterprises (OAE), employers and unpaid/contributing family workers. The first two categories capture women's entrepreneurial ventures best. Almost 31 per cent of all women workers are engaged as unpaid helpers in household enterprises and only 19 per cent run OAEs. These figures, coupled with micro-evidence from literature, show that the women OAEs remain trapped in low-scale, low-productive, low return ventures such as in rolling *bidis* and *agarbattis*, making pickles and papads, or mending clothes with a sewing machine. A substantial share (almost 70 per cent) of the women home-based manufacturing workers are engaged in low scale food processing, textiles, handicrafts, and handlooms (IWWAGE, 2020).

The post-COVID stimulus package focussed majorly on easing credit availability for the MSMEs through these schemes. Further, the emphasis of the announcements remains on easing loans and credit rather than providing access to markets, which becomes crucial in the post-lockdown scenario. It is not only the disruption in supply, but the slackening of overall demand within the economy, which can potentially lead to closures of many such small businesses, especially for women – who are anyway perceived as 'secondary earners' within a household. Increased burden of women's unpaid work due to the lockdown may also drive women to spend less time on businesses, which is also in-conducive for the needs of the business.

Self-employment only captures one half of women's work. According to the PLFS 2018-19, 47 per cent women are in wage employment. Of these, 22 per cent are in regular employment and 25 per cent work as casual labour. The impact of increasing wage employment on women's empowerment is well-established. MGNREGA attracts many women, with about 55 per cent of total person days of work created under this legislation accruing to women. This, by itself, is a positive example.

There are many ways in which livelihood opportunities can be created for informal women workers during the pandemic. Retrenched domestic workers can be skilled to become care workers, and home-based garment workers can address the ever-increasing demands of personal protective equipment and masks. ASHAs and Anganwadi workers, who are the most important public health outreach workers, should be acknowledged and compensated with adequate wages, economic benefits, and social protection. Following the principle of 'nothing for us, without us', women workers through their organisations need to be allowed to participate in both, the design and delivery of relief and recovery measures.[9]

In addition, MGNREGA wage need to be increased substantially, there cannot be a restriction on the number of days of work provided per household and it must be ensured that wages are paid weekly without delay. If all these, along with provisions such as creche facilities, shade and water are also provided adequately, will make the MGNREGA an attractive option for women. As much as 30 per cent reservation for women in NREGA work needs to be ensured as reverse migration for men in rural areas may lead to women being pushed out of worksites.[10]

Predicament of Women Farmers

Women farmers and cultivators are the backbone of agricultural production in India. Majority of agricultural labourers are women. With feminisation of agriculture, 71 per cent women workers are in agriculture and women form 39 per cent of total agricultural workers. Women today demand a 'women component plan' in the PRIs (Patel, 2007). *Permission of 100 per cent FDI in rural markets has affected women small and marginal farmers adversely*. Entry of the corporate sector into agrarian marketing has already made condition of farmers

---

[9] https://scroll.in/article/961181/covid-19-how-india-can-ensure-that-women-in-the-informal-sector-get-the-protection-they-deserve accessed on 17th June 2020.

[10] https://theleaflet.in/womens-employment-amidst-a-pandemic-what-are-we-missing/ accessed on 16th June 2020

precarious because of their monopsonistic control, where large number of poor sellers face handful of buyers. Desperate farmers are resorting to distress selling of their products to the agro-business houses. Several Indian States are facing severe drought resulting in agrarian unemployment. In this context, increase in budgetary allocation for MGNREGA, updation of skills and creation of support system of direct sell by producers to the customers through *Mahila Haats* at the block level in rural as well as urban areas are urgently required (Kelkar-Khambete, 2017).

Violence against Women and Girls

At the country level, most initiatives to address violence have been legislative. Although the legislation varies, it typically includes a combination of protective or restraining orders and penalties for offenders. *As with property rights, a formidable challenge is often the enforcement of existing laws.* Procedural barriers and traditional attitudes of law enforcement and judicial officials undermine the effectiveness of existing anti-violence laws as experienced in the #MeToo campaign against sexual harassment. Training programmes for judicial and law enforcement personnel often go a long way to change such attitudes.

Beyond training programmes, the establishment of female-staffed police stations has been effective in making them more accessible to women. For the women who have experienced violence, a range of medical, psychological, legal, educational, and state support services is necessary. To prevent violence, improving women's education levels and economic opportunities has been found to be a protective factor.

Need for psychological support and mental health services at the time of natural and social disasters must be given top priority as at the time of any crisis, girls and women are more prone to violence (Jaswal and Joseph, 2008). With the existing issue pertaining to Covid-19, there is a subsequent increase in the number of cases of domestic violence. With mandatory guidelines to stay at home and increasing economic insecurities, domestic violence has increased globally. Data from the National Commission for Women reports two times increase in gender-based violence with 116 cases on 23 March to 257 cases on 1 April 2020. The issue with the women is graver as their roles are as primary care givers. Living in close quarters and proximity to men 24×7 leads to increased violence and abuse. Non-equal relationships and added burden of the household chores puts women's health at greater risk at times of crisis. Refusing to adhere to the needs of the man might lead to extreme violence for the woman. Reporting cases of domestic violence is problematic in India as society refuses to accept domestic violence as violence. The situation becomes more intense during lockdown as the support system and resources fail to address the issue.[11]

The interventions to improve women's economic opportunities thus become even more important. To do that requires a massive media and public education campaign, which must be initiated by the students and youth (Dave, 2015).

National Mission for Empowerment of Women (NMEW)

Our youth need to play a crucial role in the NMEW. Violence against women has escalated many fold and youth need to be at the forefront of the battle to reduce such violence.

---

[11] https://idronline.org/the-link-between-lockdown-covid-19-and-domestic-violence/ https://thewire.in/women/covid-19-lockdown-domestic-violence accessed on 7th June 2020

While schemes to combat trafficking and empowering adolescent girls have received increased funds, the schemes meant for implementation of PCPNDT Act (to combat sex tests of foetus and related genocide), the Protection of Women from Domestic Violence Act have not received much allocation.

The corpus of Rs 3,000 crore under the Nirbhaya Fund has largely remained unutilised. The proposed scheme under the 'Nirbhaya Fund' envisages setting up of a National Emergency Response System with a control room under the overall control of the Ministry of Home Affairs, which will receive alerts from distressed women and take action on it.

On 8 March, 2016, the Union Budget 2015-16 had allocated Rs 653 for Scheme for Safety of Women in Public Road Transport, with an objective to ensure safety of women and girl child in public transport by monitoring location of public road transport vehicles to provide immediate assistance in minimum response time to victims in distress. Under the scheme for giving grants to States for setting up driving schools, preference is given to proposals for driving school for women.

Similarly, '***Beti Bachao, Beti Padhao***' (i.e. Save the girl child, Educate the girl child) scheme was announced with the goal of improving efficiency in delivery services for women. The aim of the scheme was to increase girl child enrollment in secondary school with a task to achieve 100 per cent re-enrollment of girls who have dropped out of school. According to the data rvealed for BBBP in the fiscal year 2016-2017, out of Rs 43 crore only Rs 5 crore was used. The report was published by the Parliamentary Standing Committee on Human Resource Development. As per further information, 'The amount of money spent on this scheme in the current fiscal year is also less than one-tenth of the Rs 59.37 crore spent on BBBP in the previous fiscal year. Against the Rs 14.28 crore provided in the budget, Rs 8.08 crore was released by the government and only Rs 5.31 crore was spent from January 2015 to March 2016 in Haryana. Similarly, out of Rs 6.36 crore released by the central government to the state government during 2014-16, only Rs 0.91 crore was utilised up to March 2016 in Punjab'.[12]

The ability of the government to draw up different schemes related to the girl child's education often shows the carelessness in understanding the social context of India. The practice of female infanticide and foeticide is prevalent. The birth of these practices stems from lack of employment opportunities for women with a skewed health system for women. Statistics proves that the unequal gender ratio leading to the skewed education system in India needs to be questioned.

Road and Rail Transport for Women

There has been continuous increase in women commuters as girls and women travel long distances for education as well as for work. Most of the working women in urban and rural areas travel in overcrowded buses and trains. In the transport sector, top priority needs to be given for women special buses, trains in all cities and stations equipped with functioning toilets. Young women of urban India have initiated a Right to Pee campaign.[13] For women street-vendors, seat-less buses and special luggage compartments in trains need to be provided.

---

[12] https://www.india.com/news/agencies/90-pc-of-beti-bachao-beti-padhao-funds-unutilised-par-panel-1948449/ accessed on 8th June 2020

[13] http://www.thehindu.com/news/cities/mumbai/women-demand-right-to-pee/article20547110.ece, accessed on 20-1-2018

Even though the governments have allocated funds for the safety of women, the data shows that several States have not utilised the Nirbhaya Fund. Along with home ministries, other ministries have also contributed to the Nirbhaya Fund with Rs 7,895 lakh to this kitty. The Women and Child Development ministry has also released Rs 1,619 lakh for the women police volunteer scheme, 'One Stop Crisis Centre scheme' and the 'universalisation of women helpline'. The data shows that the major chunk of all these allocations have remained unutilised.[14]

Domestic violence against women is the top gender-related crime, while there has been a marginal increase in rapes as well as overall crime in the country, according to data released by the National Crime Records Bureau (NCRB) for 2018. Women being trafficked were observed from the cities of Mumbai and Kolkata, according to the latest study by the NCRB, under Supreme court direction. The trend was apparent as early as in 2012 when the rate of crime against women leapt from 41.7 per cent to 55.2 per cent.

Water

The audit report of the *Comptroller and Auditor General* of India (CAG) 2018 on Accelerated Rural Water Supply (ARWS) has made a shocking revelation – that despite recurrent bouts of water-borne diseases across the country, all States are ignoring drinking water quality. Most of the State governments did not conducted water quality tests. Poor urban, rural and tribal women's major survival struggle revolves around safe drinking water. Allowing supply of safe

[14] http://164.100.24.220/loksabhaquestions/annex/172/AU1903.pdf accessed on 7th June 2020

drinking water by just private players has enhanced the hardship of common women.

The Marathwada region of Maharashtra present a very dark picture of water crisis in India. The water crisis in India is a gendered issue. As the person responsible for collecting water in both urban and rural region, the burden rests on women and drinking water is an issue that plagues impoverished women throughout the country. The increase in water crisis also results in increase of workload on women. Uma Aslekar, who works in water crisis management in Marathwada and Vidarbha regions of Maharashtra, points out that, 'water stress in the last five years has forced women to becomes the primary breadwinners in their families'.[15] Appears that women are becoming victims of double burden i.e. they have burden of the household duties and earning primary incomes.

Along with travelling long distances, the water crisis also create Sanitation issues for women, with the estimation that one in three women undergoes high risk of disease, shame, and harassment as they do not have a safe and clean toilet.

Budgetary allocation for Water Supply & Sanitation that affects women's lives greatly as consumers and unpaid and partially paid work does not mention facilities for women. This has perpetuated 'unproductive female workload of fetching water from long distance' distance', avers Indira Rajaram, who is an eminent professor in IIM, Bangalore and chair at the National Institute of Public Finance and Policy (NIPFP), Delhi. (2007). She point out that, 'water-sheds in the country need to be contoured on the Geographical Information

---

[15] https://www.livemint.com/Politics/5k07wKxfIQE6vMaDmi1ewM/Five-charts-that-show-how-women-suffer-the-most-from-water-s.html accessed on 8th June 2020

System (GIS) platform. Using space technology for mapping of aquifers, a five-year plan needs to be drawn up for creating sustainable water sources within reasonable reach of rural habitation' (Rajaram, 2007).

Energy Expenditure of Women

Reproductive work and domestic duties need major time and energy from women. In the rural and tribal areas, collection of fuel, fodder, water, looking after the livestock, kitchen gardening demand great deal of time and energy from women and girls. The 11th Plan document has acknowledged the fact, but in reality, nothing significant was done in terms of priority given to alternatives to bio-fuels that causes smoke-related illnesses, availability of safe drinking water; child care facilities and adequate public transport for women that would reduce their drudgery.

The 12th budget plan creates a very ambiguous position for women and one does not know if it will benefit or change the scenario for better in the coming years. One of the major schemes proposed during the annual budget plan was *Ujjawala Yojana* (Scheme for subsidised cooking gas cylinder to households*)*, which meant to change the lives of BPL women by providing free LPG connection to poor household. With the increase in number of connections it has still failed to address long term goal where the scheme allows only the first refill of a cylinder for free, and the consumer is expected to buy the next one at market price, while the subsidy is credited directly into her bank account. But the major issue here is that women are not able to buy the second cylinder at market price, so they switch back to the wooden *chullah (stove).* Another important issue here is the tax on sanitary napkins. It is proven that menstruation is one of the important reasons for girls dropping out of school and the government still refuses to cut on the taxes imposed on sanitary napkins. The recent budgets do not favour the issues of gender and is biased and poorly programmed and constructed.

Social Security for Women in Informal Sector

Unorganised Workers' Social Security Act, 2008 has hardly made any difference in the lives of millions of poor women in the unorganised sector due to non-implementation of the Act. Sexploitation and self-exploitation have become the norm in the informal labour markets. Condition of migrant workers is precarious and deplorable (Jha, M. and Kumar P, 2016). Ninety per cent of women are not getting maternity benefits. The design of Maternity Benefit Scheme needs to be critically examined urgently and specific details should be provided for its judicious implementation and concerned officers who are guilty of non-performance must be made accountable and punished.

The latest 2020 ILO data on the labour market impact of the Covid-19 pandemic reveals the devastating effect on workers in the informal economy and on hundreds of millions of enterprises worldwide.

Government needs to urgently guarantee reliable access to health care and housing for all. The Employees' State Insurance Scheme, a social health insurance programme for the formal sector working classes, can be universalised to cover informal workers too. Information on preventive and protective measures needs to be translated for non-literate women. It is also important to ensure that legal and policy gains made by women informal workers are not reversed. All kinds of employment, including home-based workers and domestic workers, need to be covered. But more critically, the design and delivery issues need to be addressed as well, specifically for women nformal sector workers.

Registering women as workers entitled to benefits like decent pay and welfare access would provide an opportunity for trade unions and women's organisations to rearticulate women's work and contributions. Their voices must be heard while framing solutions to Covid-19, but also to the crises of poverty, inequality, and unemployment.[16]

Elderly Women

Half-Way homes and Elderly Women's Homes are needed in every district. Pension Scheme for the old, disabled women is implemented only in 4 or 5 States such as Kerala, Gujarat, Andhra Pradesh and Tamil Nadu. Panchayati Raj Institutions (PRIs) need to be motivated to provide an extensive database on 60+ women in their areas. For widows or elderly women, creation of community-based half way homes, fully equipped with counseling facilities, temporary shelter, get-together, drop-in centres, skill building/ upgradation and technical training, is far more humane way of providing social security rather than doling out money that gets snatched from them by family bullies or wicked relatives (Siva Raju, 2011). Youth can create facilitation centers in the community for protection of rights of senior citizens.

Mahatma Gandhi National Rural Employment Guarantee Scheme (MGNREGS)

MGNREGA is the Act that supports the flagship scheme to address unemployment problem in India for the rural poor.

---

[16] https://scroll.in/article/961181/covid-19-how-india-can-ensure-that-women-in-the-informal-sector-get-the-protection-they-deserve accessed on 17th June 2020

In 2017, women accounted for 56 per cent of the MGNREGA workers,[17] but they are assigned the most unskilled and low-paying tasks. Trade unions and women's rights organisations from MP, Punjab and Bihar have repeatedly conveyed that even under MNREGA, pay disparities are reported by women. Development economists and feminists have demanded that NREGS be turned into an Earn-While-You-Learn plan through Public Private Partnership (PPP) model that creates an on-the-job training module aimed at upgradation of skills of women working at the sites.

The National Skill Development Mission (NSDM) plans to add one crore workers to the non-agricultural sector through skill training. It must reserve for women 30 per cent of the total employment opportunities thus created. Human capital formation is a must for value-addition among women employed in NREGS. The Central Employment Guarantee Council, that is supposed to be an independent watchdog for NREGS, needs to be made accountable for gender sensitive implementation of NREGS.

SHGs

Provision of loans at 4 per cent interest rate is implemented only in AP Federations of SHGs for women. No one is pressurising other State governments also to provide loans at differential rates of interest. There is an urgent need for a paradigm shift from micro-credit to livelihood finance, comprising a comprehensive package of support services including insurance for life, health, crops and livestock: infrastructure finance for roads, power, market, telecom etc. and investment in human

---

[17] https://thewire.in/176106/mgnrega-minimum-wages-women/ accessed on 20-1-2018
https://thewire.in/176106/mgnrega-minimum-wages-women/ accessed on 20-1-2018

development; agriculture and business development services including productivity enhancement, local value addition, alternate market linkages etc. and institutional development services (forming and strengthening various producers' organisations, such as SHGs, water user associations, forest protection committees, credit and commodity cooperatives, empowering Panchayats through capacity building and knowledge centers etc.).

A network of capacity building institutions need to be set up to strengthen and develop SHGs to undertake the various functions into which they are expanding, including Training of Trainers (ToT), and to nurture and mentor them during the process. Milk cooperative need to be run and managed by women. The local authorities need to facilitate meeting of SHGs of women with the bank managers, lead bank officers and National Bank for Agriculture and Rural Development (NABARD) officers.

There ought to be reservation of 10 per cent of authorised shopping areas for SHGs of women. Women's SHGs with primitive accumulation of capital ought to charge 2 per cent or below 2 per cent of rate of interest. The SHGs that manage to acquire Swarna Jayanti Gram Swarojgar Yojana (SGSY for Rural self-employment) loans ought to reduce the rate of interest to 1.5 per cent. Women-headed households (single, divorced, deserted and widows) should get special consideration while granting loans.

Women's Component Plan (WCP)

Gender audit of Scheduled Caste Plan (SCP), Tribal Sub Plan (TSP) and financial allocation of Ministry of Minority Affairs is urgently required. So far, only proclamations have been made by the State governments but except for Kerala, none of the States have implemented WCP in all development-oriented schemes and programmes. For example, in the Union Budget, 2018-19, *it appears that, 'Spending on women declined* as a proportion of the total Budget, falling from 5.2 per cent in 2017-18 (RE) to 4.9 per cent proposed for 2018-19, and allocations for the Ministry of Women and Child Development increased marginally from 0.88 per cent of the total expenditure in the revised estimates of 2017-18 to 1 per cent of the total projected expenditure for 2018-19'.[18]

These development-oriented activities where massive financial allocation is made need to specify women's component as at least 30 per cent of the total budgetary allocation within the overall financial provision. Reservation of seats for girls must be ensured for Skill Development Institutes and Model Schools for which sizable allocation is made in the budget.

Women's Rights to Education

No efforts are made by the State or professional bodies for employers' education about basic human rights of women workers. The Supreme Court directive in accordance with the Vaisakha Judgment concerning safety of women at workplace is still not implemented by most private sector employers.

Women's Representation in Governance

It is encouraging to note that more than 16 States in India have allocated 50 per cent reserved seats for women in PRIs. But fund flow to PRIs has not been streamlined even after separating budgetary allocation for PRIs made in the 2018-19 budgets. Also it is disappointing to see that States have not actually provided women's component in Panchayat funds in

---

[18] https://thewire.in/economy/women-not-likely-better-off-end-fiscal accessed on 8th June 2020

2018-19. Even if it was, was it utilised judiciously for women's practical and strategic needs?

The Ministry of Panchayati Raj reported allocations in Part B of the GBS from 2008-09 for schemes such as Panchayat Mahila Evam Yuva Shakti Abhiyan and Rashtriya Gram Swaraj Yojana, which were subsequently subsumed into the Rajiv Gandhi Panchayat Sashaktikaran Abhiyan (for empowerment of local self-government bodies) in 2012-13 and continued till 2016-17. It also reported large allocations for the Backward Regions Grants Fund in 2013-14 and 2014-15. However, it has not reported any allocations for women in either Part A or B since budget 2017-18.[19]

According to The Economic Survey, 2018, political participation of women has been low despite them accounting for 49 per cent of the population. The survey for 2017-18 tabled in Parliament said factors such as domestic responsibilities; prevailing cultural attitudes regarding roles of women in society and lack of support from family were among the many reasons that prevented them from entering politics. It has been noted that there has been substantial representation of women at local government levels but that varys from State to State. There are 13.72 lakh elected women representatives (EWRs) in PRIs (Panchayati Raj Institutions) which constitute 44.2 per cent of total elected representatives (ERs) as on December 2017.[20]

All State governments need to be made to work towards fulfillment of long standing demands of the women's groups that provisions be made in the composite programmes under

---

[19] https://www.epw.in/engage/article/union-budget-2020-21-from-gender-perspective accessed on 18th June 2020.

[20] https://economictimes.indiatimes.com/news/politics-and-nation/womens-political-participation-in-india-low-need-more-economic-survey/articleshow/62696726.cms accessed on 18th June 2020

education, health and rural development sectors to target them specifically at girls/women as the principal beneficiaries. They have reiterated that the total fund needs to be disaggregated within the total allocation and restrictions need to be placed on their re-appropriation for other purposes. Youth must come forward and support these demands.

The Indian youth must join the women's movement to press for the long-standing demand of 33 per cent reservation of seats for women in the State legislative Assemblies and the parliament of India.

Minority Women

After consistent highlighting of the findings of the Rajendra Sachar Committee Report, 2006 and several reviews after the decade (in 2006)'[21] regarding the deplorable socio-economic status of majority of Muslims in India, special budgetary allocation for socially-excluded minority communities is being made.

There are more than 70 ministries/departments that draw grants from the government. Of the 70 ministries, 57 of them have gender budget cells. But, only 34 ministries/departments have reported allocations in the GBS 2020–21.

A hugely popular scheme to provide LPG connections to poor households – has been allocated Rs 1,118 crore. Other women protection and empowerment schemes were also allotted about Rs 1,330 crore, only Rs 204.77 crore was spent of this amount; a meagre 15.29 per cent of the allocation, the media reported. For example, while the Working Women's Hostel Scheme was budgeted around Rs 165 crore, only Rs 19.72 crore was spent till 24 December 2019. For another scheme called

---

[21] http://indianexpress.com/article/explained/ten-years-after-sachar-report-no-major-change-in-the-condition-of-indias-muslims-4444809/, accessed on 20-1-2018

Home for Widows, no money was spent till 24 December out of Rs 15 crore allocated for the Ministry of WCD scheme.

Schemes such as Mahila Shakti Kendra and Ujjwala also remained underperformers. The former had an allocation of Rs 150 crore and only Rs 8.75 crore was spent. On the other hand, Ujjwala scheme had an allocation of Rs 30 crore and out of this, only Rs 8.58 crore was spent. However, it is not just the schemes for women that are lagging. According to *The Indian Express* RTI application, several other schemes where the beneficiaries belong to the minorities – Scheduled Castes, Scheduled Tribes, Other Backward Classes, and disabled people – were also found to be under performing. This includes schemes like a post-matric scholarship to SCs; free coaching of Scheduled Caste and OBC students; Babu Jagjivan Ram Chhatravas Scheme; and Hamari Dharohar scheme, among others.

As much as Rs 3,919 crore have been allocated for the Ministry of Women and Child Development. Around 64 per cent of this or Rs 2,500 crore is for pregnant women under the Pradhan Mantri Matru Vandana Yojana (PMMVY). There have been complaints of low coverage in terms of beneficiaries under PMMVY. The scheme failed to reach at least 49 per cent of the total 123 lakh mothers who are estimated to have given birth to their first child in 2017 and, therefore, it was able to benefit only 31 per cent of its intended beneficiaries. Worse, economists contend, since the total number of births in 2017 was 270.5 lakh, the number of births covered stands at 23 per cent of the total number of child births that year, and proportion of those who actually received the cash benefit is a paltry 14 per cent (Chandra 2020). Clearly, the allocations to PMMVY need to be substantially higher if the scheme aims to reach all those for whom it is intended. However, allocations alone are not enough. Following up to ensure that women who are entitled to benefit from the scheme are aware of it is needed for the scheme to be successful.[22]

Conclusion

SDG 5 aims to direct efforts of the state and non-state actors to provide structures, mechanisms, funds, and functionaries for gender equality. The Indian youth can work to ensure:

- State supported education for women at all levels, from KG-to-PG. Nutrition-strengthening PDS and nutritional mid-day meals. Healthcare facilities–Abolition of user fees for BPL population, one stop crisis centre in public hospital for women/girls survivors of violence linked with shelter homes.
- Working women's hostels, night shelters for homeless women, crèches, cheap eating facilities, public toilets. Women-friendly and SAFE public transport-local trains, Metros, buses. Housing–subsidised housing for single/deserted/divorced/widowed women. Skill training centres for women and tailor-made courses. Safe, efficient, and cheap public Transport–bus, train, metro. Water–Safe drinking water in the community centres.
- Waste Management-Technological upgradation-Occupational health and safety of recycling workers/rag pickers
- Proper electrification in the communities
- Multipurpose Community Centres, halfway homes for elderly and mentally disturbed women
- Gender parity in decision-making bodies, more women in more powerful positions.

---

[22] https://www.epw.in/engage/article/union-budget-2020-21-from-gender-perspective accessed on 18th june, 2020

Highlights of NCRB Report 2018

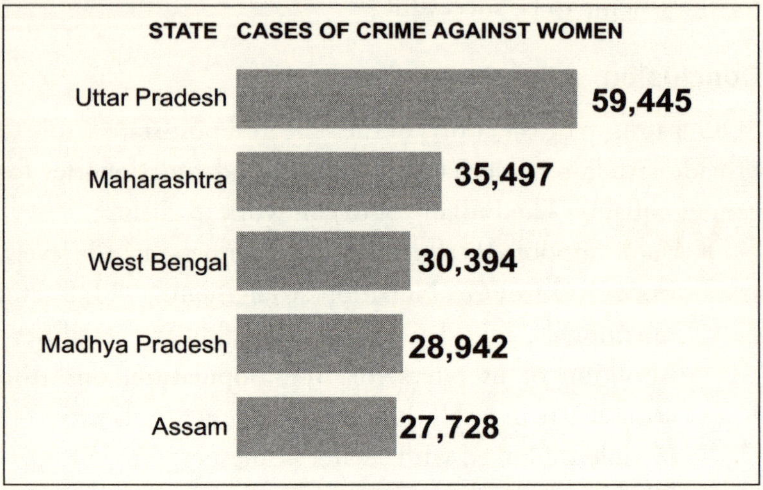

Top 5 Unsafe states for women

Overall, the Convention to Eliminate All Forms of Discrimination against Women (CEDAW) provides a useful international mechanism to hold countries accountable for meeting SDG 5. The SDG campaign offers an opportunity to attend to the unfinished business of development by fulfilling the promises made by world leaders to reduce poverty, end hunger, improve health, eliminate illiteracy, and gender parity in decision-making bodies. Gender inequality fuels many of these ubiquitous challenges and is exacerbated by them. Conversely, gender equality and the empowerment of women can secure sustainable future of women themselves, their households, and the communities in which they live and the country.

While this chapter discussed women's right and talks of eliminating all forms of discrimination against women, the upcoming chapter talks exclusively of violence against women and the role of voluntary organisations and special cells in bringing social justice to women in society to achieve the SDG.

Violence Against Women and Girls

A Barricade to Youth Development and Sustainable Development Goals

Trupti Jhaveri Panchal & Nolina Sarah Minj

I write for those women who do not speak, for those who do not have a voice because they were so terrified, because we are taught to respect fear more than ourselves. We've been taught that silence would save us, but it won't.

— **Audre Lorde**

Introduction

IN ORDER TO be able to work with youth and their response to violence against women and girls, this chapter draws learnings from the 35 years' experience of one such collaborative effort of state and civil society in India, namely the Special Cells for Women and Children. This is both an approach and a model for direct interventions in Violence Against Women and Girls, initiated as a field action project of the Tata Institute of Social Sciences, Mumbai.

These Special Cells provide psycho-social-legal services from within the Police system, through trained social work professionals, to women and child survivors of violence. Today, there are 339 such units implemented by a mix of state and civil society agencies across 14 States and one Union Territory of the country. Drawing on this experience and previous research by the Special Cells, four major categories of violence against women and girls within the 'youth' age-group, i.e. early and child marriage, honour killings, dating violence and domestic violence are discussed in this chapter. While the Indian criminal justice system has laws and policies in place to counter gender-based violence, they often fall short due to gaps in their implementation. *This book therefore argues that a multi-stakeholder approach to combat gender-based violence is an absolute necessity for India as a country, in order to realise the full potential of the fifth SDG to achieve gender equality.*

Violence and Youth in India

Violence against women and girls (VAWG) is one of the most oppressive forms of gender inequality, and a fundamental barrier to the equal participation of women and men in social, economic, and political spheres. It is the most atrocious manifestation of the systemic discrimination and inequality women continue to face, in law and in their everyday lives, around the world. It occurs in every region, country and culture, regardless of income, class, race or ethnicity (UN, 2005). It, thus, impedes gender equality and the attainment of a range of development outcomes. It is a complex and multifaceted problem that cannot be effectively addressed from a single vantage point.

The year 2015 saw a pivotal opportunity to insert the issue of violence against women and girls into future development efforts as world leaders came together to adopt a new framework for international development – the Sustainable Development Goals. SDG 5 aims to achieve gender equality and empower all women and girls. One of its key targets, and a means of achieving this goal, is to eliminate all forms of violence against women and girls in the public and private spheres. The UN states that, 'ending all forms of discrimination against women and girls is not only a basic human right, but it is also crucial to accelerating sustainable development'. (UN Women, n.d.)

Ending violence against women and girls requires a holistic approach that engages various stakeholders, especially the youth – who are involved in violence both as targets and perpetrators, in a patriarchal world order. India is slated to overtake China as the most populated country in the world by the year 2024. Moreover, in 2020 India became the youngest country in the world with 64 per cent of its population in the working age group (Business World, 2020). A substantial portion of this large population comprise girls and young women who continue to be vulnerable to violence by individuals and groups that include young men and boys. In order to achieve SDG 5, it is imperative that the younger generation understands the social construct of gender and its connections with violence against women and girls, in order to move closer to a violence-free and gender equal world, thereby unleashing their full potential.

Violence against women and girls takes various forms around the world. However, within the broad category of violence, it is domestic and sexual violence which are the most pervasive forms that cut across borders, class, caste, race, religion and socio-economic background. According to the WHO, 1 in 3 i.e. 35 per cent of women around the world have experienced physical and/or sexual violence by a partner and sexual violence by a non-partner in their lifetime (World Health Organisation, 2017).

Taking our population into context, statistics repeatedly places *India as having one of the highest rates of violence against women and girls in the world.* (Thompson Reuters Foundation, 2018). Violence against women and girls in India is deeply embedded in socio-cultural patriarchal values; it has many manifestations such as early and child marriage, dowry deaths or bride burning, female foeticide and witch-hunting, along with high prevalence of sexual assault and domestic violence

Year	2012	2013	2014	2015	2016	2017	2018
Crimes against women	244,270	309, 546	339, 457	329,243	338, 954	359,849	378,277

The annual data of the National Crime Records Bureau shows that crimes against women have been on a steady rise. While the year 2015 saw a dip in the number of reported crimes against women, a rising trend continues from the year 2016. These numbers have to be interpreted with the understanding that a large number of crimes against women go unreported. For instance, a comparison of the NFHS data with NCRB data showed that an estimate of 99.1 per cent cases of sexual violence are not reported to the criminal justice system (Bhattacharya; Kundu 2018). It is in this context of addressing violence against women from the justice and response angle, that the experience of Special Cells for Women across the country may be combed for understanding the potential for work with youth towards gender equality in India.

Special Cells for Women and Children

The Resource Centre for Interventions on Violence against Women (RCI-VAW), a field action project (FAP) of Tata Institute of Social Sciences (TISS) devoted to strengthening interventions on violence against women and girls, provides us with a vantage point on this issue.

The RCI-VAW – also a field action project unit of the Centre for Women-centred Social Work at TISS, Mumbai – emerged from and is a consolidation of the work done with the Special Cells approach across the country. The Special Cells have worked on combating violence against women and children since 1984, from within Police Stations, where professional social workers provide psycho-social and legal support to women facing violence. Although it began as a small project in Mumbai city, over the years, this approach has been expanded and adapted to multiple regional locations across India, functioning in 14 States and the Union Territory of Delhi, implemented by State and Central governments and civil society organisations. Of these units, the Tata Institute – through the RCI-VAW – directly implements 35 Special Cells and coordinates the work of 86 Special Cells in all.

The work of the Special Cells is rooted in feminist social work practice. It strategically locates social workers with/in this very State system and then harnesses the system's power in the best interests of women, to challenge men and family perpetrators of violence in the backdrop of said power i.e. this is the application of the feminist lens of empowerment/ addressing the gender-power imbalance.

Along with the feminist lens, social work principles such as acceptance, self-determination, individualisation, non-judgment, and confidentiality are an innate part of this work so that the aggrieved woman can exercise her agency. At the heart of all Special Cells' work lies a pro-woman perspective. The focus then is not only to put an end to the violence that the woman client is facing, but to aid her socially and emotionally, so as to empower her and help her attain what she wants. The Special Cells act on the premise that violence against women and girls is not a personal matter but a social issue that should be addressed in the public domain. Thereby, adhering to the feminist axiom that the 'personal is political' (TISS, 2016).

Rationale

Since its establishment, multiple evaluations and studies have been done of the Special Cells, many of them seeking to better understand the phenomena of violence. *One of the key outcomes of this is that the Special Cells now has aggregated data about the profile of its clients. Three decades worth of work, which involves interventions work with thousands of clients, has repeatedly shown that the prevalence of gender-based and sexual violence is higher with young women, that is, women between the age group of 18 - 34 years.* This is where the intersection of survivor-centric work on VAWG with State systems and work with the youth, lies, in the work of the Special Cell.

The definition of what age group constitutes the youth varies in different contexts. At present, the UN officially defines the youth as people falling within the age group of 15-24 years. In India, the National Youth Policy defined the age group 13-35 years as the youth but modified it to 15-29 years in 2014 (Ministry of Youth Affairs and Sports, 2014). However, the previous age group of 13-35 years is still used to define the youth in comparative studies. The UN also recognises that exact age groups constituting the term 'youth' can vary around the world. For the purpose of this work, we will consider the youth to be between 18-34 years, the largest client group of the Special Cells for Women.

Figure 1: The Lifetime Spiral

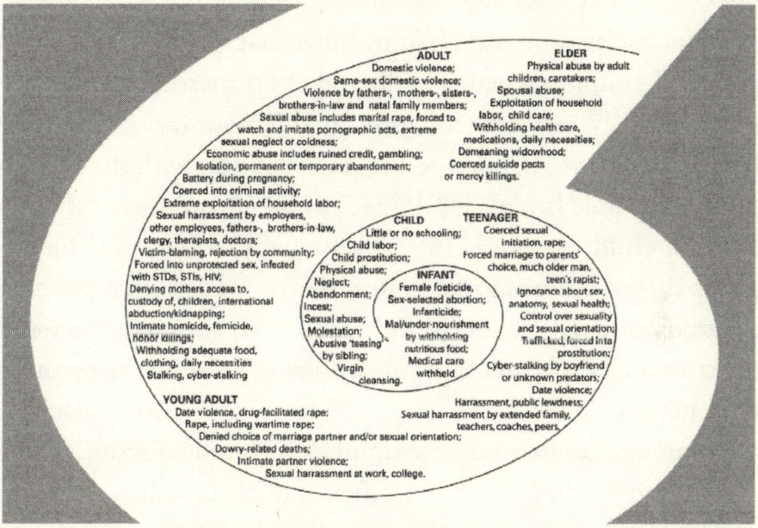

Source: Asia Pacific Institute on Gender-based Violence

The Lifetime Spiral reveals patterns of victimisation by enumerating the types of violence and vulnerabilities women and girls face. It also implicitly shows the presence of different abusers located over a woman's life course. Right from their birth, girls and women encounter numerous oppressions which continue onto childhood, adolescence, adulthood, and old age. Some of these violent phenomena are confined to one stage in the lifecycle, while some continue onto subsequent stages.

In this chapter, we discuss four major types of violence that are consistent with the above spiral and are globally recognised as occurring with young women, and also with women survivors of 18-34 years' age, with whom the Special Cells for Women have intervened. The broad categories dealt with in this chapter include: early and child marriage, honour crimes, violence in non-cohabiting, non-marital intimate relationships (otherwise known as dating violence) and domestic violence.

Early & Child Marriage

A major social issue prevalent in India that impacts millions of girls and young women is early and child marriage. UNICEF states that 27 per cent of girls in this country are married before the age of 18, making India the country with the highest number of child brides (UNICEF, 2016). According to NFHS 4 data on child marriage, the percentage of women in the age group 20-24 years married before age 18 years is 26.8 per cent as opposed to 47.4 per cent in NFHS 3, so although the trend of early and child marriage is reducing, it is not happening fast enough.

The age at marriage is significant when looking at the correlation between young women and their vulnerability to violence. Dhamija and Roychowdhary's (2018) analysis of NFHS data found that a simple delay of a year in women's marriage decreases the possibility of them being subject to physical violence. The vulnerability of young or younger women to violence, especially domestic violence, has been a common finding corroborated by many other studies. (Ahuja, 1987; Laxmi, 1990; Prasad; 1991; Bhatia, 2012; Dhamjia and Roychowdhury 2018.)

Studies also argue that women who marry early are more likely to be less assertive or are unable to challenge or stop ongoing domestic violence because of the vulnerability that comes with their age, and have less support system to exit /end ongoing violence. The younger the women marry, the more likely it is for their education to be stopped at an early age. This further increases their economic and social reliance within marriage, leaving them financially dependent on the marital family, with little social support outside. Younger women also have less decision-making power at home and about their own lives; including mobility, reproductive rights and control over finances (Roychowdhury et al., 2004, Jensen and Thornton, 2010).

Early and Child Marriage has a dire impact on many facets of the lives of girls and young women as it is a violation of their fundamental rights. Young married girls have lesser access to education and economic development, which makes them and their families more prone to poverty. The lack of education also reduces their employment opportunities, that is, if they are allowed to work outside the house. Early and Child Marriage also takes a heavy toll on their physical health and makes them more vulnerable to domestic and sexual violence, high-risk pregnancies and contracting HIV (Amnesty International, n.d.).

Early and child marriage is, thus, a gross form of violence against girls and young women. It serves as a major obstruction not only to the achievement of SDG 4 of gender equality and empowerment but also to SDG 5 on quality education, SDG 1 on the elimination of poverty and SDG 3 which promotes good health and wellbeing. It is also important to note that simply marrying off women at the legal age of 18 or older, does not eliminate the possibility that they could be forced or coerced into getting married. While there is a general concern about the legal age of marriage, there is little importance laid on women's right to marry whom and when they please, in both law and social policy. Studies show that elders often show unwillingness in allowing the youth to exercise their choice in choosing partners. (AALI, n.d.; AALI, 2010.)

In *Because the Personal is Political* – an analysis of data from two Special Cells for Women in Mumbai during the period of

July 1984 to June 1990 – it was found that 53.6 per cent of the clients who approached the Cells were married before the age of 22, and within this group 19.2 per cent were married as children before the legal age of 18. Similarly, in *Journey from Violence to Crime* – that analyses records from three Special Cells from 1990-1997 – it was found that 3.1 per cent women were married below the age of 14 years, 13.5 per cent (397) were married at 15-17 years and 30.2 per cent (884) women were married at 18-22 years. Since the Special Cells are located within the police station, it is possible that people might be wary of revealing the true age at marriage if it is younger than 18, implying that a lot more women could have had underage marriages.

In 2015, the Resource Centre for Interventions on Violence against Women published *Let them Fly*, a study on Early and Child Marriage in Haryana with Special Cells data and participants. This publication is based on the report of a study that analysed data from 472 cases of child marriage stopped by the Protection-cum-Prohibition Officers (PPOs) appointed at the Special Cells for Women & Children in Haryana for the implementation of Protection of Women from Domestic Violence, Act (PWDVA) 2005 and Prohibition of Child Marriage Act (PCMA) 2006, from the years 2009 to 2011 (Panchal and Ajgaonkar, 2015). The findings revealed that the number of girls who were married early far exceeded that of boys at 71.40 per cent. In the study, it was also found that more than half of the girls (58 per cent) dropped out of school upon getting married. In-depth interviews with parents and prohibition officers revealed other reasons for dropping out of school like sexual harassment, threat to chastity, poverty, inaccessible or distant secondary schools and lack of awareness about child marriage laws.

The authors would like to retain the use of the term 'honour crime' but acknowledge that such ideas about honour are misguided and problematic; they retain its use because of its prevalence in everyday parlance. We in the women's movement advocate the use of the word dis-honour to bring to attention that there is no honour in such VAWG crimes and they are shameful.

Dis-honour Crimes: Against Self-arranged Intimate Relationships

Dis-Honour based crimes, wherein community or family members strip, sexually and physically assault, socially boycott, forcibly separate, or even kill, one or more persons in an inter-caste or inter-religious or other socially disapproved of intimate relationship, entered into against social or familial approval, is a common form of violence against women in India. Unfortunately, society including popular media, use the words 'honour killing' to describe this phenomenon.

These killings are retaliations against women exercising their agency in choosing their sexual partners, which is looked at as 'dishonouring the family' and kinship ties.

The concept of 'honour' is deeply tied to casteism and communal, religious and ethnic pride, in which caste 'purity' is maintained through the control of women and their sexuality. Women, thus, become gatekeepers of caste, and women's bodies become symbols of caste purity, making it imperative for men to control the sexuality of women (Chakravarti, 1993). The most common 'dis-honour' crimes, then, are a patriarchal exercise to prevent lower caste men and men from minority religions from having sexual access to upper caste women.

While caste-based dis-honour crimes are more common, there are also cases where marriage between a man and a woman belonging to the same *gotra* (clan) has prompted honour killings (Shakti Vahini, 2010). As elopements and self-arranged relationships (whether co-habiting, marital or neither but still intimate/romantic) occur mostly in the prime of life, it is young women who have to face patriarchal retaliation when they marry outside of socially-sanctioned alliances. In a study conducted in 2014, 100 sample cases of honour-based killings were analysed in which 40 per cent of the girls were adolescents belonging to the age group of 14 - 19 years and 60 per cent were in the age group of 20 - 25 years (Deol, 2014). The study also noted that in most cases, the young woman's father or brothers were directly involved in the homicides, a finding that has been corroborated by another study by Shakti Vahini (2010).

The rampancy of honour crimes prove that age-old concepts of women's chastity and honour belonging to the whole family are still strongly rooted in Indian society today. These ideas become a key factor in producing and perpetuating violence against young women and girls.

As India modernises and caste and communities increasingly interact with each other, inter-caste and inter-faith marriages are on the rise. There is, thus, a dire need to introduce laws and adequate protection for young couples. *In 2011, the Law Commission of India drafted a Bill called the Prohibition of Unlawful Assembly (Interference with the Freedom of Matrimonial Alliances) Bill, 2011 but it has still not become an official Act.* The freedom to choose your own marital, sexual or other intimate partner is a crucial human right, and if the Indian state stands by its young women citizens while they exercise this right, it will only get one step closer to building a more gender-just world.

Anecdotal evidence from case-studies prepared for internal sharing and review within the Special Cells programme, implemented by TISS, shows that laws like the PCMA 2006 and POCSO Act 2012/13 are widely applied by community, family and other stakeholders – both state and civil-society – in cases of self-arranged interfaith and inter-caste relationships of young adult couples. This poses a major dilemma and strategic hindrance in interventions planning for feminist social workers in Special Cells for Women, because while they have been part of the struggles for bringing PCMA & POCSO Acts into being, they are also most restricted in survivor-centric and agency-affirming interventions' planning due to clauses of mandatory reporting, and criminalisation of young person's – including adult youth – in self-arranged relationships. RCI-VAW has made presentations on the difficulties and challenges posed by such laws and their rules for implementation in consultations such as those organised by Partners for Law in Development (Delhi) and Centre for Enquiry into Health and Allied Themes (Mumbai) in August 2017 (TISS & PLD & CEHAT, 2017).

Dating Violence: Violence in Self-arranged Intimate Relationships

The other side of the catch-22 situation in which young women find themselves is the occurrence of violence within self-arranged relationships, where there is almost no social support system left due to the choice of own sexual, marital or otherwise intimate partner. This is also the reason why in the Special Cells for Women approach, social workers have developed and use only the term 'self-arranged' for relationships that are otherwise termed as 'love affairs' commonly.

In the experience of the Special Cells' work across States since the past decade, there is evidence that there is an increasing number of women in self-arranged intimate relationships that are neither co-habiting nor marital, known otherwise as 'dating violence' – a term they choose to eschew in their work due to the non-indigeneity of it.

A rising number of youth in India are in non-marital, non-cohabiting sexual relationships. Although the term intimate partner violence includes both marital and non-marital relationships, the situation is far more complicated than what the data represents. Traditionally, as a society where family/community-arranged marriages were and still are the norm, living in/with self-arranged relationships out of free will, especially outside caste and community boundaries is taboo. Based on the growing number of women seeking support in such situations of violence, the Special Cells programme undertook research to strengthen own work in this regard.

In a 2015 research study, conducted by the Resource Centre for Interventions on Violence against Women amongst the Special Cells for Women & Children in Mumbai alone, it was found that 58 women within the age group of 18-34 years sought support from the Cells as they were facing violence in self-arranged intimate relationships that were neither cohabiting nor marital.

The study looked at the relevant cases from Special Cells located in VT, Dadar, Kandivali and CBD Belapur. These included cases from the years 2001 and 2002 and between 2009 and 2012 from Special Cells located at the Commissioner of Police Office, Dadar, Kandivali, CBD Belapur Police Stations between the years 2009 and 2012 and cases from Kurla and Vikhroli Police Stations between the years 2011 and 2012. It was found that the nature of violence in these relationships differed from that of marital ones, as women faced mental, sexual and financial violence more than physical violence. Violence, in fact, was 'disguised in the garb of love'. As many as 75 per cent of women reported sexual violence, 51 per cent were financially abused and 98.3 per cent survivors reported mental violence. Non-marital, non-cohabiting sexual relationships of young people are often kept secret from natal families which create a new set of issues for the couple, and especially women (TISS, 2015).

This means that women in such relationships are often isolated. They are emotionally more dependent on their partners and have fewer options to turn to, when subjected to violence. Being in a non-marital sexual relationship that has not received society's sanction also makes the woman even more vulnerable to violence from the rest of society. When the relationship does come out in the open, the woman tends to be blamed for entering into the relationship in the first place, and so the relationship is stigmatised more than the violence in it. This is true of unmarried adult women and situations become more complicated when adolescents are involved and become more vulnerable.

Similar findings were stated in a 2018 research study done by Centre for Enquiry into Health and Allied Themes (CEHAT) and the Municipal Corporation of Greater Mumbai (MCGM) wherein 728 cases of sexual violence were reported in three hospitals. As many as 67 per cent of these were cases of minors including 33 per cent children and 34 per cent adolescent girls.

All the cases were broadly recorded under the category of 'sexual violence/rape' in the medico-legal register, but the nature of the complaints varied. Out of 72 per cent cases that reported incidents of sexual violence, 13 per cent of the survivors were between the age group of 14 - 17 years and had been brought to the hospital as they had eloped (CEHAT- MCGM, 2018). *The above incidents points us to the law's blindness to teenage sexual consent, categorising all such instances with those that are, in fact, forced. This also results in criminalising young boys.*

The issue of elopement in India has always been a matter of contention as the impact of sexual activity before marriage or with the promise of marriage (consensual or forced) is always different for men and women in India. This is due to the patriarchal nature of the Indian society and its control over women's sexuality. Many a times, young women who engage in consensual sex, face social stigma as they are expected to be virgins until they get married. Their families file rape charges against the 'consenting' partner or pressurise women and girls to do so as they would rather see the girls as 'hapless victims' than individuals who have sexual agency. Thus, adolescence and young women in sexual relationships, unmarried women, are also subjected to violence at the hands of their natal family.

In two studies conducted by the newspaper, *The Hindu*, it was found that in 2013, from 460 cases of sexual assault that were fully argued before Delhi's district courts, a good number of the cases (189) involved allegedly consenting couples or couples who had eloped and were in court because the girls' parents had filed a case of abduction and rape against the partner (Rukmini S, 2016).

Criminalising young 'love' relationship is also highlighted in a study conducted by the students of National Law School of India (NLSIU) on the Protection of Children from Sexual Offences Act (POCSO Act) in five States – Karnataka, Maharashtra, Assam, Andhra Pradesh and New Delhi. This study makes some indicative revelations. The researchers analysed judgments on the basis of the Protection of Children from Sexual Offences Act in cases of sexual offences.

In most of these cases involving 'consensual relationship', the victim turned hostile or did not testify against the accused and the result was an acquittal. There search also observed leniency on part of the court when the victim was married or had a child from this relationship (CCL-NLSIU 2018). This reiterates that if the relationship is not solemnised into a marriage, the girl/young women continue to be stigmatised and their agency is compromised.

Based on the 2015 study cited in detail above, as well as the learnings of other interventionists in this space, RCI-VAW has consistently argued for special training of state and non-state intervention mechanism/services personnel in work with such survivors for creation of support systems and rebuilding sense of self and sexuality beyond the violence and recognising agency within such relationships. In addition, we have also advocated for special laws or legal mechanisms for justice and compensation for women facing violence in such self-arranged intimate relationships that are neither cohabiting nor marital.

Domestic Violence (within marriage)

While the Special Cells aim to address all forms of violence against women, the most common form of violence against women and girls is domestic violence. The majority of the Special Cells records disclose a telling picture of domestic violence faced by young women at the hands of their husbands and/or in-laws that has been corroborated by various researches conducted by RCI-VAW.

In the study *Because the Personal is Political* (2001) conducted between 1984-1990, out of a total of 1,581 cases, almost 75 per cent of the clients who registered cases at the Special Cells were below the age of 35 years. It was found that 42 per cent women were in the age group of 25-34 years and 30.1 per cent women belonged to age group of 18-24 years. The study looked at four different categories of violence i.e. mental violence, physical violence, desertion and non-maintenance. While all four types of violence were prevalent among the different age groups, women in the age group of 18-34 years were violated the most, both physically and mentally (TISS, 2001).

In the study, *Journey from Violence to Crime* (2001), out of a total of 2,608 cases, between 1990-1997, the trend of younger women bearing the brunt of violence continued. The percentage of women between 18-34 years facing violence increased to 65.4 per cent. It was observed that physical and mental violence were the most prevalent forms of abuse that women across all ages faced (Dave & Solanki, 2001). Another analysis of 17,962 cases of Special Cells in Maharashtra between 2003-2012 showed that women between the age group of 25-34 years faced violence the most at 42 per cent, succeeded by those between the age group of 18-24 years at 30 per cent (Panchal & Ajgaonkar 2019).

A study on the Implementation of Protection of Women from Domestic Violence Act, 2005 (PWDVA) was commissioned by the Ministry of Women and Child Development, Government of India and carried out by the Tata Institute of Social Sciences, Mumbai. The study was conducted in four States (Maharashtra, Haryana, Odisha and Tamil Nadu) on cases filed under the PWDVA from October 2006 to early 2013. The sample population of 2,466 women whose court records were perused represented women facing violence from across all age groups but more than half (around 60 per cent) of women facing violence were between the age group 18-25 years of age (819 women) and age group of 25 years to 30 years (638 women). This goes on to show us vulnerability of women and increasing number of women needing to take recourse of the law for reliefs and justice.

All these studies suggest that it is young women between 18 to 34 years who disproportionately bear the brunt of domestic violence and provide examples of the most pervasive form of gender-based violence in India.

The span of the studies across three decades also shows that the number of clients approaching the Special Cells and seeking intervention from the criminal justice system is only increasing in number. Domestic violence has far-reaching effects on women's physical, mental and sexual health. It also has grave social and economic costs that cause ripple effects throughout society. '(WHO, 2017) Studies indicate, for example, that in India women can lose an average of at least five paid work days for each incident of intimate partner violence. This fact would mean the affected woman would get 25 per cent less of her salary each time an incident of violence happens.' Such consequences further highlight the dire need to address violence against women and girls in order to attain inclusive sustainable development for all of society (United Nations, 2016).

Working with Men and Boys to end VAWG

In recent times, women's groups have been increasingly arguing that with patriarchal culture norms being the key barrier to women's empowerment, programmes must target changing attitudes among men and boys in order to create lasting improvements for women and girls.

The preceding sections of this chapter clearly show that both young men and women are caught in historically-sustained cycles of violence. At the Special Cells for Women and Children, it has been observed that most women who come seeking help principally want the violence being perpetrated on them to be stopped, and many want to reconcile and return to their partners. In such a scenario, it becomes inevitable for the social workers to engage with violent men in a constructive way. Hence, at the Special Cells, social worker's interventions are also directed at the men to challenge their beliefs and attitudes, so as to prevent violence against women.

A study conducted on women and men who were intimate partners and who sought intervention at Special Cells for Women and Children showed that men who use violence with their intimate partners are capable of change and have the capacity to show understanding and empathy (Jhaveri-Panchal, 2017). They want to love and care for their partners and not be violent to them but the societal representation of masculinity and tensions between gender roles, and the power struggles which pressurises men, make the desire to change their own violent attitude and behaviour, a struggle.

Such insights from the field reveal that working with male youth is crucially important while working on violence against women and girls. It is only through direct interventions work with men and boys that we can hope that social structures and cultural values will change in the future.

Conclusion

If violence against women and girls is so deeply entrenched in India's social fabric, then it is necessary for the state to be taking stringent action against it.

With laborious contributions from the women's movement in India, the Indian state has of late introduced appropriate laws to address this violence. These include Section 498A of the IPC, the Protection of Women from Domestic Violence Act (2005), the Prevention of Atrocities Act (1989), the Prevention of Child Marriage Act (2006), the Protection of Children from Sexual Offences Act (2012) and the Criminal Law (Amendment) Act, 2013 amongst others.

While relevant and stringent laws are in place, their implementation is greatly lacking. A 2017 Human Rights Watch report reveals that there are major gaps in the implementation of these laws. These shortcomings include: poor police response, failure to provide access to adequate health services, lack of access to effective legal assistance and lack of coordinated support services (Bajoria, 2017).

The increasing number of women who approach the Special Cells across India indicates that women want to access services and support systems, which are thoroughly lacking in our society. Some 62 per cent of women coming to the Special Cells expect a non-violent reconciliation with their husbands (Jhaveri-Panchal & Ajgaonkar, 2019). This means that women want their relationships to be equitable and non-violent and want the state to provide an empathetic and nuanced response to their needs. They want societal transformation to reach and impact their interpersonal relationships and communities.

In order to do this, there is a dire need to structurally transform the criminal justice system to ensure the time-bound and effective delivery of quality intervention services and delivery of justice. This would involve having multi-coordinated response service systems in place like the Special Cells, quality training for service providers, adequate funding and the efficient allocation of those funds and regular research studies to assess their implementation for learnings.

As the future belongs to the youth, it becomes essential to include them in preventive work on violence against women. Women's and youth organisations play an important role in sensitising and training the youth on key issues pertaining to gender and sexuality. Youth who are well-informed on these subjects early in life are bound to be more self-aware and less likely to engage in violence against women. NGOs and

INGOs like Akshara, YUVA, Empower Girls, Quest and Girls Not Brides are a few amongst many others already engaged in such consciousness raising work.

The state, the criminal justice system and organisations working on violence against women and girls and those working with the youth all need to come together and work in unison to fully realise the SD Goal of gender equality and women's empowerment. It is high time that access to quality services that address violence against women and girls become a crucial right for all women everywhere, thereby ensuring a better future for all.

The next three chapters are based on their responses as Civil Society Organisations to different issues of youth.

From Recipients to Change Agents

Participation in Enhancing Health & Sanitation in Marginalised Urban Geographies

Rama Shyam, Anuja Jayaraman,
Vinita Ajgaonkar & Neeta Karandikar

We shall not defeat any of the infectious diseases that plague the developing world until we have also won the battle for safe drinking water, sanitation and basic health care.

— **Kofi Annan**

Introduction

Overview from India

THE POPULATION OF Developing Countries can still be characterised as young. Among less developed countries, 29 per cent of the population is under age 15 and 18 per cent is aged 15-24 and for least developed countries 40 per cent of the population is under age 15 and 20 per cent is between 15-24 (United Nations 2011). It is believed that catering to the needs of the youth is important for greater economic and social development of these countries. Especially, in the movement from Millennium Development Goals (MDGs) to the Sustainable Development Goals (SDGs), the United Nations is committed to engendering youth participation as the key to realising goals related to ending poverty, promoting well-being at all ages, ensuring inclusivity in education, promoting sustainable economic growth, promoting peaceful societies and so on (Hwang and Kim 2016).

The definition of youth varies across agencies. The United Nations considers those aged 15-24 as youth (United Nations, 2009). The UN's draft National Youth Policy of 2012 defines youth population as those in the age group 16-30 years (NYP 2012). The youth policy recognises the heterogeneity of the youth within this population. That is, recognising the fact that those aged 16-20 have adolescent needs, those aged 21-25 strive to attain education and enter the labour force and those aged 26-30 aim to establish a professional and perhaps personal life (marriage). However, in this paper, the youth population is defined in accordance with the UNHABITAT definition and youth are defined as those in the age bracket of 15-32 years.

The youth today are undergoing several transformations and studies have found that today's youth have earlier and healthier entry into adolescence, spend longer duration in school, enter labour market late and delay marriage and childbearing (Lloyd 2005). As young people transition to adulthood, they take on various new roles and responsibilities and one of the most important transitions is to become productive members of the society – that is, being employed (Lloyd, Lam and Behrman 2005 chapter 5). Globalisation seems to play an important role in this transition process. In many developing countries, globalisation along with changing demographic profiles is one of the most important factors affecting transition to adulthood which not only creates new markets and brings in new technology but also influences norms and values of the society (Lloyd 2005).

Population dynamics in India: The three most populous countries in the world are China, India and USA and India accounts for 40 per cent of total global population (Office of the Registrar General and Census Commissioner, 2011). India is currently experiencing major demographic transition. Since 1980s, India has benefited from the changing age structure and growth of about two per cent per annum can be attributed to the growing working age population (Aiyar and Mody 2012). The population growth rate which was 1.64 per cent in 2001-2011is expected to decline to 0.9 in 2021-2025. At the same time, the total fertility rate is also expected to decline from 2.9 to 2.0 between 2001-2005 and 2021-2025 (Office of Registrar General and Census Commissioner, 2011).

The declining population growth rate and fertility rate in India has led to reduction in proportion of population below age 15 and increased the share of working age group (15-59 years). India can take advantage of this 'demographic dividend' resulting from this demographic transition where the large working age population can potentially bring economic growth (Parasuraman et al. 2009). Youth population is an important segment of this working age population. Therefore, livelihoods, employment and skills of the youth are bound to play a critical role in the growth process.

Simultaneously, for the first time between 2001 and 2011, fewer people have been added to the total population compared with previous decades – that is net additions to the population is declining since 1961 (Office of the Registrar General and Census Commissioner. 2011). In terms of numbers, the overall projected population in India between 2006 and 2026 is expected to increase from 1,112 million to 1,400 million (Office of the Registrar General and Census Commissioner 2011). Provisional estimates of the 2011 Census show that there are 158.8 million children between the age 0-6 years and this number has fallen from 163.8 million in 2001 (Office of the Registrar General and Census Commissioner 2011).

It is observed that the median age of the population of the world and India is increasing over time. It is projected that between 1950 and 2100, the median age of the population will increase from 23.9 to 41.9 and 21.3 to 45.8 for the world and India, respectively (United Nations 2011). At the same time, the life expectancy at birth is also expected to increase. By 2095-2100, the combined life expectancy at birth will be 81.1 and 79.5 for the world and India, respectively (United Nations 2011). This indicates that this population will be around for a longer time and hence there is a greater need to work with it while still young!

Figure 1: Percentage distribution of projected population by age group as on 1st March: 2001-2026

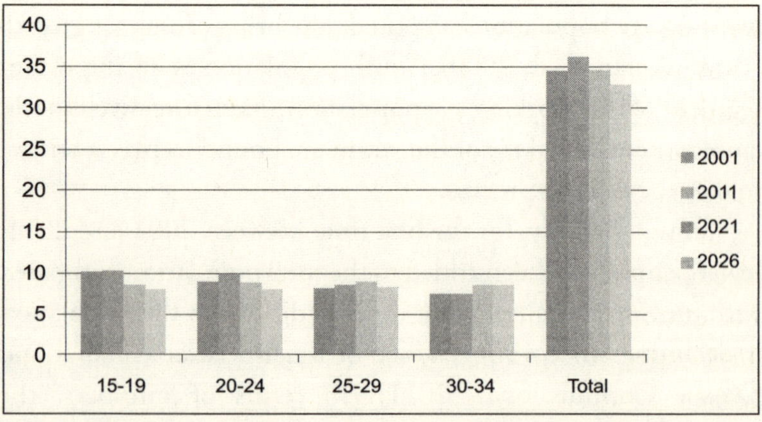

Source: Office of the Registrar General and Census Commissioner 2011

Demographic Profile of the Youth

We use the National Family Health Survey 2014-15 to study the characteristic of the youth in India. By place of residence, youth population (15-32 years) comprises 35 per cent of the urban population and 32 per cent of the rural population. There are greater rural-urban differences among those between ages 0-14. This youngest age cohort makes up 32 per cent of the rural and 26 per cent of the urban population.

The data also show that overall, in rural areas 98 per cent of the youth aged 15-17 are not married, close to 60 per cent are not married between age 18-24 and 10 per cent are not married between age 25-32. As expected, there is gender differentials with 62 per cent of the female population married versus 20 per cent of male population married between ages 18-24 in rural areas. Between ages 25-32 majority of men (82 per cent) and women (94 per cent) are married. The pattern is similar (Table 1) for urban locations, the only difference being that fewer individuals compared with rural locations are married between ages 18-24. Only 11 per cent of men and 42 per cent of women are married between ages 18-24 in urban areas (NSS 66th round).

According to NSS 66th round, educational levels among youth in urban areas, among those who are between ages 15-17, 4 per cent men and 6 per cent women are not literate. Illiteracy increases across age cohorts and is especially steep for women. As in case of rural areas, those with middle and secondary-level of education is highest for those who are between age 15-17. For example, 74 per cent of the women in urban areas aged 15-17 have attained middle and secondary level of education. More residents of urban areas have higher secondary education compared with rural areas.

Table 1: Population characteristics by marital status (urban area), 2009-2010

	Age Category								
Urban	15-17			18-24			25-32		
Marital Status	Male	Female	Total	Male	Female	Total	Male	Female	Total
Never Married	99.6	98.6	99.2	89.2	57.8	74.5	31.4	8.4	20.1
Currently Married	0.4	1.4	0.8	10.7	41.7	25.2	68.1	90.0	78.9
Widowed	0.0	0.0	0.0	0.1	0.2	0.1	0.3	1.2	0.7
Divorced / Separated	0.0	0.0	0.0	0.0	0.3	0.1	0.2	0.5	0.3
Total	100.0	100.0	100.0	100.0	100.0	100.0	100.0	100.0	100.0

Source: NSS 66th round

The Youth in India: Situation and Needs study 2006-2007 (International Institute for Population Sciences (IIPS) and Population Council 2010) identifies key transitions experienced by the youth (15 -24 years) including entry into the labour force. This study was conducted in six States including Andhra Pradesh, Bihar, Jharkhand, Maharashtra, Rajasthan and Tamil Nadu. Overall for all the States, the results indicate that close to one-third of men (28 per cent) and women (29 per cent) started working before the age of 15 and over two-third of men (68 per cent) and one-fifth of women were engaged in either paid or unpaid work in the 12 months preceding the survey. The report indicates that men were either skilled manual or machinery worker (31 per cent) or unskilled non-agricultural labourer (30 per cent). Women mainly worked as agricultural labourer (59 per cent). In terms of unemployment, 14 per cent of men and 16 per cent of women aged 15-24 were unemployed. Looking at the unemployed youths closely, not so different patterns emerge for men and women except in case of age of the youth.

Older men (age 20-24) have a lower unemployment rate compared with younger men (age 15-19) and vice versa are true for women. Youth belonging to general social category, having 12 or more years of education and belonging to the highest wealth quintile show highest rate of unemployment.

A report on the Profile of Youth in India (Parasuraman et al. 2009) uses the 2005-06 India National Family Health Survey (NFHS) and defines the youth population as those belonging to the age group 15-24. The report looks at the employment profile of the youth (men and women separately) closely and one of the findings of the report is that many youth are economically active. At the time of the study, among women, 27 per cent were employed, 7 per cent were not employed at the time of the survey but were employed at some point in the 12 months preceding the survey and about 66 per cent were not employed in the last 12 months.

Numbers were different for men. Sixty four per cent were employed at time of survey, 3 per cent were not employed at the time of the survey but were employed at some point in the 12 months preceding the survey and 33 per cent were not employed in the last 12 months preceding the survey. The report brings out the gender gap in employment. Between age 15 and 24, proportion of men employed increased from 33 per cent to 92 per cent and for women, it increased from 31 per cent to 36 per cent, respectively.

The report also shows that those residing in urban areas are less likely to be employed. They also found that among the youth, employment decreases with increasing education and wealth. Men and women are mainly engaged in agricultural and production (technical, administrative, and managerial occupation) activities. In terms of youth employment amongst Indian States, more than 75 per cent of men in Chhattisgarh and Gujarat are employed and more than half of the women are employed in Jharkhand and Chhattisgarh.

Youth, Health and Gender

Globally, adolescent and youth health concerns can be predominantly studied vis-à-vis i) nutrition ii) reproductive and sexual health (RSH) iii) mental health and iv) substance abuse.

Improving the reproductive and sexual health of adolescents is a key component of India's National Health Mission. In 2014, the Union Health Ministry launched *Rashtriya Kishor Swasthya Karyakram* (RKSK), the National Adolescent Health Programme, which expanded the scope of adolescent health programming beyond RSH but maintains

Adolescent Friendly Health Services (AFHS) in clinics as a key element of its list of programme components (Hoopes, Agarwal et al. 2016). The RKSK has rightly emphasised the importance of counseling services and support for services related to mental health conditions among adolescents and youth. The RKSK seeks to enable all adolescents and youth to realise their full potential by making informed and responsible decisions concerning their health and well-being and by accessing the services and support they need to implement their decisions (Ministry of Health and Family Welfare, 2014 in Santhya, Prakash et al. 2014).

The recent National Family Health Survey (NFHS 2015-16) data for India indicate that prevalence of anaemia among women aged 15-29 years is over 50 per cent and for men it is around 20 per cent (IIPS & ICF, 2017). Evidence from Society for Nutrition Education and Health Action's (SNEHA 2017) work with adolescents residing in informal settlements of Mumbai elicits similar patterns with 51 per cent of those (13-19 years) screened, identified with anaemia (SNEHA 2017).

A further break up of this data shows that 93 per cent of girls and 26 per cent of boys were found to be in the moderately anemic category. According to NFHS (2014-15), nutritional status of the youth (between 15 and 29 years of age) is also worrisome, with over 40 per cent of men and women (between 15 and 19 years of age) and around 20 per cent (between 20 and 29 years of age) being thin with mean Body Mass Index (BMI) of less than 18.5. Programme intervention data show that out of 1,325 young people (13-19 years) assessed using the *Child/Adolescent BMI Calculator*, 37 per cent of boys and 28 per cent of girls emerged underweight (SNEHA 2017).

On the RSH front, as per NFHS 3 data, 2.7 per cent of boys and 8 per cent of girls reported sexual debut before the age of 15 and most of the sexual activity happens in the context of marriage, this leads to early pregnancy due to social pressure. Even though contraceptive awareness is 94 per cent among girls aged 15–19, only 23 per cent of the married and 18 per cent of the sexually active unmarried girls in this group used a contraceptive once at least. All the three NFHS – 1991, 1998-99 and 2005-6 – show almost equal prevalence (59.1 per cent, 59.8 per cent and 58.2 per cent) of pregnant and mother adolescent and there is a steady increase in percentage of first pregnancy among adolescents (11.7 per cent, 12.4 per cent and 14.4 per cent) (Sivagurunathan, Umadevi et al 2015).

In addition, 34 per cent of married adolescent girls (15–19 years) reported that they suffered physical, emotional or sexual violence inflicted by their partner. There is a remarkable decline in these rates as age of marriage rises. So, early marriage also carries the risk of subjecting girls to all forms of violence (Sivagurunathan, Umadevi et al. 2015). *Talking about gender roles, the Youth report suggests that over 50 per cent of youth think it is justified for a husband to beat his wife.* However, more educated youth, those residing in urban areas, are less likely to justify wife beating (Parasuraman et al. 2009).

Mental health problems are one of the most neglected issues among adolescent. Mortality and morbidity due to mental disorders in adolescents increased and topped in recent years. A study from Goa, among 16 to 24-year-olds, shows 3.9 per cent of youths reported suicidal behaviours, with females four times more prone than males (Sivagurunathan, Umadevi et al. 2015). According to the authors, this suicidal behaviour is independently associated with factors like absenteeism, independent decision-making, premarital sex, sexual abuse, physical abuse from parents and mental disorders.

In India, suicide among adolescents is higher than any other age groups i.e., 40 per cent of suicide deaths in men and 56 per cent of suicide deaths in women occurred in 15–29 years of age. The prevalence rate of child and adolescent psychiatric disorders in the community has been found to be 6.5 per cent and in schools, it was 23.3 per cent and the *reporting systems of psychiatric disorders in children are found to be inadequate* (Sivagurunathan, Umadevi et al. 2015).

NFHS 3 data shows, in the age group 15–19, about 11 per cent of adolescent boys and 1 per cent of adolescent girls had consumed alcohol, in that 3 per cent consume it daily.

About 29 per cent of the boys and four percent of the girls use some kind of tobacco. The average age of tobacco use initiation was earliest at 12.3 years and alcohol usage at 13.6 years among adolescents. About 11 per cent of cannabis users were introduced to it before the age of 15. Initiating cannabis at this age is strongly associated with the development of Schizophrenia and spectrum disorders in adulthood (Sivagurunathan, Umadevi et al. 2015).

A review of the above statistics points out several instances of a gender-based power inequality which lies at the root of concerns related to nutrition, RSH or mental health conditions. Yet, none of our national programmes/schemes addressing health of young people have taken a particularly nuanced approach to gender and sexuality. Programme content and approach tend not to address the structural and power inequities that women and girls face, and omit the development of skills to challenge socially accepted roles and expectations around sexuality, fertility, and work (Nanda, Das, Singh, & Negi, 2013 in Daruwalla, Mishra et al 2017).

Youth Concerns:Service Provision, Engagement and SDG Connect

According to the United Nations (UN) handbook on youth (Hwang and Kim 2016), the urban population has become increasingly younger, with as many as 60 per cent of all urban dwellers worldwide are expected to be under the age of 18 by 2030. One layer of this reality is that youth are disproportionately exposed to exploitation, trafficking, and urban poverty, and they frequently live in slums and informal settlements created by unplanned and compressed urbanisation, which lack basic services and pose safety, health and security risks.

In the Indian scenario, slums are the most visible manifestation of disparities in urban areas and a stated focus of public policy, including that of the main national urban development programme as well as the National Health Mission, were 'to improve the health status of the urban population, particularly slum dwellers and other vulnerable sections by facilitating their access to quality health care' (Government of India, 2013).

According to Muller and Nair (2016), on the supply side, overall, the urban health advantage in India is considerable. In 2012, average under-five mortality in urban areas was 32.0 per 1,000, 45 per cent lower than the rate of 58.0 per 1,000 in rural areas. The population density of urban areas provides an inherent agglomeration economy in that it is easier and more cost-effective to reach people with services, such as immunisation. Investments in infrastructure and services such as water supply and sanitation are necessarily more cost-effective with higher population densities (Muller, Nair et al 2016). At the other end of this spectrum are the ill effects of urban congestion, resulting in tuberculosis and air pollution and contributing to the total burden of diseases in India (Pozzer, Lelieveld, Evans, Giannadaki, 2015).

The question is, what does it take to improve the statistics cited above or to say, improve the situation for young people? According to the World Youth Report (2003), in order to ensure the physical, mental, emotional and social health and overall well-being of young people, focus should be on:

- Creating a positive environment for promoting the right of young people to participation, development and peace as milestones on their road to better health;
- Equipping young people with adequate knowledge, self-esteem and life skills;
- Working with the ecosystem – family, service providers and community to build support;
- Enhancing the concept of gender equality between young men and young women and redressing the imbalance in the provision of opportunities – particularly for adolescent girls at risk of early marriage and consequent high-risk pregnancy; and
- Providing care and protection for all young people – whatever their health, disability, vulnerability or risk status, their age, gender, sexual orientation or class, or their ethnic, racial, religious or linguistic background – through a safe and supportive environment created and supported by appropriate legislation, clinical procedures and health services including counseling.

While it is true that a large chunk of services must invest in educating, imparting information to youth and building perspectives among related stakeholders to create a conducive environment, *the report sidesteps the critical concern of poor infrastructure and missing provisions that enable young people to practice what they have learnt.* Implications of inadequate provision for children's health and general development are connected with practical realities for children and their caregivers in urban areas. While health education and healthcare are essential complements, they can in no way be considered alternatives to provision (Bartlett 2005).

The Sustainable Development Goals come into the picture here since the Millennium Development Goals attained their aims unevenly (Hwang and Kim 2017). The erstwhile UN Secretary General, Ban Ki-moon reiterated how the SDGs encompass the unfinished business of the MDGs but go well beyond poverty eradication (World Bank-UNDP 2016). In doing so, he recognised adolescents and youth as key stakeholders to be consulted in furthering the future and achievement of the SDGs.

The SDGs lay out the inter linkages between the various issues concerning young people through specific goals (Hwang and Kim 2017). The goals relevant to the subject of youth concerns are viz. **Goal 1:** End poverty in all its forms everywhere; **Goal 3:** Ensure healthy lives and promote well-being for all at all ages – including reduced maternal mortality, greater mental health, less of substance abuse and death by accident; **Goal 4:** Ensure inclusive and equitable quality education and promote lifelong learning opportunities for all – addressing gender disparities and including persons with disabilities, indigenous peoples and children in vulnerable situations; **Goal 11:** Make cities and human settlements inclusive, safe, resilient and sustainable – ensuring access to basic services and **Goal 16:** Promote peaceful and inclusive societies for sustainable development, provide access to justice for all and build effective, accountable and inclusive institutions at all levels – enhancing participatory and representative decision-making at all levels.

The implication is that the Post-2015 Agenda for Development reflects the ambitions and vision of young people. It also means that young people can and should have a sense of ownership and play their part in the collective endeavour for achieving a more sustainable world.

In the context of urban India, this development agenda is way beyond the definition of young people as merely the 'demographic dividend'. Outlining the conundrum of the 'youth bulge', it has been posited that science and technology advance create a healthier society – vaccinations, sanitation, early check-ups through the prevention model;however, social structure does not change and the number of children in families stays large (Inayatullah 2016).

Young people challenge the patronising top-down ways in which youth policies have been framed wherein adolescents and youth are service recipients with minimum agency accrued to them.

This chapter primarily brings to fore examples of youth participation in change, essentially in questioning social structures that run contrary to rapid changes in technological innovation or economic growth. While doing so, they negotiate at home, join hands with peers and mentors and collaborate with public institutions to influence change. What still remain lacking are spaces that can nurture exchange of ideas and successes with the older generation that can create a buy-in for social transformations. The call for action would mean engaging parents and communities to trust youth to bring in positive and sustainable changes in their local communities.

On the demand side, participation of adolescents and children can go a long way in improving situations that contribute to their overall health and wellbeing. Young people are innovative and creative in problem-solving and solution-finding: they are the key to helping communities meet their subsistence needs, and in doing so, improving local people's long-term security and control over their own lives. Their participation can be looked at using the three lens assets approach wherein participatory processes include young people as i) **target groups learning together** and ii) **moving to become collaborators and finally** iii) **taking up the role of youth initiators** (DFID-CSO 2010). It is, however, not a linear process and the learning can go on while collaborating and initiating action.

Youth Participation: Experiences and Limitations

Let us look at instances of young people engaged in all these processes to transform their life situations vis-à-vis gender-based structural inequalities that impede sanitation and health, especially amidst urban marginalities. The experiences have been drawn from SNEHA's programme interventions as well as other urban interventions that have consistently valued the agency of young people in co-designing projects that are multi-sectoral in approach, jointly implementing them and disseminating learning through creative spaces.

Participation as Target Groups: Collective Learning and Questioning

As part of SNEHA's (Society for Nutrition Education and Health Action) programme on Empowerment Health and Sexuality of Adolescents (EHSAS) with young people residing in slums, the strategy is to enable adolescents to learn collectively, even as the programme invests in building an understanding of parents, teachers, communities and service providers (health, police, legal systems).

SNEHA's EHSAS programme emphasises a strategy that is multipronged in nature. It engages young people and simultaneously invests in working with related stakeholders (family, communities, school and public health systems, police) to build an adolescent-friendly ecosystem. EHSAS's strategy of improving health and wellbeing of young people is informed by the Socioecological Model and as depicted below, it includes key stakeholders within the circles of influence relevant to adolescents and youth.

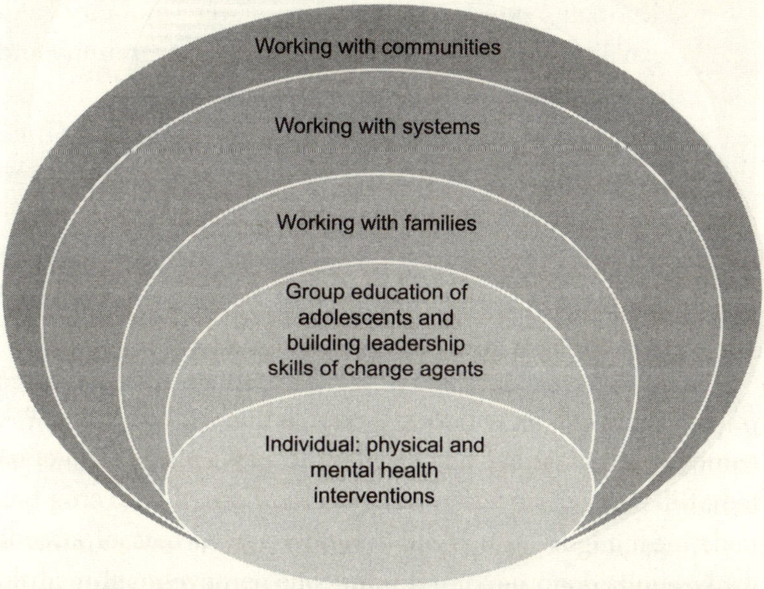

We recognise that in the NGO/Civil Society Organisation (CSO) space, it may not be always feasible to implement a multipronged programme. The best possible way to achieve this might be to build partnerships and collaboration across the CSO and public institutions spectrum, and gradually work towards convergence of efforts. In SNEHA, the EHSAS programme aims at addressing health and wellbeing of adolescents and youth (10-21 years); enabling them to become healthy, gender sensitive and responsible citizens through creation of an adolescent-friendly ecosystem. To be able to achieve this goal, adolescents/youth, communities and public institutions are being enabled to:

- Develop understanding and awareness about physical, sexual and reproductive health
- Reduce conditions of anemia
- Develop awareness about mental health and practice health/help seeking behaviour
- Negotiate power and control over mobility and sexuality across spaces of family, peers, community and institutional systems
- Work with Public Health System/Integrated Child Development Scheme (ICDS) to improve response and strengthen adolescent-friendly services
- Acquire skills to create adolescent-friendly services to address under-nutrition, mental health conditions and gender-based violence.

This is being supported by generating evidence-based impact studies that are participatory and continuously identify strengths and challenges to support public institutions to enhance services.

A qualitative evaluation is built into the programme to understand the range and possibilities of transformations in various aspects of the lives of adolescents who undergo trainings through EHSAS. Voices of the participants heard through focus group discussions, in-depth interviews, as well as informal discussions and observations of group sessions reveal impact of the programme. During one of the focus group discussions conducted after a group session on RSH, this is how 17-year-old Rajee (name changed) described menstruation and associated feelings:

> *On the two sides of our uterus there are two andaashay (ovaries) which produce one egg every alternate month. One lining of blood is created in the uterus, if there is no intercourse between male and female, then the lining of blood and the egg come out. Our feelings and emotions may go up and down in this period due to hormones. Before we knew about this, we used to react to things immediately (Kisi bhi cheese ke liye bahut jaldi bol dete the). Now that we know that these things are natural, that such emotional changes occur during this period, we are able to control our anger better. We are more careful, think a little before we say anything!*

It is interesting to see how Rajee connects menstruation with emotional changes even as her friend adds: '*we share this information with friends and younger sisters at home and in the neigbourhood. At least we get to give them "correct information."*' The emphasis on *correct information* is extremely relevant, especially in the current sphere of information overdose by virtue of exposure to information technology. It has been studied that without a conducive ecosystem, where they can discuss RSH issues, young people have been left to resort to information they gather from books, magazines, youth counselors, and through pornography, with its increasing accessibility in recent times. Those exposed to sexually implicit content on the television and internet are more likely to initiate early sex, which comes with a host of negative implications which they often find themselves unequipped to deal with (Shajahan, Rao et al. 2015).

Group education sessions on RSH have led to adolescents voicing their concerns such as '*small size of penis*' and '*unequal size of the testes*'. Girls have expressed concerns regarding '*irregular menstrual cycle*' and white discharge and have sought gynecological assistance. Additionally, peer learning has led to an understanding of gender inequalities as narrated:

> *We had watched a video, where a lady questioned why girls have to sacrifice every time. If any petticoat or bra strap is seen, they have to hide it. At the time of periods, one has to feel guilty, what if I have stained my clothes!! They have to make sure nothing is seen, they have to hide the pad while going to change. It was said in the video, there is nothing to be ashamed of. It is your body, your right. It is about my existence and I should be comfortable talking about it with boys as well so that they are aware in case I am in discomfort and need assistance.*

For the EHSAS intervention addressing anemia and need for balanced nutrition among adolescents, it has been found that group education has led to young people taking it back to families and communities. '*Earlier, we would eat Chinese bhel every day despite suffering from heartburn. Now we have given up, as we know how harmful it is. I consume home cooked food and I'm also trying to eat more vegetables and fruits to address anemia...good nutrition is important for higher iron*', says an adolescent participant. Group discussions with parents have validated this change among their children's nutritional habits: '*We no more get irritated with our children asking for money to eat junk food outside. Instead they ask us to cook at home...with the same money, the entire family can have a healthy snack and we have all started eating parathas, sometimes paalak paratha for that extra iron!*'

Some adolescents have reported that, '*now our area is cleaner. We told mummy, she told daddy and he told others*' indicating how a push from young people can motivate parents to take ownership of sanitation in their surroundings. In two other instances, while an adolescent girl counseled her mother to eat a balanced diet leading to reduction in anemia, a young boy counseled his father to reduce smoking! It must therefore be reckoned that participation of youth as target groups result in adequate information among young people and prepares the ground for engaging them as partners – drivers of change (DFID-CSO 2010).

Youth as Collaborators: Researching and Expressing Opinions

Rekha – married when 16 years old – came in contact with the EHSAS programme after a miscarriage led her to leave her marital home where she had been subjected to dowry-related harassment. The counsellor at SNEHA helped her to get back her *streedhan* (jewellery owned by her and kept back by her in laws), file a case for annulment and enroll herself for a vocational training course. The interventions helped the girl become more confident. She was bright and motivated, and was encouraged to work as a 'change agent'. Her parents were persuaded to allow her to attend a theater workshop organised for the youth volunteers. Rekha now participates in street plays on various issues concerning adolescents. She recently participated in a street play on violence against women in a *Kishori Mela* (girls' congregation) and appealed to everyone, '*Do not marry off your daughters early. Let them study, let them be independent*'.

Genuine participatory engagement is likely if children and youth are enabled to become researchers and are involved in discussions about research findings, analysis and future implications (Lansdown 2005 in Asker and Gero 2012). Evidence from the field demonstrates that the shift from young people being learners to producing knowledge goes a long way in sustaining change as demonstrated through Mumbai based

PUKAR's (Partners in Urban Knowledge and Research) Youth Research Fellowship Programme.

As mentioned in Apnalaya's Annual Report 2016-17 (Apnalaya 2017), five young boys (including Salim), conducted an in-depth research project on water scarcity in Shanti Nagar, a slum cluster in Shivaji Nagar, in the M/East Municipal ward of Mumbai and its impact on the health, livelihood and education of the residents. They conducted several interviews with officials from the Municipal Corporation of Greater Mumbai (MCGM), local representatives – MLA and corporator, NGOs, and the local community. Their survey findings were presented to a larger audience in the form of a published research report. They conducted five presentation meetings in the Shivaji Nagar community, highlighting (a) the linkage between unavailability of potable water and the vicious circle of intergenerational poverty; (b) how their research can help in solving the issue; and (c) the need for such research.

Some of the key findings articulated by this group in their report are:

- *The fact that there is no continuous supply of potable water in the slums, caused students to either miss schools or reach late resulting in being reprimanded by teachers;*
- *With the primary responsibility of managing household chores lying with girls, inadequate access to water resulted in them dropping out of school since their attendance regularity takes a toll;*
- *No water supply in school toilets meant girls would drop out of middle and high school as managing menstruation with no water was most difficult.*

Since 2014, the EHSAS programme has been organising a one day youth festival –*Yuvanaad* – engaging young people to express themselves through creativity. In January 2018, this platform was taken over by youth volunteers to a large extent with a youth convening committee taking charge. By 2020, we have seen how the process has been completely taken over by the youth with the NGO just bearing the responsibility of mobilising financial resources. A researcher observing the organising process in 2018, mentioned, '*during the discussion that followed, it was clear that there was one leader amongst the youth, who was not just taking decisions but helping others to come to a decision, encouraging those voicing different opinions, prompting others to ask questions and seek clarifications. Others, boys as well as girls, were vocal even as all of them were making a conscious effort to engage in discussion with the few who were presumably new entrants, and were a little subdued. Decisions were taken fast, people volunteered for various tasks while weighing their other commitments and responsibilities. The group ensured that nobody was burdened with too many responsibilities and nobody was left out either.* It has been observed that the dynamism of these processes reiterated how young people want to build stable democracies, sustainable economies and societies based on equity (Inter American Development Bank 2009 in DFID-CSO 2010).

Youth as Initiators: Interface with the Ecosystem and Strengthening Demand

While the movement from target group to becoming collaborators may be a long journey involving agency-building processes and creating buying-in from families and communities, the leap to initiating action may take lesser time. We have seen that in one of the EHSAS programme locations, adolescent girls who went through a workshop on self-transformation could easily take up the issue of safety and mobility in their community. They quickly moved to undertake a safety audit mapping safe/unsafe spaces and engaged with community members and police to present the data collected and seek support for redressal. Their understanding of gender-based violence and its interlinkages with access to sanitation facilities led them to chart out specific action points:

- *A wall needs to be built near the local nullah, and more garbage bins were required in the community;*
- *Letters need to be drafted to be sent to concerned officials – elected representatives and the sanitation department at the municipal corporation;*
- *The demand letters need to be signed by community members implying a door-to-door visit to present the contents to community elders,*
- *We need to organise a community rally to galvanise public support for the issue.*

The perception of safe access to sanitation facilities is mired with insecurity associated with public toilets. As cited in a study conducted in Mumbai, when asked about personal experience of any particular crime associated with use of public toilets, nearly a fifth of the women surveyed (22 per cent) reported being subject to eve teasing, and another fifth (20 per cent) to a variety of other crimes such as assault (12 per cent), robbery (8 per cent) and indecent exposure (1.5 per cent). The biggest source of insecurity was 'eve teasing', that included whistling, passing explicit comments, singing lewd songs, and inappropriate touching (Belur, Daruwalla et al. 2017). The study findings are echoed in an instance of youth initiative from the urban slums.

Archana Reddy is one of the very few non-Muslim families that chose to remain in an otherwise Muslim-dominated slum pocket in Jogeshwari East, torn asunder during the post Babri Masjid Bombay riots of 1992-93. When she was 16 years old, she learnt about issues of RSH and hygiene and went on to become a youth volunteer with a community-based Non-government Organisation (the NGO, Apnalaya), promoting gender equal access to public toilets in her community.

During the NGO-organised Peace Week, it was Archana's idea to paint the community toilet, clean up the surrounding and send out a strong message that '*a toilet is a basic sanitary need...we girls feel disgusted when we see comments and phone numbers soliciting sexual favours scratched on the walls of the women's wing*'. The otherwise quiet young woman – now 20 years old – feels that she would not have been able to climb up the scaffolding and paint the toilet if she had kept away from the soccer practice and sessions on gender rights. '*The NGO's team ensured that we participate and express our voices...now we have taken up the ownership of organising community events. I'm not very vocal, but a doer and I have the space to lead just like that.*'

When Sadiya came for an NGO-organised workshop on Child Friendly Spaces (CFS) methodology, she had already crossed certain milestones. She had learnt a bit about the Indian Constitution, knew that sanitation in her community was a joint responsibility of the Municipal Corporation and people and was aware of whom to approach to address grievances. She was soon part of a *Bal Panchayat* (Children's Governance Committee). When the Kranti toilet – one of the only two community toilets for a population of 5,991 – was rendered defunct – as nobody could cross the garbage heaped on the way to the toilet – *Bal Panchayat* members Nasreen and Sadiyas sprang into action.

'*For over a year I used the community toilet without any electricity and doors, and was always dependent on someone else to take me to the toilet. Due to such danger I used to defecate at the dumping ground which was full of druggies as well but we had no option*', Sadiya says.

First, they wrote letters to the Solid Waste Management (SWM) Department requesting them for a BMC Janitor who is supposed to clean that area every day. After getting the area cleaned, they also got a street lamp installed right outside the toilet. Nasreen and Sadiya's actions have inspired many others from the *Bal Panchayat* to file complaints in the SWM Department of M-East Ward for either construction or repair of public toilets (Apnalaya 2016-17).

Engaging the Ecosystem

In all the above experiences, it is evident that while working on health and wellbeing of young people, it becomes imperative to engage with the ecosystem – families, communities, service providers. Despite positive instances cited in this chapter, creating this support system can pose one of the biggest challenges owing to the unequal power relations between i) parents and children, ii) collective community codes and individual 'aberrant' actions, and iii) public authorities/service providers and citizens from marginalised groups. At the end of this long journey, even if the ecosystem becomes friendlier, inadequate provisioning in facilities can result in frustration just as in case of an assessment of ARSH clinics in Surat.

Data showed that service utilisation was comparatively very low among boys and only for few services even among girls. Only 1.9 per cent beneficiaries were boys. Service utilisation was done mainly for STI/ RTI counseling (96.83 per cent), IFA tablets (59.23 per cent) and Immunization (81.53 per cent). Inadequacy of infrastructure, materials, human resources, referral linkages, monitoring and supervision was observed. SWOC (Strength-Weakness-Opportunities-Challenges) analysis revealed that the staff was empathetic towards the needs of adolescents but lack of IEC (Information, Education and Communication) material was identified as a major challenge to prepare an action plan. Demand generation was identified as the critical pathway (Desai, Moitra et al. 2017). This strategy addresses the complexity of gaps that can impede improvement in youth health and wellbeing.

Discussion and Recommendations

In this narrative, we have traversed through the contours of the youth profile in India and dwelled upon some of the critical challenges in improving health and wellbeing of young people in a well-rounded manner. Nevertheless, we cannot wish away the largely unchartered territory of structural inequalities – based on gender, caste, religious, economic fault lines – which impact youth access to provisions and services. In our bid to restrict the experiences of youth participation to issues related to Water, Sanitation and Hygiene (WASH), we have had to overlook critical questions of the responsibility of governance structures in ensuring that human rights are protected at all costs. Having said this, the paper does provide key insights into engendering participation of young people in improving their life situations.

'I was married when I turned 16, bore two children and yet was determined to learn. I negotiated at home – with my parents, my husband and my in-laws. Here I am today, skilled to earn a living, supporting my children and my family…and have encouraged my sister-in-law to study and aspire, acquire knowledge and skills and then make a choice, be it with marriage or any other decision in life', says a female programme participant from SNEHA's EHSAS programme.

The story of the female programme participant from SNEHA's intervention among youth from some of the most marginalised urban communities depicts the power of the skills she has acquired to negotiate and is also a call to action to address issues of young people. It covers issues that are echoed in India's Youth Development Index Report (RGNIYD 2017). *The report admits that gender discrimination and inadequate civic participation pose two of the most challenging structural issues in youth development.* Though the narrative tone of the report once again reiterates youth as the demographic dividend and young girls as prospective mothers, it does take cognisance of pertinent issues such as teenage pregnancy and morbidity related to substance abuse.

The concern is that the indicator definition of health and wellbeing in the report does not touch upon adolescent issues of pubertal changes, the need to express openly, emotional and psychosocial upheavals, sexual and reproductive health concerns. It does not accrue any significance to a supportive ecosystem rooted in family, communities, and public institutions including education, healthcare, and judicial-legal systems – all necessary precursors to a healthy transition into youth-hood.

Against this backdrop, it becomes essential to understand the psychosocial demography of young people who inhabit urban geographies. These are mostly informal settlements housing a large migrant population that aspires towards economic improvement, while clinging on to cultural values of conformity to family hierarchies and patriarchal gender norms. Within such socio-economic structures surrounded by deprivation, an adolescent raises her/his key concerns as lack of communication with parents/family, inadequate knowledge/exposure regarding health conditions coupled with inadequate access to health infrastructure (including mental health support) and quality education that can hone cognition and skills. These provisional concerns are compounded by sexual harassment of girls in private and public spaces and/or substance abuse and consequent fallout in the form of sexual harassment, mental health conditions and lack of support networks.

The situation for young people is aggravated by limited response from public institutions – health, police, schools – that do not recognise the agency of adolescents as significant. It must be reckoned that though the response may be limited, public institutions in India are now bound by legal procedures that have very well outlined the key aspects of:

- **Investing in nutrition of adolescents** (ICDS Sabla under the Ministry of Women and Child Development and *Rashtriya Kishor Swasthya Karyakram* (RKSK) under the Ministry of Health and Family Welfare).
- **Investing in life skills and Reproductive and Sexual Health** (RSH) of adolescents (ICDS Sabala), Adolescent Reproductive and Sexual Health (ARSH) under the National Health Mission.
- **Investing in safety and protection of children and adolescents** (Protection of Children From Sexual Offence, POCSO) Act 2012.

The probable approach could be a programme that adopts a gender-transformative approach to build perspectives of young people, their parents, community stakeholders and public institutions (health, police, education, civic representatives) to come together and improve conditions of health (physical, sexual and mental) and gender inequality. Primarily, the programme believes in the responsibility of the society and the state to ensure an adolescent-friendly ecosystem. Placed within the broader paradigm of youth development, the programme echoes the key aspects included in the Global Youth Development Index and Report (Wight 2016). The report, published by the Commonwealth, draws upon two fundamental arguments posited by Martha Nussbaum (2012) and Amartya Sen (1985) to substantiate youth development viz.:

- The *Human Rights* approach that endorses civil liberties, political participation, education and employment;
- The *Capabilities* approach that lists good health, adequate nutrition, adequate shelter, opportunities for sexual satisfaction and choice in reproduction, and mobility.

While the *Capabilities* approach emphasises enhancement of human abilities, the *Human Rights* approach focuses on the conditions or pre-requisites that would induce such enhancement. Based on this theoretical framework, the Report has progressed to aggregate a complex of 18 indicators to arrive at the Youth Development Index (YDI). The YDI has five domains and among the global youth population, it measures: (i) Levels of education, (ii) Health and well-being (iii) Employment and Opportunity, (iv) Political participation and (v) Civic participation.

There exists very limited information citing comparisons of youth across contexts (rural-urban; social backgrounds), especially for WASH. The authors recognise that there is much left to study in terms of understanding and appreciating the role of young people in transforming societies. The subject warrants more qualitative studies to substantiate best practices and evidence.

Conclusion

All these interventions mentioned with adolescents have been striving to build capabilities of young people and is now poised to intensify the sporadic efforts to strengthen the ecosystem that will support young people to remain healthy and attain their full potential. It must be reiterated that while educating young people will prepare them for future wellbeing, engaging them to participate and evaluate services and programming meant for them will actually strengthen the demand to improve provisions and services that will enhance their capabilities and expand their freedom to choose development. It has been observed earlier how the key health concerns of young people are interlinked in a way where any approach must be interdisciplinary in nature and therefore must be conceived through consultation.

It becomes imperative that all youth participation programmes are modeled on a child-friendly, interdisciplinary curriculum that focuses on life skills, community service activities and peer-to-peer interaction (UNICEF 2012). Additionally, an integrated focus on working with parents and service providers will help transforming social structures that underlie impediments to participation, especially of young women. This eco-systemic approach will sustain efforts in a way that young people feel supported in their initiatives, even as they have the opportunity to concentrate on building individual capabilities to enhance well-being in future.

Going forward, such programmes have been able to deepen youth participation and dedicated cohorts have been formed to transfer knowledge and skills to younger adolescents, negotiate change at home and facilitate positive transformations in their communities.

Beyond Skilling

Alternative Praxis of Livelihood for Urban Poor Youth

Alicia Tauro & Sachin Nachnekar

Recognising that the future growth of India will depend on greater skill development, the National Policy for Skill Development aims to create a skilled workforce of 500 million by 2022.

— **MM Pallam Raju**

Introduction

EXCEPT IN ANCIENT times, there has never been as much emphasis and attention on the youth as there is today in the world. This is largely due to a rise in the share of the youth population to the total population in the world and in India. Globally, the youth population or the population between the ages of 15-24 stands at about 18 per cent of the total world population. In India, the population of the same age group is about 28 per cent of the total population of the nation (Census, 2011). Moreover, India being one of the youngest nations worldwide, about 65 per cent of the total nation's population is below the age of 35 years and is said to have the youngest average age of population at 29 years by the beginning of the next decade. At the same time, more than half of the population falls within this category, this age group also faces immense problems of job insecurity, serious and varied health issues, lack of educational and training opportunities and a high lack of representation.

This chapter locates itself within the targets of SDG 8 which is 'Decent work and economic growth', with a special emphasis on work opportunities and safe work conditions, especially for urban poor youth. One is to create adequate work opportunities and smoothen transitions from education to work for youth by facilitating access to holistic skill development comprising technical as well as soft skills training through localised centres. This would also mean, to strengthen the education as well as the working ecosystem to ensure there is a strong backward and forward linkage.

Another important goal is to create well paid jobs and safe working environment. According to the Global Employment Trends for Youth 2017 put out by the International Labour Organisation, in 2017, 39 per cent of youth employed in work in the developing world lived in moderate to extreme poverty. This means that while they were engaged in some form of employment they were still living in poverty, often referred to as the 'working poor'. According to the same report, around 95 per cent of employed youth worked in the informal sector without any forms of social security or protection.

In addition to Sustainable Development Goal 8, this paper also touches upon SDGs 4 – Quality education, SDG 10 – Reduced Inequalities and SDG 11 – sustainable cities and communities. Urban poor youth are unable to access quality education due to poor quality public education system, heavily priced college private education and also fewer scope and credibility of part-time and distance learning education. This makes them fall back and due to several other conditions like inability to access basic services and everyday struggles for water, sanitation, young people are unable to continue and stay in education. As a result, they drop out of studies and are unable to get proper jobs in the formal sector. They are easily absorbed into the informal sector, take up self-employment and then the cycle of the 'working poor' continues.

This chapter seeks to understand the current situation of education and employment opportunities for urban poor youth and the inequalities they face in accessing them. The primary reason is limited access to and low quality of education, coupled with frequent evictions and insecurity on the home front which lead to youth dropping out of school at a young age. Inevitably, they are absorbed into informal jobs with low level of education, formal training and are unskilled. These jobs are unable to pull them out of poverty and the cycle continues.

The second reason is a mismatch between skills learned from education and those required for employment. This has resulted in a huge section of the youth population being *unemployable.* As per the India Youth Development Index and Report, 2017, about 67.6 per cent of the unemployed youth possessed secondary-level and higher education.

Finally, the biggest reason for youth unemployment in India is that there is low job creation. India has experienced 'Jobless Growth' in the past few years, where despite growth in GDP and the economy, very few or no jobs have been created. The rate of creation of jobs deteriorated substantially during the period 2013-14 through 2015-16. Jobs grew at a meagre 0.2 per cent per annum during this period, although real GDP grew at a faster rate of 7.8 per cent per annum, as per a report by *Live Mint.*

At the same time, this chapter also looks at the skilling policies and the approach taken by governments to work on youth empowerment, livelihood and development. A limited education policy, dilution of child labour laws, short-term part-time courses for skill training, an absence of soft skills and holistic vocational training has rendered the youth, specifically the urban poor youth living in slum communities, into a group of no more than unskilled labourers performing labour-intensive tasks.

Having understood the current scenario and the limited approach towards youth development through skilling, an alternative praxis is provided to youth development, through the work of Youth for Unity and Voluntary Action (YUVA). YUVA's work with the most marginalised communities through the Integrated Community Development (ICD) model and through the processes of youth-led development have been able to foster democratic values and a sense of responsible citizenship among the youth. This has been done through formation of youth groups and youth networks that work towards youth self-development and development of the communities they live in.

The chapter concludes with insights on the way forward for holistic youth development based on praxis and experience. Localising skill training, implementing vocational training in a holistic and an integrated manner and not in isolation, emphasising on education and non-formal training to build careers, and finally creating more decent jobs for youth and breaking the cycle of poverty are some of the ways in which we can truly view youth as 'partners in development' and co-creators of a better society.

By 2025 India's working age population will grow to 87 million, says a Morgan Stanley report. According to 'World Population Prospects: The 2015 revision' Population Database of United Nations Population Division, India has the world's highest number of 10 to 24-year-olds, despite having a smaller population than China, which has 185 million young people. Youth (15-24 years) in India constitutes one-fifth (19.1 per cent) of India's total population. As much as 64.3 per cent will be India's working age population (15-59 years) and only 12.5 per cent will be India's proportion of old people (60+ years) in 2025 against US's 56 per cent.

India is projected to record the highest number of births in the 9 months since coronavirus was declared a pandemic in March, with more than 20 million babies expected to be born in the country between March and December 2021, according to a UNICEF report in May 2020.[1] This will stretch the country's already stretched healthcare resources further, it is feared.

Despite this massive youth population, so far India has scored very low on youth development indicators. India ranked 133rd out of 183 countries in the Global Youth Development Index in 2016, compiled by the Commonwealth Secretariat. Sri Lanka, Bhutan and Nepal, India's neighbours scored far better at 31, 69, and 77 respectively. The report shows that India lags considerably in the domains of health, education and employment for youth. This chapter focuses on education and employment of youth.

Approaching the third decade of the new millennium, the education and employment scenarios in India seem pretty bleak. Education is being increasingly privatised, and

---

[1] https://www.indiatoday.in/india/story/20-million-babies-india-highest-births-coronavirus-declared-pandemic-1675274-2020-05-07

affordable government education is of poor quality and often, even inaccessible.

Education has already become distant for millions of Indian children, with online classes. Even the national capital government, proud of its nearly 7,000 schools in the city has said educating has become a difficult process. As recently as in July 2020, a PTI report said approximately 15 per cent of the students enrolled in Delhi government's 1,100 schools have not been 'traceable' since the lockdown was announced. The report quoted Delhi education minister Manish Sisodia. The State-run Delhi schools have over 15 lakh students enrolled. When this is the state of affairs in the nation's capital city, one can imagine how difficult 'education' has become in 2020.[2]

Livelihood too, is the major need for a youth population. And yet, youth are three times as likely as adults to be unemployed (ILO, 2017). It is widely recognised that people need work to sustain themselves and their families when they come of age, and hence the International Labour Organisation mandates Right to Employment and also the Rights at Work, as a set of core fundamental principles to protect the rights of the workers at their workplace. The Indian Constitution, too, recognises the Right to Life in Article 21 as a Fundamental Right with the unwritten right to employment.

Finally, the Sustainable Development Goals, 2030 also recognise Decent Work and livelihood as one of its goals. 'Targets under Goal 8 in particular, as well as several other goals, recognise the centrality of youth employment challenges, and open pathways for consistent and focalised action on decent jobs for youth, and youth development overall.' (ILO, 2017.)

---

2 https://www.livemint.com/companies/news/delhi-govt-ropes-in-school-managements-to-trace-students-missing-since-lockdown-11597141893641.html

Under the umbrella of employment issues, unemployment, underemployment and un-employability are at the heart of the matter. In order to address these, the policy-makers have seemingly resorted to the panacea of *skills*. This word 'Skills' has even become one of the most talked-about schemes for the Youth – the Skill India Mission. 'In 2009, GoI launched the National Skill Development Policy (NSDP) with a target for skilling 500 million people by 2020. (National Youth Policy, 2014).' *In reality, by mid-2020, industry reports suggest this 500 million has remained a number in policy papers.* While skilling young people is important for them to upgrade their skills and meet the market demands, in this chapter the authors argue, that it is not enough. Young people need more than just skills for employment, and certainly much more, for developing themselves and harnessing their potential.

This is imperative all the more for urban youth in poverty. According to the Arjun Sengupta committee report (2009), 93 per cent of India's economy is in the informal sector. Global trends suggest that in developing countries, 19 out of 20 youth are engaged in informal work. The growing informal sector and the higher participation of youth in informal work is proof of perpetuating poverty and uncertainty for youth. The list of skills with the ministry being provided to youth are also indicative of a 'manufacturing and industrial orientation', leaving out skill development in all other sectors of the economy and does not ready the so-called 'trained' young people for work in the formal sector of the economy, nor does their attained 'skills' obtain them formal employment.

Against the backdrop of this macro scenario, Youth for Unity and Voluntary Action (YUVA) is a development organisation that works with urban poor youth, helping them with a sustainable livelihood through vocational training, bringing youth back into formal education, promoting democratic values through value-based trainings, and above all providing an impetus for youth participation through networks for development.

An illustration from YUVA's work with youth provides the reader with an example of an alternative praxis for engaging with the issue of young people's livelihoods and working towards more sustainable ways to develop strong, confident and proactive youth with a sense of democratic citizenship alongside being a contributor to the nation and the economy.

Youth for Unity and Voluntary Action (YUVA) has been working in slum communities in Mumbai, Navi Mumbai, Guwahati, Nagpur, Bhopal, Nashik and with issues of urban poverty for over the past 35 years. YUVA has also been closely working on urban governance and policy, as well as environment sustainability.

Urban Youth living in Poverty: the Context

According to a global poverty assessment report by the World Bank titled 'Poverty and Shared Prosperity' (2018), an estimate of about 16.7 per cent of youth workers live on income below US$1.90 a day, which is the extreme poverty threshold. Most of them are also primarily employed in the informal sector. These youth working in the informal sector, typically in cities, come from marginalised slum communities. Their everyday lives are a struggle owing to a lack of the most basic amenities of water, sanitation and housing. YUVA has typically worked in slum communities which are unrecognised by the government, prone to eviction and have the lowest Human Development Indicators of health, education, income and standard of living.

Youth from marginalised sections of urban India lack access to basic facilities of nutrition and health, sanitation, lack of quality education, unemployment and lack of political representation and participation. What's worse is that these inequalities are allowed to persist through systems and structures. *Despite umpteen policies for child and youth development, they do not penetrate to those who need them the most.* The chain of weak mothers giving birth to malnourished children, who continue to be ignored by the system and grow up to be unhealthy, incapable youth and continue the same vicious cycle for yet another generation.

For example, the problem of malnutrition is a severe issue in India. The Integrated Child Development Services (ICDS, a scheme that was set up in 1975) mandates for anganwadis to be in place in all areas so that the cycle of malnutrition can be broken and children, mothers, pregnant women and adolescent girls can receive appropriate nutrition, vaccinations, and health education and awareness. In the last 45 years, its success has only been partial. Moreover, in recent years, there have been severe fund-cuts and budget slashes for the ICDS and so the existing anganwadis, that are already inadequate, do not function properly, resulting in high malnutrition rates perpetuating the cycle of ill-health and poverty.

Just like health, education also remains an area which requires immense amount of work in the context of developing nations. The Right to Education Act, 2009 in India has made education a justifiable right for every single individual. The preceding schemes of Sarva Shiksha Abhiyaan (SSA) and inclusive education ensure universalisation of primary education and inclusivity of children with special needs. Above 12 years old, the RTE act continues to be inadequate and only covers free and compulsory education for children within the ages of 6-14 years.

College education and higher education is not only costly but of low quality too. A report (2016) by Oxfam International states, 'When talented young people cannot afford to pursue secondary or tertiary education, their talents are not nurtured and the societies they live in suffer from a reduction in innovation and the loss of their potential contributions. For youth who manage to enter higher education, the challenge is not only cost, but also quality.' As a result, in India today, young people continue to drop out of formal education due to unavailable, unaffordable, inaccessible education, go on to do short-term skill training courses provided through the Skills Mission and allied schemes.

A report by the Ministry of Statistics and Programme Implementation (MoSPI, GoI, 2017) on the education of youth in India also reinforces this same trend. 'Despite significant improvements in increasing primary school enrolment in some regions, *the Millennium Development Goal of achieving universal primary level education by 2015 could not be achieved.* Moreover, such improvements have not necessarily been followed by an equivalent transition to secondary education, vocational training, non-formal education or entry into the labour market, especially for girls and young women' (Youth in India, 2017).

The third important area as identified in the Youth Development Index parameters is livelihood. This area is extremely pertinent to youth. Yet, globally, too we see a different trend. 'Youth makes up 25 per cent of the global working age population, but account for 43.7 per cent of the unemployed. This means that almost every other jobless person in the world is between the ages of 15 and 24.' (Concept Note, Breakout session: Poverty, Inequality and Youth Empowerment in Urban areas, 2016). The Skill India mission in India tries to work towards providing livelihoods. It provides skill training to youth and tries to link it with job placement.

However, the kind of salaries offered is in the range of Rs 5,000 to Rs 9,000 per month, according to the Maharashtra government's base employment wage/minimum wages circular.[3] So across the country, different States offer different base minimum wage for the same skill set. In comparison, a person in the informal sector engaging in street vending, hawking or doing house-work easily earns an average sum of Rs10, 000-12,000 per month.

Thus, we need to re-examine this minimum wage structure for skills offered by even the government departments, as youth are not going to be motivated enough to learn the skill offered and then find a job that pays less than what they can receive doing something else. Also, while several training centres are being established, they do not cover tribal areas and remote villages. Such youth are thus kept away and the benefits of development are inaccessible to them.

At the time the Skill India Mission was introduced, there were amendments made in the child labour act and the new act 'Prohibition and Regulation of Child labour Act, 2016' allowed for children's work in family enterprises/ businesses. This regulation makes it even more difficult for youth from marginalised sections to break through and enter higher education or any other employment as they are legally encouraged to work in family enterprises such as agriculture, shop floors, and small industries. Such youth, then, are never motivated to leave to pursue education and get stuck in the rut of informal family trades.

---

[3] https://mahakamgar.maharashtra.gov.in/Images/pdf/minimum-wages.pdf

The inequalities in the standards of quality health, education and employment are further accentuated on account of external factors like evictions. Evictions are often done in the name of development, and are often thrust upon the dwellings of the urban poor. Evictions are not just the act of taking down governmentally-defined 'illegal' houses, but they uproot families, communities and cause irreversible damage to people's lives often times to such an extent that affects them for generations. In other words, it causes generational poverty and further widens inequalities. Matthew Desmond, author of, *Evicted,* states that 'Evictions don't reflect poverty, they cause it... Evicted families lose their homes, their communities, their schools, and even their jobs and possessions. Evictions have now become a way of life for thousands of families who bounce between temporary shelters, short-term leases, and unstable nomadic lifestyles.'[4] Thus, evictions are a system of perpetuating of urban inequities and maintaining structures of suppression and informality.

These sub-standard basic provisions of health, education and employment along with harsh realities of evictions lead to further reducing inequalities for the urban poor youth. In such an era of growing differences and systems that perpetuate these kinds of inequalities, the agenda of the Sustainable Development Goals, the New Urban Agenda and other such initiatives towards development makes sense. The motto of the SDGs 2030 is 'Leave No One Behind' which entails that development should penetrate every corner of the world, thereby, leaving no one behind from reaping its fruits. However, national realities are far behind such goals.

---

[4] https://inequality.org/great-divide/read-evicted-matthey-desmond/ Inequality.org blog post (2017), Josh Hoxie.

Current Youth Development Paradigme: An Analysis

The whole idea of skills and vocational training has come with the objective to reduce poverty, give second chance to drop-outs and keep youth out of the streets and doing something meaningful. Considering the 'demographic dividend' angle of reaping benefits of a young population, the Indian government set up the National Skills Development Council (NSDC) in 2009 as the apex body at the central level to coordinate the 17 relevant ministries. Developing the skills of the youth would also mean preparing them to be part of a skilled workforce, which would in turn attract a lot of FDIs and investment into the country.

However, a decade of observation of youth accessing these skill programmes show, these youth have not been adequately prepared for the workforce. They have received a poor education or have dropped out mid-way. *The short-term nature of skills programme is not enough to equip them to take up jobs and keep them.* Moreover, the kind of jobs generated in the formal market is inadequate to match the ever-expanding number of skilled and semi-skilled youth. They, thus, get absorbed into the large informal economy that is typically characterised by low wages, lack of security, long hours and lack of any formal protection.

A paper reviewing skills development for youth in India quotes data from the World Bank database which says that nearly one third of total employees are casual labourers and 43 per cent are low-end self-employed (World Bank 2012b: Figure 1.2). Only 17 per cent of total employees receive regular wages or salaries. Casual workers and the self-employed together account for more than 90 per cent of rural workers and about 50 per cent of urban workers.[5]

---

[5] https://home.hiroshima-u.ac.jp/~cice/wp-content/uploads/publications/15-2/15-2-10.pdf

The Indian government has claimed to have spent about Rs 90,000 crore on Youth Development schemes and policies every year or 'approximately Rs 2,710 per young individual per year, through youth-targeted (higher education, skill development, health care etc) and non-targeted (food subsidies, employment etc) programmes' (National Youth Policy, 2014). The government says, a major proportion of this was spent in imparting Skills and Training. Yet, unemployment continues to rise since these skills do not seem to get translated into work.

'Jobless growth', a concept that has been aptly used for the Indian economy, reflects its condition, where the economy has been growing but the number of jobs created are very few. What could be the reasons for this? *Who are the youth majorly left out in these national level missions? Where does the failure lie?*

One of the core reasons is that skill training is unable to penetrate the marginalised communities and areas where youth live in poverty. Skilling programmes through NSDC are largely implemented in universities and through big organisations. For the youth coming from small communities and *basti*s (slums) these structures are intimidating and often, inaccessible. They also do not have the leisure to spend so much time in training and money in travelling to the training. Most organisations tied to NSD programmes have targets of students to reach, therefore, have a tough time finding students and have to hire mobilisers and other local organisations to bring them some students.

The next is the profile of skills offered through these courses. Most of them are part of the industrial and manufacturing sector and have limited scope to be part of the formal sector. Even if they, after the training, are given a job in a formal company, they are hired on contract for low pay for many hours and at distant locations. These skills imparted can, therefore, be seen as perpetuating and, are in fact, expanding the informal sector since the jobs they translate into do not have social security, job security or any leave and accident covers.

Thirdly, skill training is implemented in isolation, *without understanding and targeting the systems at work which act as barriers* to youth to access these skills. These systems could be patriarchy restricting women from work and skills, lack of core skills and confidence among youth with limited exposure, and finally, at the front-end after the training period is complete, there is no follow up process to ensure that the young person does get a job and is able to keep and grow in his/her job.

Finally, there is no mention of strengthening the education system or helping build aspirations of youth to pursue something based on their aptitude. It is more of helping them get a 'job' and not really giving any impetus for them to think beyond. Pursuing a career is very different from just doing a job. Even though youth have limited exposure and may think of certain careers as inaccessible due to financial constraints and other reasons, it is a challenge of how the system – society and government – can make these affordable, available and therefore, accessible to them.

Alternative Praxis for Empowerment of Poor Urban Youth

YUVA's Model

Working with youth cannot be done in isolation; it has to be a combination and integration of several elements in order to truly be effective. The right blend of services, associations and advocacy is what makes up the youth work at YUVA. When one looks at the theme of livelihood and youth holistically, a lot of back and foreground needs to be built. *This is one of the biggest drawbacks of the current policy on skills; it is being implemented in isolation, without having any foundation built, nor a clear goal to reach.* It's more like a continuum along which we should view employment.

The present Skills policy lacks connect with nurturing healthy children and youth, retaining them in schools and colleges, enhancing quality of education in these institutions through people's participation, providing skills and vocational training, developing core skills/soft skills which are most important and lacking in today's youth, to drawing linkages with job markets locally, boosting youth participation and ownership through youth-led movements.

Considering the inequalities facing urban poor youth, it is important to work at multiple levels in order to empower youth through their participation. YUVA works with a lifecycle approach, at multiple levels of intervention.

First it starts with the very essential need of human beings – food. Youth from marginal settings are malnourished. They are stunted and wasted. There is high incidence of anaemia among adolescent girls (government and NGO data over the years). For this, YUVA works closely with systems like Anganwadis to ensure that the adolescent girls' support programme runs smoothly, and their nutrition needs are taken care of. For the rest, with the help of Youth campaigns on strengthening the Public Distribution System, affordable food of good quality is made available to the community, and mal-practices of corruption in the ration shops of the PDS system is curtailed.

Next is education. School education is free; however, college education is not only expensive but also lacks quality. YUVA intervenes by facilitating scholarships by connecting with individual, institutional and other donors to meet the fees expenses. Youth leaders also take on the process of admission enrolments through online modes.

In order to facilitate the process of transition from education to livelihood and also to ensure employability through some hands-on training and vocational skills, skills training are imparted. Courses for skills like beautician's, tailoring, computers are taught in tandem with the NSDC guidelines and format. However, what makes these different is that these skill trainings have been supplemented by training on life skills and parallel non-formal education. Most youth and young people entering skill training courses are school or college drop-outs. They are unable to go back to school or even attain proper jobs due to lack of certificate and degrees.

Moreover, the present education system in India is incapacitated to provide them with essential skills of critical thinking, decision-making, communication, and forming their own opinions about themselves and their worlds. The importance of life skills has been underlined by many social scientists, and have also been echoed by the world bodies. One such definition is provided by UNICEF which defines life skills as, 'psychosocial abilities for adaptive and positive behaviour that enable individuals to deal effectively with the demands and challenges of everyday life'.

'They are loosely grouped into three broad categories of skills: cognitive skills for analysing and using information, personal skills for developing personal agency and managing oneself, and inter-personal skills for communicating and interacting effectively with others.' Through these participatory life skill modules, Yuva tries to help them develop these essential skills which form the basis of any kind of good vocational training model. These have helped many of them, particularly the girls and young women, negotiate in their spaces for social access to jobs, further education and also defer their marriage.

Alongside these vocational services, a process of youth empowerment is run simultaneously. Greater emphasis is laid on life skills, core skills and sessions on rights, laws, and the constitution which are regularly implemented through the vocational centres and the community resource centre, a centre which is open to anyone irrespective of age, run by the youth. It is here where the youth learn through the sessions, but more through peer to peer interaction. Processes like regular film screening, cultural activities, workshops, and exposure visits help them to think critically and engage differently with realities around them. Youth groups are formed to sustain the process of youth transformation and inculcation of democratic values. Campaigns and networks are run through these youth groups, which help them for their own development and also contribute to the development of their community and city.

All of these processes have helped youth become more confident, inspired them to continue their education if they've dropped out, build their aspirations and life goals, and also made them more responsible and vigilant citizens. Many of the youth emerging from these processes have not just got themselves a job, but are pursuing a career. They have dreams to transform and make a difference by the work they do. Many of them are interested in becoming social workers, IAS and IPS officers, joining the police, armed and military forces, and even entering into politics to make changes at the policy level.

Understanding these aspirations of the youth also makes service providers reflect on how they can help translate the Sustainable Development Goals at the grassroot level, especially goal 4.7 which reads, 'by 2030 ensure all learners acquire knowledge and skills needed to promote sustainable development, including among others through education for sustainable development and sustainable lifestyles, human rights, gender equality, promotion of a culture of peace and non-violence, global citizenship, and appreciation of cultural diversity and of culture's contribution to sustainable development'. (Sustainable Development Goals, 2030.)

When Yuva talks about youth as becoming change agents and taking on the agenda of transforming the world, it asks if just a course on skills training for a job is enough. Youth is that period of life where one experiences tremendous transition, a mix of anxiety, hope, creating an identity, confusion and chaos, at the same time, fending for family, earning through a job, all of which have to be addressed with limited means, typically for a poor youth living in the city. Does a skills training course prove to be enough? How can a service provider, be it the government or a non-profit, supplement skills with developing a relationship which can prove to be empowering for youth? How can the true potential of youth be harnessed by allowing them to take charge and only facilitating the process instead of treating them solely as receivers?

Following is an illustration of youth work in a community called Ambujwadi in Malwani, Mumbai. It is a success story which points towards how youth group building and regular youth processes can bring sustainability to youth livelihoods.

Case study 1

Vocational training centre: Ambujwadi, Malwani

Ambujwadi is an informal settlement in the area of Malwani. It is an unrecognised slum, and hence is devoid of basic amenities of water, sanitation, etc. It is located far away, along the edge of the periphery of the city and is thus distant from transport facilities. Education institutions and health centres, too, are located at a fair distance from the community. The total population of the community is 50,000 plus. Of this, youth between 15-29 years account for 27.6 per cent of the population. The sex ratio is 917, similar to the national average (YUVA Project baseline survey, 2014).

In this settlement, people are engaged in different sectors of informal work such as domestic workers, building and construction workers, masons, carpenters, electricians, home-based work (imitation jewellery-making, beads and artificial stone works), and some are in contractual labour as security guards, peons, etc. Many of the people have small businesses and factories in the house or near the house in the *basti*. Youth in these families continue the family business by working at the stall or in the factory, shop, or restaurant or do home-based work, household chores or child care. This group of youth are invisible due to social confines and mentality towards women that keeps them within the confines of their home.

Apart from this, there is also another big proportion of youth who fall within the NEET category i.e. youth not in Education, Employment or Training. The Yuva survey found that reasons for drop-outs of youth from education and training were – 17 per cent dropped out due to marriage, while 61 per cent dropped out because they were not interested. Another big and very astonishing fact was that, about 45 per cent of this age group were non-earning, and a majority were women.

A vocational centre is run in Ambujwadi, as an entry point for youth to launch themselves with professional skills so that they can look for a job outside the community or start their own business. This is particularly for girls, who are not even allowed to leave their house, but parents allow them to come for the course since it is nearby, and some skills to pursue as a hobby. Once they enrol for skills training, they are also simultaneously initiated into processes of life skills, rights trainings, and experiential learning.

They are introduced to the youth groups – Malwani Yuva Parishad (MYP) and Nakshatra girls group. These youth groups lead many campaigns such as strengthening Public Distribution System, identity of the community on the Development Plan, to stop violence against women, claiming spaces and transforming them into safe spaces for children and youth, promote good food and urban farming for healthy eating habits, clean water campaign, toilets and sanitation campaigns.

By associating with these networks, it has been observed that a majority of the youth are back in education, or learning some skills, or working. As a result of these processes, more than 150 young people have been brought back into the fold of education, out of which many are completing graduation and some have enrolled for Masters' courses. About 200 youth have got jobs and are continuing and advancing in their field. Youth who have taken the beautician's vocational and skills training, too, have got jobs in reputed parlours like Loreal.

They feel a sense of identity and membership in the group, and thus become an example of youth leadership to others. They are also connecting others to the process. All these youth continue to meet together on Sundays and days of holiday to plan further agenda and also discuss and share their problems and concerns. They even go and perform street plays in different places to raise awareness on social issues.

Way Forward & Conclusion

A holistic approach to dealing with this issue is to reduce inequalities (SDG 10) and facilitate universal access to basic services including quality education (SDG 4), thereby creating safe, sustainable, just and inclusive cities and communities (SDG 11). This, when supplemented with appropriate skill training and availability of job opportunities, will ensure a base support for youth as well as a smooth transition into the transforming world of work and systematically reduce the inequalities faced by the urban poor youth.

Livelihood training, job readiness and skills are essential steps to employment. However, these must be supplemented with core skills training, life skills, exposure and peer learning, as also linkages to the market and creating more jobs. This will ensure that the livelihood process completes a full circle and enters sustenance. This is true, especially for youth living in marginalised communities, where information is also an expense and so they are not abreast of the world happenings.

Many may not even have ever ventured out of their lanes or the community. How does one get skills and livelihood training to reach even these youth at risk or youth who live along the fringes of society? Localising and decentralising training and skills centres to have branches even in *basti*s can prove to be one of the solutions. In this way, young people do not have to travel far and can access training.

Yet, it may be observed, especially in the case of girls, they may not even come to the training centre located at one end of the community, as their social access is very restrained. How does one overcome this problem to really reach to these invisible youth at risk? Partnering with local NGOs to implement localised training could help. YUVA has been working in Ambujwadi for more than 15 years. It is much easier for a YUVA worker to establish rapport and increase credibility of the centre than for some alien organisation to do the same in this area. Local NGOs know the families and support systems; they can counsel the youth and their families to convince them. Additionally, they can also do the follow up processes to ensure sustainability.

Moreover, organising youth and bringing them together, from the YUVA experience, has been one of the strengths of youth work. In this process, youth must feel a sense of ownership and accountability to the processes. This is key to the work; if it doesn't happen, they will just remain recipients or beneficiaries of the process and it will not translate into empowerment of youth for a sustainable youth-led development process.

Youth are active agents of the nation, and they must be treated as equals in the change process. Therefore, strengthening youth networks and youth groups will ensure a sense of responsibility among the youth to take charge of issues of drop-outs etc. and conduct these processes independently. Once youth groups are capacitated, there will not be a need for any NGO to collaborate; these community groups themselves will coordinate the processes.

While this is essential at the field level, it is equally essential at the macro level to build greater jobs and opportunities for the youth. The job market for decent jobs has increasingly shrunk. It is imperative that jobs and careers that help youth realise their potential more fully are explored and created. Without this, the much talked-about youth 'dividends' are only going to turn into mechanised products of industries, lacking any critical thinking skills and motivation to do something for the betterment of themselves and for society at large.

Creating Level Playing Field

Participatory Action Research for Gender Equality and Youth Development

Anita Patil-Deshmukh,
Payal Tiwari & Sunil Gangavane

We know things with our lives and we live that knowledge beyond what any theory has yet theorised.

— **Catherine McKinnon**

Introduction

SDG 4 OF THE world's goals talks about inclusive and quality education. This goal has ten different targets to be achieved by the countries. In India, Participatory Action Research has gained prominence due to its efforts in promoting Quality Education at all levels. It serves as an important tool in raising the voices of Indian youth, put up their concerns, present their thoughts and opinion.

Many social organisations believe that the marginalised youth are the repository of indigenous knowledge which is of great value. If given an opportunity, proper access and right platform, these youth can transform their everyday experiences into a systemic, learning one. It is also looked at as an avenue to work effectively with communities. During the community work, the insider's lens that the youth wear as researchers makes them look at their own lives more critically, using an alternative lens.

Research-based initiatives, as part of quality education, creates organic knowledge which often makes a significant contribution to the development of sustainable and inclusive societies and nation. It is worthwhile to invest in making a research fellow see himself/herself transform into not only a good researcher, but also a critical thinker who can then take an initiative to ask, consult, build perspectives, collaborate with people and make a difference in the existing situation.

Partners For Urban Knowledge Action And Research (Pukar) is a Mumbai based non-government organisation that started in early 2000s as a research collective. Inspired by Prof Arjun Appadurai's writings on 'Right to Research', the organisation was established to create a space for cross-disciplinary discussions that extend beyond the academic circles in the city. PUKAR, the acronym for the organisation in Hindi, means 'clarion call' and the objective of the organisation is to call upon the youth, especially from the marginalised sections of society, to engage in discussions on social transformation through participatory and democratic research rooted in their communities, using systematic inquiry and documentation as intervention.

The organisation started its flagship programme 'Youth Fellowship' in 2005 to engage and empower the youth from communities across the city of Mumbai as praxis of Professor Appadurai's writings on right to research.

In his paper, Appadurai (2006) questioned the inherent power in traditional research methodologies and explored the democratisation of research, using PUKAR as a case study. The programme has since evolved, borrowing from various alternate pedagogies on how community-based participatory action research can best be contextualised, based on the communities and the participants of the programme.

It is important to diversify the knowledge and co-produce, so as to include the experiences of those who continue to be on the fringes of society, because their voices are often not accounted for in the development discourse. This leads to a continuum of oppression and seclusion faced by vulnerable communities. To amalgamate these narratives and bring attention to their concerns, their voices need diversified forms of communication, which needs context-specific tools and strategies and calls for diverse methodologies that are suitable for each community.

Doing so is imperative as these voices have faced a systemic exclusion from learning spaces on grounds of caste, class, gender, ethnicity and religion that has led to an invisibilisation of diverse epistemologies in understanding our complex socio-political surroundings. Therefore, the programme conceptually uses a cross-pollination of various alternate pedagogies that reconceptualise the traditional process of knowledge creation.

Exploring the politics of knowledge production, PUKAR questions what 'knowledge' is, who produces it, who owns it and whose knowledge matters? With a focus on the marginalised during the co-production of knowledge, PUKAR specifically works with youth intersecting across caste, class, gender and ethnicity and brings the voices of the youth from the subaltern communities to the centre of the discussion.

PUKAR focuses on youth (18 – 35 years) as India is a young country with the highest youth population. PUKAR believes that youth today cannot merely be recipients of knowledge rather they have to be critical thinkers who are informed about the multi-faceted complexities that shape our socio-cultural context. Importance of this has also been globally recognised, which is imperative in attaining Sustainable Development Goals.

Critically thinking youth will challenge the status quo and unequal relationship, and also work for their and their community's wellbeing. To work towards youth development and gender equality, it is important to work with youth from marginalised ghettos in the city and document the processes of urbanism from the lenses of youth. PUKAR's Youth Fellowship Programme works specifically in lower income communities and with marginalised groups and deconstructs the heterogeneous category 'youth' to include the voices of 'all'.

Youth Fellowship Cycle: Process Documentation

The framework of Youth Fellowship is based on questioning 'accepted' knowledge and bringing indigenous knowledge into the development discourse.

Through the Youth Fellowship programme, barefoot researchers document and advocate to understand diversity in experiences, grounded in lived and shared realities. Additionally, it questions the inherent power in traditional research methodologies; using community- based participatory action research, with a focus on reflective learning to understand self and society for societal transformation. According to Anita Patil-Deshmukh et. al (2016), the Executive Director of PUKAR, the Youth fellowship programme is based on privileging indigenous knowledge located within each community, anchored in their lived experiences and creating distinct knowledge about the city which is perhaps seldom possible in the high end, strongly academic research-based institution.

The Fellowship cycle is of 11months, and provides an opportunity for community-based youth to engage in participatory action research and explore the issues of their own lives and communities through the lens of a researcher. The participants conduct research in groups of 8 to 10 members, as that provides them the support and confidence to take on subjects related to their lives that they so closely introspect upon. Participants who embark on the journey of becoming 'barefoot researchers' are often first-generation learners or school dropouts. However, the programme encourages those who are denied access or do not access learning spaces because of larger socio-political and cultural issues.

To make the processes participatory and inclusive from diverse contexts, all sessions are conducted in vernacular languages and are activity based. The selected groups undergo an intense course work comprising perspective-building sessions on social reality by academicians, activities, practitioners, media people and journalists to include multiple voices and learning techniques. The group conducts research on a topic that is necessarily rooted in their lived reality and goes through a series of workshops on research methods, data collection tools, perspective building, community visits and understanding one's own self.

The research study that is co-authored by the group and is an outcome of the group processes is used for advocacy in the same community from where data was gathered. This aspect of action research is critical to a fellow's journey in the YF cycle. Advocating the findings and creating awareness in the community is intervention through documentation. *The most powerful aspect of intervention remains in the heart and minds of Fellows, who go beyond the boundaries in exploring their communities, think, re-think, create new vision and transgress the fellowship programme into the lives of youth in the city.*

Outreach

At the onset of the programme, the communities that face multiple oppressions are approached for the fellowship cycle. Such as:

- M-East Ward - Since the 1960s, M-East ward has been home to migrant populations that immigrate to the city from different parts of India, as well as those that have been resettled from slums in the city's centre (TISS 2015). The ward has the lowest human development index in Mumbai (24 out of 24 wards in Human Development Indices) (MCGM 2010).
- Sex Workers and HIV positive groups.
- Adivasi/ Dalit groups/Religious minority – Fellowship in its 12-year long journey has consistently worked with barefoot researchers from Adivasi and Dalit groups, and Minority religious groups on the issues faced by marginalised castes and communities, especially women.
- LGBTQIA+– sexuality, identity and gender remain core areas of work in the fellowship programme. Resource persons who identify as gay, transgender or queer take sessions on gender and sexuality during the programme, using personal narratives as political issues and talking about intersections.
- State Wards/ Observation Home – The fellowship cycle has been reconceptualised and contextualised in accordance with those who are considered *wards of the state* and reside in protection/observation

homes. Considering the vulnerability of the groups, the programme uses needs based and here and now approaches of facilitation. Additionally, the fellows undergoing the training are also trained in research methods and data collection.

- Women's groups – The fellowship cycle works with women's groups on issues related to poverty, social exclusion, governance, safety and violence.

Experience Sharing as Perspective Building

In her book, *Teaching to Transgress,* Bell Hooks (1994) describes the importance of sharing of individual experiences in learning spaces. Through the exercise, she talks about the value in uniqueness of each voice, despite the privilege of the one sharing it. This instils communal awareness about diversity of those present in a learning space. While there is a focus on experience-based learning, Hook's understanding is not merely restricted to the participants but also the facilitator, as it enhances the processes of learning. PUKAR's Youth Fellowship programme borrows from feminist pedagogy's idea of challenging the traditional learning methodologies and using experience as theoretical knowledge.

Asserting feminist pedagogical values during PUKAR's workshops, the facilitators are also participants who share their personal narratives as well. This makes the narrative-sharing process non-coercive for the participants and everyone is able to express their vulnerability. The participants learn that being vulnerable is also being powerful and everyone, including those in positions of power is human first, who have multiple identities that shape their experiences.

The YF programme starts with orientation workshops that are residential in nature. In the beginning of the programme, pertinent social concepts are introduced to the groups for which the fellows are invited for residential workshops. The nature of residential workshops provides space for participants to interact with each other in informal settings. This is an important space for many participants who are women, allowing them opportunity to interact with a diverse population of participants. The residential workshops are an opportunity for youth to come out of the confines of their homes, *basti*s (slums) or communities, especially those who face a restriction in mobility. This space is useful for group-building processes, which is an important aspect of group research.

To be able to share narratives in informal setups that are not facilitated or supervised helps the participants in being reflective and feeling comfortable in sharing their own stories in a larger group during the group process. In addition, the process also includes activities such as writing one's autobiography and drawing one's *river of life* as reflective methodologies. Being introspective and reflecting upon our own life stories is an important part of CBPAR. This helps the participants in selecting a research topic that is rooted in their community and is a part of their collective everyday experience.

Deconstructing these epistemologies is a process of self-actualisation that for participants is liberating, as they begin to understand self, society and their community from a nuanced perspective where their collective experiences are connected to a larger social structure. The sessions on social realities then do not become an abstract course work that is highly jargonised, but a process of self-actualisation and helps in understanding one's own location and the social constructs that shape our everyday interactions.

Engaged Pedagogy as Theory and Praxis

Even while the fellows are engaged in data collection and report writing, the groups remain conversant with the facilitators through group meetings that take place in the communities. The Fellows discuss issues with facilitators in smaller groups, in their communities, in the presence of their community members. This makes the Fellow comfortable in the process. This 'comfort' is important in the process, given that writing and being a part of a learning space in a diverse group can be challenging for first time learners. Facilitators actively engage with Fellows, using *empathetic listening* to understand the problems that the Fellows might not always be vocal about. *Additionally, the team of facilitators often comprise those who have undergone the Youth Fellowship cycle themselves as barefoot researchers.* The voices and experiences of these facilitators help in understanding the programme, the Fellows and evolving the Fellowship cycle into a more participant friendly and learning oriented way.

Believing strongly in Paulo Freire's methodology to treat the learner as a co-creator of knowledge, Fellows are encouraged to build upon that knowledge through their research techniques and community engagement. While they engage with the community during the data collection phase, the Fellows learn about research ethics where emphasis is on understanding that *humans are not data sets.* The participants are taught the importance of asking questions in a sensitive, polite manner, importance is given to people's right to their own privacy and their right to not participate in any research proceedings, keeping the information about respondents safe and keeping their identity anonymous. They are taught ways to seek and record consent – oral, written, visually-recorded or audio-recorded.

Gender Equality in Youth Development

Theory that does not resonate with the collective, in the voice of the collective, by the collective and for the collective cannot truly be used to represent the collective consciousness. Women form an integral part of this collective. The absence of women's voices in group process and documentation presents only half the narrative. To bring the voices of the other half, research done by women on issues faced by women in their communities need documentation, visibility and advocacy. For the past several years, Youth Fellowships has seen a relatively higher participation of women vis-à-vis men, the ratio being 60:40. While the increased participation can be an outcome of strategic outreach, more and more documentation about women's lives in the communities can help understand gender and urbanism from a bottom up approach. As stated before, PUKAR's intervention tool of participatory research makes the researcher self- aware and a critical thinker, while this might not change their circumstances drastically; the process empowers them and gives them the skills to document their own stories and their shared realities in their communities using systematic data collection techniques.

When youth is empowered, they talk about their own communities, using evidence-based data and critical thinking skills. In the context of Mumbai, PUKAR has been working with youth across the city who have been stigmatised because of their marginalisation. This stigmatisation translates into their reduced access to resources and opportunities. Over the years, PUKAR has seen multiple documentations that have been a window into the everyday lives of youth in communities strewn across the city.

For example, groups in the programme have used documentation to give voices to their mothers, whose lives they felt are often neglected and thus remain unknown. This is a study of the 'Manipotwali' women who travel across Mumbai, selling combs, makeup and trinkets. The participants who documented their lives were the daughters of Manipotwali women, who belong to the 'Vaidu' community, a nomadic tribe that migrated from Andhra to Mumbai that was traditionally engaged in collecting medicinal herbs.

Muslim youth from across Mumbai have over the years given us extremely thought-provoking insights into their lives and everyday interactions with their families and those outside their communities. Muslim girls, after reflecting on their daily lives, together decided to document the impact of alcoholism in their families and on the restrictions in mobility and their personal negotiations. Similarly, Muslim girls have also documented interviews of Islamic religious leaders to understand the connection between the *burqa* and the *Quran.* The process required the girls to critically understand religion. Interviewing the religious leaders who hold significant power and exercise control over the community gave the girls confidence and empowered them to go beyond socialisation. These reflective, participatory and critical lenses help youth, especially girls, to learn and unlearn, using evidence-based data.

Another group from a religious minority, who have been ghettoised in Mumbra, have documented the multiple facets of marginalisation and how they face stigmatisation because of where they reside. The documentation involves an in-depth analysis of these spaces, negotiations and interactions where they face differential treatment. Another group of girls from the same community have documented taboos around menstruation. Post the completion of the Fellowships, this group, based on the findings of their study, have been engaged in raising awareness about menstrual cycle, facts and myths and creating a space to talk about menstrual cycle. Another youth-led group comprising girls and boys have used participatory mapping to understand the locations and demystify the reasons of women feeling unsafe in accessing the local trains and its impact on their daily routine, additionally giving suggestions to relevant stakeholders.

While academic circles and development discourses discuss marginalisation, the documentations that emerge from lived experiences can provide practitioners with detailed understanding of ground reality. In M-East ward, PUKAR has been consistently engaging youth from various community-based organisations in the Community Based Participatory Action Research(CBPAR). A group of Muslim boys from this ward, during the process identified the issues plaguing their neighbourhood. Using detailed interviews and surveys with respondents most of who are women, this group that called itself '*Aashayein*', writes about how scarcity of water in their *basti* negatively impacts access to schools. Their study takes the reader through the lanes of M-ward where water connection is a privilege, available water is extremely dirty and its effects on the health of the residents. They have documented how the time spent on filling water cans coincides with the time when the children and youth of the community have to go to school.

The problem of safe water has existed in the ward for many years now, but the in-depth engagement of youth with this problem during the phase of data collection and advocacy (2017-18) has made residents take cognisance of it. The group has been actively engaged in talking about the issue at various platforms. Similarly, a group of boys from a community in Jogeshwari that face high cases of drug addiction in youth have documented how access to public spaces has been getting cramped over the years, effecting spaces for youth to engage in sports. All the members of the group enjoy playing football and wanted to document reducing spaces and changing patterns of the city. The process of documentation also brought insights into the conditions of available playgrounds, negative effects of lack of open spaces on youth and gendered access to available spaces.

The constant dialogue with participants on gender as a perspective can be seen in majority of the research studies. This Fellowship focuses on gender as an important theme and uses various workshops and activities to engage the participants on understanding gender, using it as a lens while conducting research and being reflective about how the discourse on gender is connected to their lives.

While questioning gendered spaces and accessibility, the discussions in the group involve questioning their own biases, stereotypes and generalisations in their close-knit circles. Questioning, learning and unlearning; being accountable to each other and to the Fellowship programme and incorporating the values of engaged pedagogies in a Fellow's research and advocacy is the essence of the outcome of the Fellowship cycle. These forms of engagement help understand the process of urbanisation and development discourse from the lenses of youth, the communities that form this city and the youth whose voices are not homogeneous, the differences in these voices and the context shaping these differences needs attention.

Through these documentations, barefoot researchers, most of who are women, begin to explore the themes of gender-based issues in their individual contexts, challenge hegemonic, patriarchal, class-oriented spaces and structures using their own lives and indigenous knowledge as theory. This not only redefines gendered understanding of community, relationships, infrastructure and social reality but also helps them re-conceptualise the feminist movement to include subaltern experiences and theorise as knowledge. This also throws light on identifying the need to deconstruct 'youth' as a category and work with *the marginalised among the marginalised.*

Conclusion

Target 4.5 of the SDG 4 particularly aims at eliminating gender disparities in education and ensure equal access to all levels of education and vocational training for the vulnerable, including persons with disabilities, indigenous peoples and children in vulnerable situations.

Youth from vulnerable communities, with different gender and sexual orientation, different disabilities seldom get any opportunity to enhance their skills and knowledge based on action research.

Along with the theoretical understanding of the subjects, hands on-experience of carrying out action research activities in the grassroots communities has proved to be a good source for social cohesion. Such models of education is the need of the time, as it provides avenues to marginalised youth who are school dropouts or have little chance of completing their formal education, to engage with an experiential learning space. Such interventions not only serve to bridge them to the main society, but also sow the seeds of interest to take up further education.

To achieve target 4.5 and the goal 4, it is imperative to build participatory group work, leadership and critical thinking capacities of the youth. Such educational interventions provides enhanced confidence to re-enroll into the mainstream. We need such youth leaders who have created a repository of knowledge that emerges by and from their everyday lived experiences to transform the society and support the nation in its journey of development.

While training youth on the diversity in contexts, differences in accessing education systems must be given cognisance. Given the diverse socio-cultural and political difference of each community, the access to learning opportunities varies. While training the youth in transforming the nation, the first step is to bring the youth, including those from the marginalised communities, to the same level of education, using equitable measures. Strategies for engaged pedagogies must constantly be changed, invented and re-conceptualised. In order to work with youth from varied communities, not only do their paradigms need to shift but also the way they think, write and speak.

Knowledge creation about these equitable measures and revised strategies, identifying vulnerable youth and pedagogies that have been useful in working with them must be documented and shared with stakeholders and the communities. Additionally, there is a need to create spaces for youth that include, celebrate and value narratives based on lived realities, especially representing the voices of the marginalised and the vulnerable.

This chapter is a documentation of PUKAR's engagement with youth using community based participatory action research and the pedagogies and processes that PUKAR borrows from to best implemented CBPAR. The programme has sofar been a fruitful engagement with the community youth and has received recognition from academic institutes where the programme now runs as a course or in similar capacity.[1] The programme in 2017 received accreditation from Tata Institute of Social Sciences Centre for Lifelong Learning as a

---

1 The youth fellowship cycle has been replicated in BMN College of Home Science: SNDT University as a part of the course work for a select batch

certificate course in Community Based Participatory Research and Action. The Youth Fellowship cycle continues to evolve each year, based on the groups and their specific needs from the programme; finding inspiration in works and writings of barefoot researchers, scholars, academics, communities, team PUKAR and those who have found peace in working with and for the people.

The Youth Fellowship cycle can be summarised by quoting Paulo Freire:

> … *To begin always anew, to make, to reconstruct, and to not spoil, to refuse to bureaucratize the mind, to understand and to live life as a process – live to become…*

The in-depth documentation of its flagship programme and the thought process, values and ideologies behind it can be replicated in similar contexts in other youth-centred programmes across the country. SDG 4 commits for quality education and access to lifelong learning spaces through which youth can be enabled to acquire knowledge about their human rights, gender equality, power of peace and sustainable development. The programme is unique and adaptable to every context.

The last chapter on Creating Spaces for Lifelong Learning Skills in Youth discusses the importance of lifelong learning and the need to upgrade oneself to be able to meet new challenges of life. The ability to keep learning is significant to growth and development.

Creating Spaces for Lifelong Learning Skills

Intervention to Generate Sustainable Workforce of the Future

Saigita Chitturu

Anyone who stops learning is old, whether at twenty or eighty. Anyone who keeps learning stays young.

— **Henry Ford**

Introduction

YOUTHHOOD IS KNOWN to be a process of growth and development. Young people are frequently addressed as problematic, so much so that it appears this is what we want them to think of themselves. But are they problematic?

All generations of youth have been identified with problems. The history of human race shows that young people are always struggling for or against something. A changing world means changing values, trends and norms. Young people are merely participating in these changes, just as adults do. A large proportion of the world's youth are enjoying success and doing well for themselves and their societies. This aspect goes unrecognised and young people's presence is felt only when it is a problem, when they go out of bounds. Thus, young people are not problematic, but this is what is seen most in their existence. Negative labels of this nature are not a true commentary on them. The positive qualities like volunteerism, commitment, dynamism, willingness to sacrifice, sensitivity, and receptivity to new ideas, courage, potential for creativity and growth, must necessarily be considered in devising appropriate youth policies and programmes.

A fresh look at the conventional approach underlying the policy and programmes in dealing with youth issues is recognised by society and educators. Is it recognised by policy-makers with top-down policies? At the same time, emphasis on maintenance of productivity is to be encouraged.

Young people are known to be playing an important yet challenging role in the development of any society. In every country, it is the youth who are more radically influenced by social changes. The values and beliefs of old people are set, unlike those of youngsters whose ideals are in the state of formation. Coupled with this, the questioning attitude fostered by education and the corrosive effect of education on conservatism make young people more liberal in their attitudes. They are the section of all societies who are ready to change, willing to innovate and improvise, adaptable to fluid situations and most willing to learn.

This chapter reviews the current status of youth development and the core skills necessary to engage youth meaningfully in a future of work life. Drawing from the experience of working with National Youth volunteers of NYKS and NSS, India's most popular youth-based programmes, the paper discusses the ongoing need of training and academic intervention to facilitate smooth transition of young men and women into the world of work.

The young volunteers associated with the two youth schemes constitute a large segment of India's population, with a majority coming from rural backgrounds. Access to higher education and relevant training has generally been a challenge to them. Many a times, without adequate skills and training these young people enter into the world of work and are unprepared. Harnessing potential of these young groups by providing them appropriate space for learning different skill sets at different points of time proves useful not only in upgrading their knowledge and skills but also meeting future challenges.

While much of the discussion in India on skill development is around employability-related skills, acknowledgment of relevant and practice (soft) skills like interpersonal skills, people skills, leadership, life skills etc. is missing and needs to be paid equal attention. There is no strong policy framework for these associated and very necessary skills.

A qualitative study was carried out with some youth volunteers across India in the year 2018. One of the objectives of the study was to examine their understanding of 'lifelong learning' and its relevance in sustainable development. The second objective was to understand the relevance of 'soft skills' like leadership and interpersonal skills in the lives of young people.

It is observed that the need and relevance of lifelong learning in the context of sustainable national development needs a careful look in the policy document. Integration of different soft skills along with employability-related skills set is a must to accommodate every need of every young person's future and to challenge every challenge at professional and personal level.

This chapter has attempted to examine and highlight all such critical issues in the perspective of skill building and lifelong learning framework of skill development in India.

According to the Study on Evaluation of NSS in India, 2009, *'Youth work has a great deal to do with personality development of young people. It might be said that youth work is to prepare the youth to be the instruments of change. While such institutions as family, schools, religious organisations, etc, are basically conservative and usually tend to preserve the status quo, youth work can and should progressively lead youth towards constructive social change. Therefore, it is not wholly a matter of transference of skills. It also involves training young people to work through groups of their own.'*

Youth Programmes and Services in India

Post-independence, in India, youth groups have been involved in social transformation and other developmental activities more seriously. Involvement of youth in the Gujarat movement in 1974 and Bihar movement in 1975 are some of the examples. Sewa Mandir in Rajasthan, Gram Vikas in Orissa and CINI-Child-In-Need Institute in West Bengal, Sangham Kshetriya Vikas Samiti in Uttar Pradesh tends to focus on traditional artisan crafts; Asha for Education[1] and some more examples of voluntary youth groups are working as catalysts to bring change in the society by being actively engaged in economic, social and political processes of change.

However, the full account and exhaustive directory of voluntary youth groups working in the field is yet to be

---

[1] https://shodhganga.inflibnet.ac.in/bitstream/10603/14299/7/07_chapter%202.pdf accessed on 20th June, 2020

documented. At the government level, one attempt to involve non-student youth has been made by opening nation-wide, Nehru Yuvak Kendras. Youth organisations working in the field of social service represent the efforts of the voluntary sector. A large number of such organisations are mobilising youth energies for constructive activities and community work. They operate at different levels and represent a variety of interests and groups.

A similar intervention at the community level is done by college-going youth through the National Service Scheme (NSS) programme. They are large in numbers and work locally as well as nationally. Bharat Scouts, NCC, RSP, Guide etc. are few more examples of Youth Services and Schemes which are equally popular and recognised in India.

Progress in a country of India's size and diversity depends on participation and full involvement of all sections of its people. It is also an acceptance of the fact that to ensure accelerated growth, great social justice and modern self-reliant economy, its youth resources must be marshalled properly. For this purpose, they must be exposed to the social realities and the pressing problems that India is confronted with, for being and becoming active partners in national progress and development.

Youth should be made aware of the different plans and youth-related programmes of the government, both at the micro and macro level, for deriving and entailing maximum benefit out of them. Along with awareness and knowledge, skills are also necessary to keep this momentum alive. This may help youth to steer well and keep a good balance between work and life. This involves skills like leadership skills, life skills and those skills which are geared towards leading a successful life and not just aiming to gain employment.

The education system in India, with its major focus on classroom teaching, seldom exposes students to the world outside and to the skills necessary to equip them to meet the challenges of life. Programmes like the NSS, RSP, NCC, Scouts etc present a third dimension of the standard education system and play an important role in shaping the personalities of students, by providing them appropriate opportunities and skills to grow. Change of attitude, improved leadership and people skills are some of the distinguished features of these programmes.

Population of India

India's population is among the youngest in an ageing world. By 2022, the median age in India will be 28 years; in comparison, it will be 37 in China and the United States, 45 in Western Europe, and 49 in Japan. India's working-age population has numerically outstripped its non-working age population. A demographic dividend, said to have commenced around 2004-05, is available for close to five decades. This is an extraordinary opportunity. There are however, two caveats.

Key Caveats

First, India's population heterogeneity ensures that this window of demographic dividend becomes available at different times in different States. While Kerala's population is already ageing, in Bihar the working age cohort is predicted to continue increasing till 2051. By 2031, the overall size of our vast working age population would have declined in 11 of the 22 major States. Second, harnessing the demographic dividend will depend upon the employability of the working age population, their health, education, vocational training and skills, besides appropriate land and labour policies, as well as good governance. India will gain from its demographic opportunity only if policies and programmes are aligned to this demographic shift.

There is consensus now that among other factors, it was the demographic dividend that powered respectively the Asian economies of Japan, China, and South Korea to spectacular growth. More significantly, in each case, the underlying pattern was fairly similar i.e. countries will benefit from the economic potential of their youth bulge when and where they succeed in providing good health, quality education, and decent employment to their entire population; and not to segments defined by socio-economic status, geography, or historical legacy.[2]

A May 2020 modelling study conducted by the Ipas Development Foundation, India, a non-profit dedicated to preventing and managing unwanted pregnancies, concluded that around 1.85 million Indian women could not terminate an unwanted pregnancy due to lack of medical abortion drugs or availability of contraceptives or public and private abortion health facilities.[3]

Also, the United Nations Children's Fund (UNICEF) has predicted that India would see the birth of more than 20 million babies this year. Of the total 116 million babies expected to be born worldwide, the highest number of births was predicted in India followed by China (13.5 million), Nigeria (6.4 million), Pakistan (5 million) and Indonesia (4 million).[4]

The above statistics has set an alarm bell ringing for India. Are we prepared as a country to accommodate these numbers?

---

[2] https://www.thehindu.com/opinion/lead/youth-can-be-a-clear-advantage-for-india/article30897179.ece accessed on 14th June, 2020

[3] http://www.kashmirtimes.com/newsdet.aspx?q=104136, accessed on 18th August, 2020

[4] https://www.femina.in/trending/in-the-news/india-may-record-20-million-births-this-year-says-unicef-157049.html

Do we have robust plan, systems or mechanism in place to ensure wellbeing of this new-born population?

Lifelong Learning Opportunities and Skills

Lifelong learning has been an integral part of Indian culture. The ancient Indian religious tradition and culture have accorded prime importance to the acquisition of knowledge and upheld the virtues of learning. Notwithstanding the gradual modernisation of society and the emergence of multiple channels of learning, the first formal recognition of lifelong learning came in 1966 when the Indian Education Commission (1964-66) made the following observation:

Education does not end with schooling, but is a lifelong process. The adult needs an understanding of the rapidly changing world and the growing complexities of society. Even those who had the most sophisticated education must continue to learn; the alternative is obsolescence... Thus viewed the function of adult education in a democracy is to provide every adult citizen an opportunity for education of the type which he wishes and which he should have for his personal enrichment, professional advancement and effective participation in social and political life (Report of Indian Education Commission, 1966, more than fifty years ago).

However, the process of developing a nationwide policy framework for lifelong learning has been rather slow in India and seems to be linked to external stimulus. Currently, 'lifelong learning' is often used as an umbrella term to cover basic literacy, post literacy, continuing education and extension programmes of different organisations, refresher/continuing courses of professional bodies, private institutions and business houses; but not conceived as an overarching framework of learning.

This is mainly due to an absence of inter-sectoral linkages among different sectors of education and recognition and validation of prior learning. Besides, the lack of coordination between the two national bodies dealing with adult education and skill development viz: the National Literacy Mission and the National Skill Development Mission and overlapping of their functions has also put hurdles in the path of development of a comprehensive national policy on lifelong learning.

While the National Skill Development Mission has recognised the importance of skills and knowledge as the driving forces of economic growth and social development for any country and emphasised the need for promoting lifelong learning, maintaining quality and relevance according to changing requirement of emerging knowledge economy (National Policy on Skill Development, 2009); the National Literacy Mission continues to focus on just literacy, mainly due to massive number of non-literates in the country. Imparting skill training and providing avenues for skill up gradation has not received much attention of the National Literacy Mission. Anyway, the NPSD is a decade old and the NLM is 30 years old; and both need to be reworked under the 2020 changed circumstances globally.

As Prof SY Shah, of the International Institute of Adult and Lifelong Education, India, points out, '*Lifelong learning has been an integral part of Indian culture, but the most populous South Asian country is yet to develop the following (a formal) framework for lifelong learning*'.

Learning is inevitable and unavoidable. It happens all the time. Most people associate learning with formal education at school, college, university etc. Generally speaking, it is true that a formal education and the resulting qualifications are important. However, this kind of education is only one kind of learning. Along with this, there are many other opportunities to further your knowledge and develop the skills you need throughout life. Lifelong learning is about creating and maintaining a positive attitude to learning, both for personal and professional development. Lifelong learning enhances our capacity and understanding of the world around us, which in turn improves the quality of life (https://www.skillsyouneed.com/learn/lifelong-learning.html). Lifelong learning skills are critical to sustain and succeed in professional life by changing and adapting to the change happening around us.

Since Independence, the higher education system in India has been found wanting in its effort to prepare students to face the challenges of life, even though this has long been acknowledged to be the aim of education. The reality is that a great deal of knowledge acquired in the college remains peripheral to the personality structure of the student. Students may learn a great deal in order to pass examinations and to get through college, without actually changing their personalities in any important way. Much knowledge is quickly forgotten and the individual, as a person, may not change much by forgetting, any more than what she/he may have changed initially from the learning. Efforts have to be made in educating and training them for future.

The university system continues to face the challenge of preparing students for life, by helping them, as individuals, to discover the means of continued learning, which involves a change in the individual's personality. This will occur to a greater extent if freeing of students' imagination takes place. For this to occur, it is necessary to open the individual to experience, encourage creativity and spontaneity.

Much of the conventional education provided in colleges (and in schools) is concerned with suppressing spontaneity and to build up the highest possible degree of obedience. Much of this may be necessary, but then how can one release or encourage the imagination to bloom? In India, the struggle to meet the basic purpose of education continues in the twenty-first century in a more challenging environment than ever before, on account of factors like immense spurts in knowledge, easy access to knowledge by modern means of communication, fast pace of social, economic and political changes, increasing commercialisation, consumerism, erosion of moral values, and so on.

Institutions of education and training should open new vistas and offer unique opportunities for lifelong learning and training for the individuals to become instruments of change and development, with a value orientation to instil an obligation of community service, while promoting self-growth in the youth.[5]

Knowledge and Skill Society

Knowledge and skills have great impact on today's globalised and digital world. In other terms, knowledge economy or the knowledge society has replaced the industrial society and has great implications for learning and educational systems across the globe and throughout the lifespan. The world also expects '21st century competencies' which includes 'deep understanding, flexibility, and the capacity to make creative connections' and 'a range of so-called soft skills' including good team-work. They are known to be driving forces for economic activity, prosperity of individuals etc. Industries and societies are looking for quantity and quality of learning; thereby these factors have become central to all successful education systems, with the accompanying concern that traditional educational approaches are insufficient. Education and learning systems, for which knowledge and skills are their core business, is clearly right at the heart of such a mega-trend.

[5] *An Evaluation of National Service in India*, TISS

Lifelong Learning (LLL) is Continuous Education (CE), including designs and strategies of organisations. It is a key tool of speeding up to adapt to modern technologies. It is an ongoing education and learning process, in formal, non-formal and informal forms, from cradle to grave, making knowledge the tool to improve quality of life.

LLL is providing or using all types of learning opportunities in an individual's life to encourage the continuous development and enhancement of the knowledge and skills that are occupationally required and also for personal satisfaction. Many benefits are ascribed to CE that includes individual, community and country economy. CE leads to skills, academic and personal developments. We live in a world where individuals should possess the abilities to understand, explain and process the information, so we should identify and value different kinds of learning and education (Marjan, 2014).

Youth Employment

The number of people unemployed around the world stands at some 188 million. In addition, 165 million people do not have enough paid work, and 120 million have either given up actively searching for work or otherwise lack access to the labour market. In total, more than 470 million people worldwide are affected.[6] Predicting a grim picture of India's employment scenario, a report jointly prepared by the Asian Development Bank (ADB) and International Labour Organization (ILO) has estimated that the youth unemployment rate of the country is likely to be at 32.5 per cent in case the spread of coronavirus

---

6 https://economictimes.indiatimes.com/news/international/world-news/global-unemployment-projected-to-rise-by-around-2-5-million-in-2020-un-report/articleshow/73480520.cms2019 accessed on 20th June

is contained within six months of the start of the rigorous containment measures. As per the report, over 61.13 lakh Indian youth are expected to lose their jobs during the year 2020 in case the spread is contained within six months, For the past decade, India's youth unemployment rate has been hovering around the 10 per cent mark. Youth unemployment rate refers to those in the workforce who are aged 15 to 24 years and without a job, but actively seeking one. Generally, youth unemployment rates are higher than the adult unemployment rates, and India is no exception: youth unemployment in India is significantly higher than the national unemployment rate.[7]

The youth bulge is a common phenomenon in many developing countries, and in particular, in the least developed countries. The conventional approach for dealing with youth bulge is to make young people job ready. The idea is that young people's skills – or more broadly, human capital – needs to be increased to enhance their productivity in the labour market. The 2007 World Development Report, Development and the Next Generation, lays out the policy agenda by focusing on five key life transitions: learning, work, health, family and citizenship.

Three 'lenses' are used to focus on the policy discussion: opportunities, capabilities and second chances. Basic skills and access to secondary and tertiary education, are needed to create opportunities, while ability to seize opportunities can be enhanced through better information, access to credit and other factors. On the other hand, when outcomes are negative – for example, poor decisions lead to low levels of education or

---

7 https://www.statista.com/statistics/271330/unemployment-rate-in-india/accessed on 20th June, 2020
https://www.freepressjournal.in/business/indias-youth-unemployment-rate-for-2020-at-32-report#:~:text=India's%20youth%20unemployment%20rate%20for%202020%20at%2032%25%3A%20Report on 18 August 2020

exposure to communicable diseases – young adults may need access to services that can help them re-start their economic and personal lives. The 2007 WDR emphasised, both the skills upgrading and the institutional setting for improving economic outcomes for young people.[8]

Although Government of India has stressed the goal of increasing employment opportunities and eventually eradicating unemployment from the country, unemployment remains one of India's biggest challenges. Awareness about the difficulties of eliminating unemployment has, over the past three decades, led the successive governments at both the Central and State levels to formulate and implement schemes for promoting employment.

As per the findings of the 'State of the Urban Youth, India 2012: Employment, Livelihoods, Skills,' a report published by IRIS Knowledge Foundation in collaboration with UN-HABITAT, India is set to experience a dynamic transformation as the population burden of the past turns into a demographic dividend, but the benefits will be tempered with social and spatial inequalities. Also Covid-19.

Need for Skills

The Economic Survey 2019 called for additional jobs to keep pace with the projected annual increases in working age population. A workforce that is well educated and appropriately skilled is needed. UNICEF 2019 reported that at least 47 per cent of Indian youth are not on track to have the education and skills necessary for employment in 2030. The projected demographic dividend can turn into a demographic disaster if an unskilled,

---

[8] http://blogs.worldbank.org/developmenttalk/youth-bulge-a-demographic-dividend-or-a-demographic-bomb-in-developing-countries

under-utilised, and frustrated young population undermines social harmony and economic growth. While over 95 per cent of India's children attend primary school, the National Family Health Surveys (completed up to 2015-16) confirm that poor infrastructure in government schools, malnutrition, and scarcity of trained teachers has ensured poor learning outcomes.

Even while India aspires to become a knowledge economy, millions of young people are getting left behind. The national capital has now demonstrated that when meticulous attention is paid to equity and quality across government schools, huge numbers benefit, with encouraging learning outcomes. High quality education achieves gender parity and propels people forward into more productive lives. A coordinated incentive structure prompting States to adopt a broadly uniform public school system focusing on equity and quality will yield a knowledge society faster than privatising school education can accomplish.

Most districts now have excellent broadband connectivity. Irrespective of rural or urban setting, the public school system must ensure that every child completes high school education, and is pushed into appropriate skilling, training and vocational education in line with market demand. Deploying new technology to accelerate the pace of building human capital by putting in place virtual classrooms together with massive open online courses (MOOCS) will help prepare this huge work force for next-generation jobs. Investing in open digital universities would further help yield a higher educated workforce.[9]

Most employers these days wish a mix of skills and values in the employees they want to hire. While technical skills will always be important, soft skills have become the most sought

---

9 https://www.thehindu.com/opinion/lead/youth-can-be-a-clear-advantage-for-india/article30897179.ece accessed on 14th June, 2020

after skills in employment today. According to *an analysis of 2.3 million Linked in profiles for The Wall Street Journal,* nearly 58 per cent of employees who touted stellar communication skills were hired over the course of a year, making it clear that soft skills is more than just a buzzword in the job market these days. Policies should ensure that education system prepares young people for the skill demands of employers through outreach programmes, soft skills training, life skills programmes, technical training etc.

According to ILO, the global youth unemployment rate was 13.0 per cent for the period 2012 to 2014. Overall, two in five (42.6 per cent) economically active youth were either unemployed or working, yet living in poverty. As of 2014, 73.3 million youth were unemployed which accounted for 36.7 per cent of the global unemployed. (ILO, Global Employment Trends for Youth 2015, 2015, p.6, http://goo.gl/QphyAv.)

Youth employment is now a top policy priority in most countries across all regions. At the international level, it is being translated into the development of a global strategy for youth employment and embedded into the 2030 development agenda under Sustainable Development Goals. With a growing multitude of country-level initiatives involving many actors and institutions from the public and private sectors, focus now turns to forging partnerships for policy coherence and effective coordination on youth employment (Youth in India, 2017).

National Policy on Skill Development

This policy envisioned the establishment of a National Skill Development Initiative. Its mission has been to empower all individuals through improved skills, knowledge and recognised qualifications to gain access to decent employment and ensure India's competitiveness in the global market.

The aim of skills development in the country is to support rapid and inclusive growth through: a) enhancing individual's employability and ability to adapt to changing technologies and labour market demands. b) improving productivity and living standards; c) strengthening competitiveness; and d) attracting investment in skills development.

Although the term 'lifelong learning' is used in the Indian policy, there is no definition or description of the concept. It is mentioned in some of the UN objectives and measures to be taken within skills development.[10]

Youth are at the epicentre of the United Nations' newly adopted 2030 Agenda for Sustainable Development – as future leaders of the agenda. Developing capacity of the future workforce is an important agenda which the Government of India has taken on. The policy document talks about creating skill development ecosystem and framework and providing opportunities for lifelong learning. This includes incorporation of skilling in the school curriculum, providing opportunities for quality long-term and short-term skill training, by providing gainful employment and ensuring career progression that meets the aspirations of trainees.

The Mission Also Seeks To

Create an end-to-end implementation framework for skill development, which provides opportunities for life-long learning. This includes:

> *Incorporation of skilling in the school curriculum, providing opportunities for quality long and short-term skill training, by*

---

[10] http://uil.unesco.org/fileadmin/keydocuments/LifelongLearning/en/india-2009-abstract-lll-strategy.pdf

providing gainful employment and ensuring career progression that meets the aspirations of trainees.

Align employer/industry demand and workforce productivity with trainees' aspirations for sustainable livelihoods, by creating a framework for outcome focused training.

Establish and enforce cross-sectoral, nationally and internationally acceptable standards for skill training in the country by creating a sound quality assurance framework for skilling, applicable to all Ministries, States and private training providers.

Build capacity for skill development in critical un-organized sectors (such as the construction sector, where there are few opportunities for skill training) and provide pathways for re-skilling and up-skilling workers in these identified sectors, to enable them to transition into formal sector employment.

Ensure sufficient, high quality options for long-term skilling, benchmarked to internationally acceptable qualification standards, which will ultimately contribute to the creation of a highly skilled workforce.

Develop a network of quality instructors/trainers in the skill development ecosystem by establishing high quality teacher training institutions.

Leverage existing public infrastructure and industry facilities for scaling up skill training and capacity building efforts.

Offer a passage for overseas employment through specific programmes mapped to global job requirements and benchmarked to international standards.

Enable pathways for transitioning between the vocational training system and the formal education system, through a credit transfer system.

Promote convergence and coordination between skill development efforts of all Central Ministries/Departments/States/implementing agencies.

Support weaker and disadvantaged sections of society through focused outreach programmes and targeted skill development activities.

Propagate aspirational value of skilling among youth, by creating social awareness on value of skill training (National Skill Development Mission-A framework for Implementation, Government of India).

Although the major objective is to 'Ensure Inclusive and Equitable Quality Education and Promote Lifelong Learning Opportunities for All', it is interesting to note that not much has been emphasised on creating lifelong opportunities or developing soft skills set, related to sustaining work life and job, in the policy document.

As a policy document it stands to be very comprehensive. However, the implementation part of it – which is so critical – is not paid much attention to. The presence of multiple stakeholders in India, coupled with a lack of coordinated policies, has resulted in no standardisation of procedures or outcomes. The government today does not even have a unified definition of 'skill'. A 2013 paper of the Institute of Applied Manpower Research (IAMR) questioned the basis of the government's target of skilling 500 million people by 2022 without this definition (http://www.thehindu.com/opinion/op-ed/the-nuts-and-bolts-of-skilldevelopment/article7020970.ece). And seven years later, this target still remains a dream.

Jobs are constantly changing and evolving and therefore employability skills. People skills such as honesty and integrity, adaptability, problem solving, responsibility, teamwork, openness to grow and learn with change, ability to work with others in a professional manner etc. are some of the critical tools and traits that are needed to succeed in the workplace. These are some of the key aspects that can be learnt, cultivated, developed, and maintained over lifetime.

Link between Skill Development & Sustainable Development Goals

Sustainable Development Goals based on three dimensions of Development, namely, Economic, Social and Environmental are viewed as extensions of the UN's Millennium Development Goals (MDGs), with sustainability parameter added to each MDG to be implemented in the post-2015, era along with a set of all new goals which were ignored in the MDGs. This is a new, universal set of goals, targets and indicators that United Nations (UN) member states are expected to use to frame their agendas and political policies over the next 15 years.

The SDGs are a set of 17 specific goals offering special focus on important areas related to sustainable development that require urgent and extensive attention at present and in the near future. The SDG framework undertakes to provide systematic solutions to the obstacles identified in case of the MDGs like inequality, sustainability, institutional resourcefulness, implementation efficacy, environmental deterioration, etc., (UN 2014a).[11]

According to the UN agency in India, India's economic progress over the last decade has been remarkable. India's progress globally has been accompanied by rapid internal change. The Government of India played a key role in shaping the Sustainable Development Goals. The challenge now is to translate the SDGs into concrete action.

---

[11] http://www.un.org/sustainabledevelopment/news/communications-material/

Several of the ambitious programmes launched by the government directly contribute to a number of SDGs: The Clean India campaign; The End of Open Defecation by 2019 Campaign; Pradhan Mantri Awas Yojana or the Prime Minister's Housing Scheme; The Make in India Campaign; the 100 Smart Cities Initiative; Health Assurance for All; and the Prime Minister's Financial Inclusion Scheme, among others. Emphasis has been placed on Skill Development and Entrepreneurship to ensure a direct focus on youth.

Goal 4 of the SDGs – Ensures Inclusive and Equitable Quality Education and Promote Lifelong Learning Opportunities for all.

It aims to ensure that all people have access to quality education and the opportunity for lifelong learning. The Goal goes beyond school enrolment and looks at proficiency levels, the availability of trained teachers and adequate school facilities, and disparities in education outcomes.

Target 4.4 under 'Goal 4 of the SDGs' says that By 2030, substantial increase in the number of youth and adults who have relevant skills, including technical and vocational skills, for employment, decent jobs and entrepreneurship.

GOAL 4	Targets
4.1 By 2030, ensure that all girls and boys complete free, equitable and quality primary and secondary education leading to relevant and effective learning outcomes	4.1.1 Proportion of children and young people: (a) in grades 2/3; (b) at the end of primary; and (c) at the end of lower secondary achieving at least a minimum proficiency level in (i) reading and (ii) mathematics, by sex

4.2 By 2030, ensure that all girls and boys have access to quality early childhood development, care and pre-primary education so that they are ready for primary education	4.2.1 Proportion of children under 5 years of age who are developmentally on track in health, learning and psychosocial well-being, by sex 4.2.2 Participation rate in organised learning (one year before the official primary entry age), by sex
4.3 By 2030, ensure equal access for all women and men to affordable and quality technical, vocational and tertiary education, including university	4.3.1 Participation rate of youth and adults in formal and nonformal education and training in the previous 12 months, by sex
4.4 By 2030, substantially increase the number of youth and adults who have relevant skills, including technical and vocational skills, for employment, decent jobs and entrepreneurship	4.4.1 Proportion of youth and adults with information and communications technology (ICT) skills, by type of skill
4.5 By 2030, eliminate gender disparities in education and ensure equal access to all levels of education and vocational training for the vulnerable, including persons with disabilities, indigenous peoples and children in vulnerable situations	4.5.1 Parity indices (female/male, rural/urban, bottom/top wealth quintile and others such as disability status, indigenous peoples and conflict-affected, as data become available) for all education indicators on this list that can be disaggregated
4.6 By 2030, ensure that all youth and a substantial proportion of adults, both men and women, achieve literacy and numeracy	4.6.1 Percentage of population in a given age group achieving at least a fixed level of proficiency in functional (a) literacy and (b) numeracy skills, by sex

4.7 By 2030, ensure that all learners acquire the knowledge and skills needed to promote sustainable development, including, among others, through education for sustainable development and sustainable lifestyles, human rights, gender equality, promotion of a culture of peace and non-violence, global citizenship and appreciation of cultural diversity and of culture's contribution to sustainable development	4.7.1 Extent to which (i) global citizenship education and (ii) education for sustainable development, including gender equality and human rights, are mainstreamed at all levels in: (a) national education policies, (b) curricula, (c) teacher education and (d) student assessment
4.a Build and upgrade education facilities that are child, disability and gender sensitive and provide safe, non-violent, inclusive and effective learning environments for all	4.a.1 Proportion of schools with access to: (a) electricity; (b) the Internet for pedagogical purposes; (c) computers for pedagogical purposes; (d) adapted infrastructure and materials for students with disabilities; (e) basic drinking water; (f) single-sex basic sanitation facilities; and (g) basic hand washing facilities (as per the WASH indicator definitions)
4.b By 2020, substantially expand globally the number of scholarships available to developing countries, in particular least developed countries, small island developing States and	4.b.1 Volume of official development assistance flows for scholarships by sector and type of study

African countries, for enrolment in higher education, including vocational training and information and communications technology, technical, engineering and scientific programmes, in developed countries and other developing countries	
4.c By 2030, substantially increase the supply of qualified teachers, including through international cooperation for teacher training in developing countries, especially least developed countries and small island developing States	4.c.1 Proportion of teachers in: (a) pre-primary; (b) primary; (c) lower secondary; and (d) upper secondary education who have received at least the minimum organised teacher training (e.g. pedagogical training) pre-service or in-service required for teaching at the relevant level in a given country

The 21st century is truly the era of the 'learning society' – continuous learning is necessary, it is believed, if economic development is to be ensured.

There is a flood of information everywhere. The young people of today require reading much more than their forebears, to fulfil their obligation as responsible citizens as well as meet their personal and social objectives. The country can compete with developed countries only if it creates a strong culture of reading among its youth. Without a regular reading habit, the advantages accruing from literacy, or what is learnt in school, may be quickly frittered away (Shukla, 2010).

While attaining formal qualifications remains crucial for grasping new employment opportunities, Redecker & Punie (2013) say that informally acquired skills will have to become better recognised. Mechanisms must be put in places that allow people to obtain formal recognition for their professional expertise by upgrading their skills with adequate and targeted training. In particular, the experts foresee that ICT will play an important role in facilitating lifelong learning opportunities. The majority of experts believe that, in 15 years' time, a range of sophisticated learning tools and programmes will be available, making it easy for people to upgrade their skills and pro-actively drive their professional careers.

Methodology: A Qualitative study was carried out with youth volunteers across India in 2018. The objectives of the study were:

To examine their understanding of lifelong learning and its relevance to sustainability of work.

To understand relevance of soft skills like leadership and interpersonal skills in their lives.

Findings

According to the respondents, lifelong learning is a skill which can be cultivated and developed over a period of time. The ability to learn is considered to be one of the strongest skill amongst other soft skills that exist. Lifelong learning, according to the volunteers, refers to upgradation of self from time to time through various medium, for eg. through trainings, workshops, academic intervention etc. Respondents have said that learning is needed to react, behave and act appropriately upon situations. Learning throughout life makes an individual perfect in the sense it helps them to analyse every experience of life, good or bad. These skills and techniques are needed by every individual to make their lives better which continue till the last breadth.

Skills have the potential to transform lives by transforming life chances and driving social mobility. Possessing higher skills enables and guarantees a person to play a fuller part in society, makes him more cohesive, environmental-friendly, more tolerant and more engaged. Only by assuring that everyone has got the opportunity to gain skills that the benefits of renewed growth can extend to the society. Learning and skill development is not always about qualifications in India; we do recognise informal and non formal learning as a major component of learning.

Many are of the opinion that learning never ends and that technical skills, people skills, life skills are all essential requirements of life. It is a continuous process that can last throughout a person's entire life, from early childhood education to post-working age. The attitude towards learning makes it easy to learn other necessary skills to support life. It keeps oneself motivated. It helps in getting ideas on how to tackle life's issues. In this rapidly changing environment, it is the only safeguard to keep young people steady, vibrant and sustainable at work.

Discussion

Skills and values are key levers to achieve sustainable development goals. The idea of sustainable development is based on the vision of inclusive societies in which all citizens have equitable opportunities to access effective and relevant learning throughout life, delivered through multiple formal, non-formal and informal settings.

According to Redecker C, Leis M, Leendertse M, Punie Y, Gijsbers G, Kirschner P, Stoyanov S and Hoogveld B (2011), with the emergence of lifelong and life-wide learning as the central learning paradigm for the future, learning strategies and pedagogical approaches will undergo drastic changes. With the evolution of ICT, personalised learning and individual mentoring will become a reality and teachers/trainers will need to be trained to exploit the available resources and tools to support tailor-made learning pathways and experiences which are motivating and engaging, as well as also efficient, relevant and challenging.

Along with changing pedagogies, assessment strategies and curricula will need to change, and, most importantly, traditional E&T institutions – schools and universities, vocational and adult training providers – will need to reposition themselves in the emerging learning landscape. They will need to experiment with new formats and strategies for learning and teaching to be able to offer relevant, effective and high quality learning experiences in the future. In particular, they will need to respond more flexibly to individual learners' needs and changing labour market requirements.

Online and Distant Learning during Covid-19

According to ILO Policy Brief, 2020, India and many countries worldwide have arrived at paralysed 'regular education' and training provision. This unprecedented situation has affected all learning at all levels. Basic and secondary education, initial and continuing training and work-based learning have all come to a stop. It has upturned course schedules and attendance, disrupted teaching and learning, frustrated examinations and assessments, delayed certification and will affect the immediate and future careers of millions of learners. It has also reinforced existing inequalities, affecting workers and learners around the globe.

The shift to online or distance learning during the pandemic is seen first and foremost as an emergency response. However, the crisis also provides an opportunity for the development of more flexible learning solutions that make better use of distance learning and digital solutions. Three important policy issues must be addressed to create long-term positive impacts and develop greater resilience. First: human and financial resources have to be mobilised to ensure universal access to digital infrastructure, tools and modern learning technologies. Second, college managers, teachers, trainers and learners themselves need training and support to engage in distance and online learning. Third, education and training providers have to revise teaching and learning models to make the best use of digital resources and tools.

However, in the vocational and skills sector, there is evidence that the major challenge for institutions has been to remain operational, to establish communications with and between teachers and students, and to still provide their services to the community, despite having suspended face-to-face classes.[12]

Important Lessons Learnt during Covid-19 Pandemic

Pandemic has thrown at us new challenges and problems which people never imagined in life. The coronavirus disease has offered India a valuable lesson on the importance of self-reliance and self-sufficiency, it taught every individual to be self-reliant and self-sufficient. It taught individuals to self-regulate and allow for delayed gratification. Another significant aspect of this situation was the change in the way people cooked, ate, preserved and wasted. Food wastage in many households had reduced. People seem to have put a thought on planning meals and how much waste they produce. Very important lessons of personal hygiene, maintaining

---

[12] ILO CINTERFOR – Inter-American Centre for Knowledge Development in Vocational Training/Covid-19 and the World of Work, accessed 30 September 2020.

cleanliness not just at home but around, proper sanitation practices were learnt.

The challenges for Lifelong Learning are also three-fold:

- promoting a rapid and more fluent transition from school to work in order to reduce the barriers between the worlds of work and education;
- facilitating re-entrance to the labour market, especially to tackle long-term unemployment; and
- focussing on permanent re-skilling to enable all citizens to keep their competences updated and quickly respond and adjust to possibly fast-changing work environments.

In the working sector, soft skills are important to employers. Employers are concerned about the ability of a person to self-manage, solve problems, ability to work as part of a team, more coherent and consistent, better coordinated and integrated, ability to display leadership skills, communication skills, analytical and critical skills etc. The gifts of being able to relate well to others, imparting positive feelings, making the environment a peaceful and productive one, 'people skills' are the minimum requirements for employment.

National Skill Development agencies and various training institutions, skill sectors have been set up to impart vocational, technical–all employability related skills. There is a tendency to focus on vocational and initial education more with less emphasis to fully engage with the implications of an emphasis on lifelong learning for other arenas (Field 2000: 21-34). Even as these policies adopt the ethos of lifelong learning as learning over the life course, there is a need to slot in the learning pursuits within a specific time frame within the formal education system. *The policy document thus needs to be fine-tuned further and fitted to new circumstances in the world.*

Clear gaps have also been seen between the level of ambition articulated in SDG 4 and levels of national and international commitment to develop feasible, robust monitoring tools. Just like the contested meaning of 'life skills' in EFA Goal 3, the lack of a common definition of 'relevant skills' in Target 4.4 and of 'skills to promote sustainable development' in Target 4.7 also undermines the global monitoring of SDG 4.

A key lesson from the monitoring of EFA Goal 3 revolves around the fact that in the absence of a clear definition of 'life skills', international monitoring was stymied. Thus, the precise skills noted in each SDG 4 target require careful definition with clear measurement guideposts (https://www.un.org/%20 millenniumgoals/pdf/Think%20Pieces/4_education.pdf). A country like India needs to give special attention to clarity in definition as this is likely to be the guiding force for all future policies on youth skills.

There is hardly any data to map the implementation of the sustainable development goals in India. While the government is concentrating on employability-related skills and in that sense largely on technical skills, which is very important, the nation may be losing focus on the core skills necessary to drive these skills and also which is basic to any sustainability work (https://www.unicef.org/lifeskills/index_7308.html).

Research suggests that hard skills contribute a mere 15 per cent to one's skill success as compared to 85 per cent that comprises soft skills. It is exactly at this point where 'hard' and 'soft' skills meet.

Hard skills are often related to general intelligence – there is a component to them that's fixed and consistent throughout a students' academic history. However, it cannot be said to be same in the case of soft skills – they are flexible and may be developed through commitment and systematic practice.

Up until recently, soft skills were almost unprecedented, and for several they were deemed as unimportant, particularly in terms of their use in academia. However, today, the student experience is richer and more varied than it's ever been.

This is a mirrored image of the talents that employers are searching for in employees to make sure their commercial survival during an ever-changing and global world – it's the search for the right candidate, with the right skills.

People need help in the transition as they start a new job, and also need support to increase their skills so they can stay in work and move up the ladder. According to Debbie Hance of the Association of British psychologists, 'There's a saying that hard skills will enable you to perform well in academia and in interviews, but its soft skills that get you the job'.

One way to increase the sustainability of employment is to help people improve their skills, so that they can progress from short-term, entry-level jobs to better jobs and fortunately these skills can be identified, harnessed, and strengthened. Ideally, it is a mixture of soft and hard skills that helps individuals to develop and maintain sustainable careers.

Capacity building and learning LLL skills which includes relevant skills like social skills, life skills, leadership skills, interpersonal skills, problem solving skills, communication etc. are essential and need a proper place in the policy document. Secondly, it cannot be viewed in isolation and needs to be integrated well into the education system. Market, industries and companies should be made aware of the relevance of the life skills.

Education and Success in SDGs

Youth is a social category, a heterogeneous group, a phase of lifecycle between childhood and adulthood which is most productive part of human growth. At this phase, the youth is most energetic and if he/she channnelises his/her energy well, it will lead to the development of nation. The country has just about begun to realise the potential of youth who are willing to challenge the old societal rules and norms and to address issues such as gender inequality, poor education, unemployment, casteism etc.

Education is key to employment. Lack of proper education and employment among youth has resulted in an increase in crime and individuals indulging in unhealthy health practices. The migration issue is another after-effect of lack of proper education, skills and employment, especially in the rural parts of the county.

A Reflection on the National Education Policy, 2020

The recently announced NEP, 2020 has attempted to revamp the existing structure, pedagogy, curriculum, language of instruction, keeping Sustainable Development Goal 3 in mind. It aims to achieve 100 per cent youth and adult literacy. It has addressed issues of school drops outs, life skills, digital technology, vocational education at early stage, providing multiple subjects at school education, teacher training, research etc. It talks of establishing several monitoring bodies, credit bank system at higher level of education etc. However, some gaps in the policy are clearly evident.

While the document emphasises on the 'what' of the policy, the 'how' part is clearly missing. It is merely a guideline, a framework, a proposal without any legal status.

Secondly, the policy does not discusses enough on adult education and synergy between various ministries like the Skill Ministry, Youth and Sports etc. Its inter-connection with the Right to Education is not clearly known. Experts speak about the challenge of spending 6 per cent of GDP on education; equally difficult is to remove the coaching culture in the county.

In the area of skilling, there is a requirement of aligning the vocational training curriculum with industrial needs. Also, it is noted that encouragement and promotion of 'Entrepreneurship Culture' among youth and women will multiply the process of employment generation.

Indian society which is extremely diverse and is plagued with the age-old systems of class, caste and structural inequality is one of the major obstacles for the country's development. Youth born in this millenia are or can be easily equipped with tools to change India's society into one that matches a 21st century democracy. The new education policy skirts round these issues.

It is evident that for a productive youth workforce, it is necessary that they are healthy. Along with the promotion of their physical well-being, it becomes essential to meet their mental well-being needs. Attention to special nutritional and health needs of female youth is the need of the hour.

Furthermore, instilling constitutional values among youth and encouraging their participation in community services through accredited voluntary work will lead to the creation of morally responsible citizens.

Given that youth comprises 34.8 per cent of total Indian population and has huge potential to contribute to the progress and development of the nation, it becomes imperative to understand their needs and provide a conducive environment for their growth. Also, in the modern era, and especially in terms of achieving the 17 Sustainable Development Goals, a country can't progress by excluding its most productive force. India is a country with a vibrant youth population but it can reap expected returns only when they are empowered. The 21st century has seen young global leaders like Malala and Greta talking on issues of climate change, gender equality etc. We need such young leaders in our country. Only film stars cannot be the nation's youth icons.

Changing social realities through development and creating a just society with the support of every member of the society is the need of the hour. A convergence of Civil Society Organisations and the government to co-create empowering spaces where local youth take leadership and act on the issues affecting them and others in their communities is critical. Concerted efforts to build capacities of youth across India will help India to walk on the path of achieving Sustainable Development Goals.

Annexure I

Case Study of a Volunteer

Profile of the volunteer: 25 years old, male from Mumbai city. He was interviewed by students of TISS.

How and when did the idea of volunteering arise in your mind?
Volunteering became a part of my life at a very early age. I started volunteering at the age of four, in a Ganpati Pandal and then in every local event, as in selling papers in Baba Satsang. So that is how it started and eventually grew as a profession.

In my school in particular, I was never allowed to participate in activities and events, due to some of their reasons. So I could never take part in sports and dancing, and then would wonder that what it is that I could do. While in Class XI, I entered into volunteering for the reason that nobody else (classmates) joined it. I thought, this might become a reason at least that no one would send me back or stop me. So, I entered finally! (Cute smile on the face). We managed our college gathering and then I identified that a skill in management is required. I have volunteering skills! Now I should be participating in event management. Then I started doing it and specialised in that field. We took part in every big event while in XIth and XIIth standard.

When did you start participating in social service events?

At a very younger age I didn't knew where to put efforts and time and hence I would participate in religious events, but when I came to know where I should be contributing, it has mostly been the social ones. Then the cause of participation crystalised and became very specific. For example, events where rallies were to be done, we used to do it.

Then it became concrete when NSS role started. I was a volunteer there and then was chosen as a district leader, where I used to handle 24 colleges. It was a huge responsibility. My field and area got bigger. So I continued with it and got a President's award in 2012.

While in NSS, another parallel field of action was growing in me and it was Disaster Management. An accident took place in 2005 where I fell from the height of a 1-storey house and people thought I was dead. The site had nails and glass and so blood spread all around. I got injuries in the spine and my breathing stopped and so people thought I was dead. But a First Response team saved my life. This was the first incident I had encountered.

In 2009, a man fell from a platform and went under a running train. People, however, saved him and it reminded me of my situation. I then took it as a necessity to work in this field because of the need. We researched into it and entered into civil defense as a volunteer. We trained around 2,000 to 3,000 children.

I started training myself in civil defense, with the police and also fire brigade. By now I had taken it as my career because I had entered into the social sector. I did not know about MSW and so, while in NSS I started working with NYKS. In 2015, I came to know about the Gandhi Fellowship programme, which is one of the top five in the country. I got selected there and now started to work in the education sector.

For two years we worked with the government schools. I got a complete understanding of the domain… as to how the sector runs in the grassroots level. So I understood that domain, and the fact that education is linked to every issue. Gandhi Fellowship works in the manner that I had to work at every level, including in a process of community inclusion.

It is an exercise where our homes get locked and we don't have a penny in our pockets, then we are sent to live in a community where we have to find a place to reside and beg for food and other necessities, for a month. I got to learn many things there, and eventually, I developed the strength to do this.

Then I worked in the Ministry of Drinking Water and Sanitation as a consultant. They posted me in Palghar District, Ahmednagar and other districts in the State. I got to understand the functioning of the government. For ex, the coordination between the States and the centre-State relations, Gram Panchayat, etc.

In the course of time, in disaster management with the civil defense authorities, two of my friends have died. One died in a road accident and other due to electric shock of a geyser. Then I questioned myself–that I had been working in the disaster management for about seven years and here people's lives could be saved. My friends need not have died. I asked myself, what exactly am I doing? I am playing a safe game! I had been provided a car, salary and travel allowances by the government but then too, I was not performing responsibly.

I then resigned and started my own enterprise called 'The Resilient Foundation' where we give training in disaster management. Thereby, we impart resilience skill through emergency- preparedness training.

There was a drastic shift in your attitude towards community services, mainly because of the circumstances and the opportunities you got. How would you inspire a person who has not been through it and does not know the importance and nature of work?

There were many instances in my life when I tried to commit suicide. At this point of life, my teachers played a very important role in my life. They have been my mentor at times when I thought I could never come out these difficulties and this must be the end of my life. I approached my teachers for help. I believed, I should be talking to those who have a larger perspective of life and have much more experiences than me.

There was this incident where in college days, ragging used to happen, and a bunch of boys came and hit me. This happened regularly and I used to cry a lot. Once, I went to my teacher's house and cried! Then she said something that I could never forget. She said,'Till when are you going to cry? Go and fight!' That transformed me. I started changing myself. Started to talk in the manner they used to talk and would make my own gangs. This was the time when my attitude changed a lot.

Communicating with them should be a resolve to approach the youth in order to shape their idea about this work. As I have been through difficulties and found solutions by communicating with my teachers, maybe we can approach the youth to make them understand the nature of work and their potential.

How good is it to bring every youth under one banner? Does it not negatively affect an individual's other set of responsibilities?

What significance and importance does this work of volunteering for social service have in one's personal and social life?

Every person has a role in society! Not everyone can be put under one banner, neither should they be given the same responsibilities. They are, in fact, in a very good position if they responsibly carry out their duties and perform their part. Besides, for a person to feel meaningful, one does not have to find a purpose in life in his workplace. So here, we are providing this platform for people to volunteer and contribute something to the society. So in this field of volunteerism, self-satisfaction in exchange of contribution has become the new transaction, and the NGOs provide people such platform. So, one can achieve happiness and satisfaction away from their places of job-related workplaces.

What were the experiences and its challenges that you have faced while in this journey? How did you tackle them?

Since childhood, almost everything has been challenging for me. Even going to school was very difficult, with a half trouser and bare feet. So, from going to school to being beaten up in college days, everything was challenging! So the only way I tackled them was by communication. Communicating with those who are more experienced than me was the solution.

The NYP 14 does not really talk about education and skill development in rural Indian societies, their current status, their needs and their challenges. So what is your call on it? What do you feel is the government and the NGOs doing about it and what is the remaining gap?

Mostly, urban areas have been in the forefront of the focus of the government.

The villages are being transformed into semi-urban and then urban cities, mainly because of urbanisation. The concept of 'village' is a great idea, in fact. But it has just been kept in theory and not practical. People talk about resilient cities and not resilient village. So I think that when we talk about this policy, we should talk about the role of villages, their contributions and their value. Also, there is a need to strengthen them through various programmes.

NSS has considered both the rural and the urban areas, and has spread its reach almost everywhere. I believe, in rural areas, NSS has been very successful because it is the only way through which the children there have been able to realise their potentials and have participated because of the opportunities it gives. NSS has been able to cater to the needs of the children's development in rural areas, mainly because of its programmatic approach. The NCC and the NYKS have also been making efforts, but the NYKS has many leakages. For instance, there is only one district coordinator in NYKS unlike NSS which has at least 2 to 3 coordinators in a college. Also, the NYKS fails to count the number of volunteers and maintain contacts.

How has been the civil volunteerism efforts and to what extent have they been successful in implementing their policies? What is their role today and what are the areas of concern in today's times?

When we went to Ratnagiri, we assessed the area and we did a programme on disaster management. The need there was completely different. The children there needed life skills. So we learnt that disaster management was not their first need. Secondly, we identified that the young people there have a fascination towards Mumbai. So, they – without completing their education – leave for Mumbai to earn and end up getting into cheap labour work. So we understood that it was really important that we make them realise their own capacities and create opportunities for their own selves.

Developing aspirations and skills is the key to cater to the different needs of the different sections of the society.

Most from amongst today's youth, who wish to serve the nation, either go in the military or to the civil services, which in turn at least provides them financial stability and many provisions and allowances.

So how does the field of volunteerism cater to the needs of an individual willing to participate, in terms of job prospects?

We look at this issue as a trap. For example, 'social service' is such a sector wherein if you do something and then get some appreciation or an award, you tend to repeat the same behaviour in order to get the same amount of satisfaction and pleasure. So, one gets engaged in the same repetitive activity wherein the aspect of a youth, overcoming that phase, ceases and then the youth does not really give increasing efforts in different things. So one gets trapped in that cycle and does not grow. Likewise, after having tried to solve many immediate problems, people tend to enter into activism, and activism is a trap. It is not a bad thing but it is a trap.

So, we always tell people that,'identify your traps and try to overcome them'.

Should there be independent and parallel NGOs working besides the government despite the latter being completely responsible for the community services and public welfare?

Does the requirement for NGOs and Volunteerism mean inadequacy in government's role?

How does this parallel existence affect the polity and society of India?

Definitely there must be NGOs. There are some who work against the government and some who strengthen the government's role by implementing its policies and programmes. The civil society organisations help and support the government. It is very important that these civil societies coordinate with the government and help them reach its desired results.

How would you inspire today's youth? What message would you like to give them and what lessons would you want them to learn in life?

It is like– what you feel you like– you should choose it as your career. But one questions one's self is what I am doing right? Talking on a structural level, keeping ideology aside, a pragmatic approach is needed. Multiple perspectives should be open to one and one should be open to different options and choices.

So, make pragmatic efforts and keep yourself open to multiple perspectives – would be the message I would like everyone to get.

What do you think is the role of Youth in attaining the Sustainable Development Goals?

Young people have a very important role in SGDs. They can and should collaborate with adults and attain every goal of the agenda. It is necessary to raise the development parameters of our country at par with other nations of the developed world.

Conclusion

World is currently going through an unprecedented phase due to Corona crisis. The way people lived, organisations functioned, and students acquired education etc. has changed in a matter of few months. The skills that were relevant a few months ago have been replaced by digital skills in many domains.

Even in post-Corona phase, experts predict that there will be a major disruption in many facets of life. This is just one example to cite how important it is to adapt to the changes and mould ourselves into the new normal. But this needs a lot of re-skilling or up-skilling. So, Lifelong Learning is no more just a 'good to have' trait but the world today is showing us that *Lifelong Learning is the need of the hour* to fit in and survive in the current context.

'Youth are immature and irresponsible.' This is a very often-heard statement from various people from different generations in our society. Is it a generalisation based on a few wayward youth they have encountered with? Or, are people misreading youth's energy, enthusiasm and risk-taking traits as immaturity? Answer could be yes. But we can see immature, irresponsible, easily-gullible people in other elder generations too who are involved in violence, illegal activities etc. Nonetheless, the fact remains that youth is a powerful force and if channelised properly, they can be a huge asset to a nation. If we examine, we can find ample examples around the world where younger cohorts played active role in political and social movements.

A right mix of education, skills and attitude are necessary to gain good employment. Unfortunately, in India, lack of proper education and employment among youth has resulted in an increase in issues of crime and individuals indulging into unhealthy health practices.

The migration issue is another after-effect of lack of proper education, skills and employment especially in the rural parts of the county. In the area of skilling, there is a great need to align the vocational training curriculum with industries' needs. Also, it is necessary to note that encouragement and promotion of 'Entrepreneurship Culture' among youth and women will multiply the process of employment generation.

Indian society today is plagued with the age-old systems of class, caste and structural inequalities, and is misogynist and patriarchal, is one of the major obstacles for the country's development. The youth born in this millennium are or can be easily equipped with tools to destroy the evils of

India's socio-cultural practices. Youth, as an important phase of lifecycle, is the most productive part of human growth. The country is gradually realising the potential of youth who are willing to challenge obsolete but still clung-to societal rules and norms and to issues such as gender inequality, poor education, unemployment, casteism etc.

It is evident that for a productive youth workforce, they ought to be physically, mentally and emotionally healthy. Given that youth comprises a huge percentage of the total Indian population and has huge potential to contribute for the progress and development of the nation, instilling constitutional values in them and encouraging their participation in community services through accredited voluntary work will lead to the creation of morally responsible citizens. A convergence of Civil Society Organisations and government to co-create empowering spaces where local youth take leadership and action on the issues affecting them and others in their communities is critical

Equally imperative is to understand their needs and issues and provide an appropriate environment to bring out their potential for their growth. Also, in the modern era, and especially in terms of achieving the 17 sustainable development goals, a country can't propagate and proliferate by excluding its most productive force. India, a country with a vibrant youth population, can reap expected returns only when they are empowered.

The 21st century has seen young global leaders like Malala and Greta talking on issues of climate change, gender equality etc. We need such young leaders in our country. Efforts to build capacities of youth across India will help the nation to walk on the path of achieving Sustainable Development Goals.

References

Changing Narrative

State and Non-state Sector's Role in SDG & Youth

Agarwal, Pawan (2006), Higher Education in India: The Need for a Change, ICRIERWorking Paper No. 180, June.

Albert J Mills, Gabrielle Durepos&Elden Wiebe 2010. *Encyclopedia of Case StudyResearch.* Sage Publications, Inc.

Andrew V Beale. *The School Counselor*, Vol. 32, No. 1 (September1984), pp. 68-71, Published by: American School Counselor Association.

ArietiSylvano (1975), Creativity and Its Cultivation: Relation to Psychopathology and Mental Health. *American Handbook of Psychiatry* Volume 6, pp.737-40.

Batson CD (1995). *Prosocial motivation: Why do we help others?* In ATesser (Ed.), *Advanced Social Psychology*. New York: McGraw Hill.

Baudrillard J (1995). *Simulacra and Simulation.* Ann Arbor: University of Michigan Press.

Baynoli, Mark and Michael McKee (1991). Voluntary Contribution Games: Efficient Private Provision of Public Goods, Western Economic Association *Economic Inquiry* 29: 354.

Borghans L, Duckworth A L, Heckman JJ and Ter Weel B (2008). The economics and psychology of personality traits. *Journal of Human Resources*,43(4), 972-1059.

Brennan M A (2006). The development of community in the west of Ireland: A return to Killala twenty years on. *Community Development Journal*, 42(3), 330_374.

Carl Benedikt Frey, Michael A Osborne, (2016) The Future of Employment: How Susceptible Are Jobs to Computerisation?Oxford Martin School, University of Oxford,

Oxford OX1 1PT, United Kingdom Department of Engineering Science, University of Oxford, Oxford OX1 3PJ, United Kingdom Publications.

Casimir Raj M 2015. Contemporary Youth in India: Prospects, Problems and Perspectives, Vol 5 Issue 7 Aug 2015, *International Multidisciplinary Research Journal, Indian Streams Research Journal.*

Catalano R F, Berglund, M L Ryan, J A MLonczak, H SandHawkins, Development in the United States: Research findings on evaluations of programs. *Annals of the American Academy of Political and Social Science*, 591, 98-124.

Cheon J Woong (2008). Convergence of a Strengths Perspective and Youth Development:Toward Youth Promotion Practice. *Advances in Social Work*, 9, 176-190. http://journals.iupui.edu/index.php/advancesinsocialwork/article/view/5/202.

Dictionary.com (2018, November 12) NEET Definition. Retrieved fromhttps://www.google.com/search?q=Dictionary#dobs=NEET

Dewan Sabina (2018, May 21). Only 4.75 Million Join India's Workforce Annually, Not 12 Million as Claimed. Retrieved fromhttps://www.

indiaspend.com/only-4-75-million-join-indias-workforce-annually-not-12-million-as-claimed-70548/

Dolan P (2006). Assessment, intervention and self-appraisal tools for family support. In P Dolan,J Canavan and J Pinkerton (Eds.), *Family support as reflective practice* (pp. 196_213). London: Jessica Kingsley Publishing.

FE Online, New Delhi. 'With an average age of 29, India will be the world's youngest country by 2020' March 26, 2017. https://www.financialexpress.com/india-news/with-an-average-age-of-29-india-will-be-the-worlds-youngest-country-by-2020/603435/

G Hurlburt (2017). How Much to Trust Artificial Intelligence? *IT Professional*, vol. 19, no. 4, pp. 7-11

GhoseAjit K (2004). The Employment Challenge in India. *Economic and Political Weekly November 27.*

Ginzberg E, Ginsberg SW, Axelrad Sad Herma JR (1951). *Occupational choice: An approach to a general theory.* New York: Golumbia University Press

Hindustan Times, 65% Indian youngsters show early signs of depression: Study. (Apr 26, 2017.) Retrieved from https://www.hindustantimes.com/health-and-fitness/65-indian-youngsters-show-early-signs-of-depression-study/story-9JJoIWNn0FsRINKcHFYnwM.html

Hoppock R (1976). Occupational information (4th Ed.). New York: McGraw-Hill

https://www.indiatoday.in/education-today/news/story/800-engineering-colleges-to-shut-down-aicte-1037426-2017-09-04

Huber M S Q, Frommeyer J, WeisenbachandSazama J (2003). *Giving youth a voice in their own community and personal development.* Thousand Oaks, CA: Sage.

India 2017 OECD Economic Survey Strong reforms are boosting inclusive growth, *Economic Survey of India* 2017. OECD, Economics Department.

KaI Zhou (2016). Non-cognitive skills: Definitions, measurement and Malleability. Background paper prepared for the 2016 Education for people and planet: Creating sustainable futures for all. *Global Education Monitoring Report*, United Nations Educational, Scientific and Cultural Organisation.

Law Ben M FandShek Daniel T L, Validation of the Beliefs Against Volunteering Scale among Chinese Adolescents in Hong Kong, *Social Indicators Research*, Vol. 100, No. 2 (January 2011), pp. 287-298 Published by: Springer

Living in EU: (n d) [European Union Website], Retrieved from https://europa.eu/european-union/about-eu/figures/living_en

Massumi Brian (1987). Realer Than Real: The Simulacrum According to Deleuze and Guattari, Copyright, 1 (Fall), 90-96

Mental illness, Symptoms & Causes. 2015, Oct. 13, Mayo Clinic website Retrieved from https://www.mayoclinic.org/diseases-conditions/mental-illness/symptoms-causes/syc-20374968

Metz Edward and Youniss, James. A Demonstration That School-Based Required Service Does Not Deter-but Heightens- Volunteerism . PS: Political Science and Politics, Vol. 36, No. 2 (Apr., 2003), pp. 281-286. American Political Science Association

National Service Scheme. Retrieved from Government of India website https://nss.gov.in/

National Youth Policy (2014) [Website of Ministry of Youth Affairs and Sports Government of India] Retrieved from https://yas.nic.in/national-youth-policy

Nehru Yuva Kendra Sangathan. Retrieved from retrieved from Government of India website http://nyks.nic.in/

Pearson Coverage Report (2015) Employability of Students: All India. Pearson Voice of Teacher Survey 2015.

Petras James. Volunteerism:"*Economic and Political Weekly,* Vol. 32, No. 27 (Jul. 5-11, 1997), pp. 1587-1589.

Pierre G, Sanchez Puerta M L, Valerio A and Rajadel T (2014). STEP skills measurement surveys: innovative tools for assessing skills.Petras, James Volunteerism: *Economic and Political Weekly*, Vol. 32, No. 27 (Jul. 5-11, 1997), pp. 1587-1589.

Pittman K, Irby M, & Ferber T (2001). Unfinished business: Further reflections on a decade of promoting youth development. In P L Benson & K J. Pittman (Eds.), Trends in youth development: Visions, realities and challenges. Boston: Kluwer.

R N Nadar. Contemporary Issues and Challenges inthe Indian Education System. ADMIFMS International Management Research Conference 2018. *IOSR Journal of Business and Management* (IOSR-JBM) p-ISSN: 2319-7668, PP 86-91.

Raj.M.Casimir (2015): CONTEMPORARY YOUTH IN INDIA: PROSPECTS, PROBLEMS AND PERSPECTIVES, Indian Stream Research Journal, 1, 12, Vol, V(https://www.researchgate.net/publication/281707329_CONTEMPORARY_YOUTH_IN_INDIA_PROSPECTS_PROBLEMS_AND_PERSPECTIVES).

Roger C (2008). Youth Participation in society. *Asia European Journal*, 5, 469-477. http://www.springerlink.com/content/9657153742702697/

Roshni Chakrabarty, February 6, 2018. 93 per cent MBA graduates are unemployable: Problems with management education in *India*

IndiaToday.inhttps://www.indiatoday.in/education-today/featurephilia/story/mba-education-problems-328626-2016-07-11

Shek D T L (2007). Conceptual framework underlying the development of youth.

Shukla, A, (2010). 'First official estimate: an NGO for every 400 people in India'. Retrieved 15 January 2012.

Retrieved from: http://www.indianexpress.com/news/firstofficial-estimate-an-ngo-for-every-400-people-in-india/643302.

Singh Sunitha and Gopalkrishna Gururaj. August 2014. Health behaviours & problems among young people in India: Cause for concern & call for action. *Indian Journal ofMedical Research* 2014 Aug; 140(2): 185–208.

Statistia : Statistics Portal (2018) India: Total population from 2012 to 2022 (in millions). Retrieved from https://www.statista.com/statistics/263766/total-population-of-india/

Stedman's Medical Dictionary © Wolters Kluwer Health. Retrieved from https://www.medilexicon.com/dictionary/39451 on 2018, November 12.

Suicide Data, Mental Health, World Health Organization report 2016 retrieved from http://www.who.int/mental_health/prevention/suicide/suicideprevent/en/

The President's Summit For America's Future (1997) [website] Retrieved from https://clintonwhitehouse3.archives.gov/WH/New/Summit/

The surveys can be found on the Labour Bureau's website, http://labourbureau.nic.in/. Until 2015, the surveys reflected data gathered from 2,000 enterprises in textiles, leather, metals, automobiles, gems and jewellery, information technology, and transport. In 2016, the survey was expanded to cover 10,000 enterprises across manufacturing, construction, trade, transport, education, health, hotels and restaurants, and information technology and business process outsourcing.

The surveys until 2015 can be found on the Labour Bureau's website of Government of India (2018, March 12) Retrieved from http://labourbureau.nic.in/

The Sustainable Development Goals Report 2018, retrieved from https://unstats.un.org/sdgs/report/2018/overview/

The World Development Indicators is the World Bank's premier compilation of cross-country comparable data on development (2016). International Bank for Reconstruction and Development/the World Bank 1818 H Street NW, Washington DC 20433.

United Nations. About the Sustainable Development Goals. Sustainable Development Goals. https://www.un.org/sustainabledevelopment/sustainable-development-goals/

Visaria P (1998), Unemployment among youth in India, Level, Nature and policy Implications. International Labour Organisation, Employment and Training Papers, 36, Institute of Economic Growth, New Delhi.

Volunteerism definition and meaning Collins English Dictionary Retrieved from https://www.collinsdictionary.com/dictionary/english/volunteerism

What Are Cognitive Skills, Anyway? Learning Rx (n d) Retrieved from https://www.learningrx.com/brain-training-101/what-are-cognitive-skills/Date

Woetzel Jonathan, Madgavkar Anu, Gupta Shishir (2017). India's Labour Market, A New Emphasis on Gainful Employment, Mckinsey Global Institute, Mckinsey and Company.

World Health Report, 2001. Mental Health: New Understanding, New Hope. World Health Organization, Geneva.

Worldometers (2018, November 12) [Africa Live Website] Retrieved from http://www.worldometers.info/world-population/africa-population/

Zech Charles E (1982). Citizens Willingness to Assist as Volunteers in the Provision of Local Public Goods: A Case Study of Volunteer Firemen in 70 West German Cities, *American Journal of Economics and Sociology* 41.

Fostering First Generation Micro-entrepreneurs

Opportunities and Challenges

Demographics of India(n.d.).In Wikipedia. Retrieved on December 11, 2017, from https://en.wikipedia.org/wiki/Demographics_of_India

Gurnani SP (2016). *Women Entrepreneurship: Emerging Dimension of Entrepreneurship in India.* New Delhi: Educreation Publishing.

Hariharaputhiran S (2011). Entrepreneurship Challenges and Opportunities in India. *Asian Journal of Research in Social Science& Humanities.* 1(2), 82-91.

The Global Entrepreneurship and Development Institute (2018). Global Entrepreneurship Index. Washington DC.

UNICEF report titled GBC-Education 2030 Skills Scorecard (www.gbc-education.org).

The Puzzles and Contradictions of the Indian Labour Market: What Will the Future of Work Look Like? Sher Singh Verick ILO and IZA.

Global Employment Trends for Youth 2020: Technology and the Future of Jobs (GET Youth 2020).

CMIE's Consumer Pyramids Household Survey (consumerpyramidsdx.cmie.com/) accessed on 14th June, 2020.

Teachers and Society in Mumbai and Hong Kong

Comparative Perspectives for Quality Education

Aiyar SA (2019). 2010s: The decade is ending on a sour note for Indian economy. *The Times of India.*

Batra P (2013). Teacher Education and Classroom Practice in India: A Critique and Propositions, in S Chunawala& M Kharatmal (Eds.). The *Episteme Reviews*, volume 4, Research Trends in Science, Technology and Mathematics Education, HBCSE, TIFR, NarosaPublising House, 2013.

Batra P (2017). Inertia in teacher education and the need for judicial intervention. *Learning Curve*. February 2017 pp. 25-28.

Bereday GZF (1964).*Comparative method in education*. Calcutta: Oxford and IBH Publishing Company.

Bhorkar SS (2017). From supplementation to supplantation: expansion and role of private tutoring in urban Maharashtra, India. Retrieved from https://hub.hku.hk/handle/10722/252472

Borwankar V (2018, Feb 18). IB and Cambridge-affiliated schools are leaping in popularity. *The Times of India.* Retrieved from https://timesofindia.indiatimes.com/city/mumbai/ib-cambridge-affiliated-schools-leap-in-popularity/articleshow/62976078.cms

Bray M (2004). Methodology and Focus in Comparative Education. In M Bray & R Koo (Eds.), *Education and Society in Hong Kong and Macao: Comparative Perspectives on Continuity and Change* (pp.237–250). Hong

Kong: Comparative Education Research Centre The University of Hong Kong, Kluwer, Academic Publishers.

Bryman A (1988). *Quantity and Quality in Social Research.* New York, NY: Routledge.

ChatterjeeS(2017). India's youth–A blessing or a curse. Retrieved from https://www.huffpost.com/entry/indias-youth-a-blessing-o_b_9288120

Cheney GR, Ruzzi BB &Muralidharan K (2005). A profile of the Indian education system. Retrieved from http://www.ncee.org/wp-content/uploads/2010/04/India-Education-

Choudhary R (2020). COVID-19 Pandemic: Impact and strategies for education sector in India in *The Economic Times.* Retrieved from https://government.economictimes.indiatimes.com/news/education/covid-19-pandemic-impact-and-strategies-for-education-sector-in-india/75173099

Comyn P (2020). *TVET and skills development in the time of Covid-19.* Retrieved from https://gemreportunesco.wordpress.com/2020/04/28/tvet-and-skills-development-in-the-time-of-covid-19/

Costa P Guntupallu, Rana MV & Trieu H (2006). *China & India: A comparative study of the manufacturing and services industries,* Retrieved from http://www.umich.edu/~ipolicy/IEDP/2006china/4)%20China%20and%20India,%20A% 20Comparative%20Study%20of%20the%20Manufacturing.pdf

Creswell JW (2012). *Educational Research: Planning, conducting, and evaluating quantitative and qualitative research.* New Jersey: Pearson/Merrill Prentice Hall.

DNEP(2019). Draft National Education Policy. Retrieved from https://mhrd.gov.in/sites/upload_files/mhrd/files/Draft_NEP_2019_EN_Revised.pdf

Doughery S & Herd R (2007). Growth prospects in China and India compared. *The European Journal of Comparative Economics 4(1)*, 65-89. Retrieved from https://www.researchgate.net/publication/5163974_Growth_Prospects_in_China_and_India Compared.

GOI(2017). *Youth in India 2017.* Retrieved from http://mospi.nic.in/sites/default/files/publication_reports/Youth_in_India-2017.pdf

GOI (2019). School Education Quality Index. Retrieved from https://niti.gov.in/sites/default/files/2019-09/seqi_document.pdf

GOI (2019). *SDG India Index 2019-2020.* Retrieved from https://niti.gov.in/sites/default/files/SDG-India-Index-2.0_27-Dec.pdf

Grace HC, Huang & Gove M (2012). Confucianism and Chinese families: Values and practices in education. *International Journal of Humanities and Social Science, 2(3).* Retrieved from http://www.ijhssnet.com/journals/Vol_2_No_3_February_2012/2.pdf

Henry N (2018). *The Ferment – Youth Unrest in India.* Macmillan.

Kingdon GG (2007). The progress of school education in India. *Oxford Review of Economic Policy*, 23(2). 168–195.

Kumar K (2019). Teaching in the times of consumerism. *The Hindu.*

Lodico M, Spaulding D &Voegtle K (2010). *Methods in educational research: From theory to practice, 2nd edition.* San Francisco, CA: Jossey-Bass.

MenonSB & Mathew R (2016): Teacher education in universities: A case from India. In B Moon (Ed.) *Do universities have a role in the education and training of teachers? An international analysis of policy and practice* (pp 149-68), Cambridge: Cambridge University Press.

MerriamSB &Tisdell EJ (2009). *Qualitative research: A guide to design and implementation.* San Francisco, CA: Jossey-Bass.

Mohanty SB (2015). High Quality teacher training in advanced education systems. *Journal of All India Association for Educational Research, 27* (1), 1-37.

NUEPA (2016). Teachers in the Indian education system- How we manage the teacher workforce in India. Retrieved from http://www.niepa.ac.in/New/download/Research/Teachers_in_the_Indian_Education_System.pdf

Pathak A (2018). A sick society that manufactures failures – the true face of education of India. *The Wire*. Retrieved from https://thewire.in/education/the-true-face-of-indias-education-system

Pathak A (2020). The Pandemic and Absurdity of 'Online Teaching' in *Mainstream Weekly*. Retrieved from http://mainstreamweekly.net/article9405.html

Ramachandran V,Beteille T, Linden T, Dey S et al. (2017). *Getting the right teachers into the right schools: managing India's teacher workforce (English)*. Washington, DC: World Bank Group.

Rao N & Chan CK (2010). *Understanding the Chinese learner and teacher today*. Retrieved from http://www.fe.hku.hk/cerc/Publications/yhk_1_4_13-15.pdf

Roy K (2019). Examining the Draft National Education Policy, 2019. *Economic & Political Weekly*. Retrieved from https://www.epw.in/engage/article/examining-draft-national-education- policy-2019.

Sarangapani PM (2010). Comparative education research: Why it is missing and why we need it. *Journal of Education Planning and Administration 24() 4: 363-378. 2010.*

Singh RP (2011). Comparative Education: A Neglected Discipline in India. *Journal of Educational Planning and Administration, XXV* (3), 249–255.

Sweeting A (2008). Teacher professionalisation in Hong Kong: Historical perspective. In DJohnson & RMaclean (Eds.). *Teaching: Professionalisaton, development & leadership* (pp.45-65). New York NY: Springer.

The Hindu (2020). E-education no child's play, teachers putting tremendous efforts in online classes: HC. Retrieved from https://www.thehindu.com/news/cities/Delhi/e-education-no-childs-play-teachers-putting-tremendous-efforts-in-online-classes-hc/article31454616.ece

UNESCO (2015). The Incheon Declaration and SDG4 – Education Framework for Action. Retrieved from https://www.sdg4education2030.org/education-2030-framework-action-unesco-2015.

UNESCO (2017). Unpacking Sustainable Development Goal 4, Education 2030 Guide. Retrieved from https://www.right-to-education.org/sites/right-to-education.org/files/resource-attachments/Unesco_Guide_to_unpacking_SDG4_2015_En.pdf

United Nations (2015). *Transforming our world: The 2030 Agenda for Sustainable Development.* Retrievedfrom https://sustainabledevelopment.un.org/post2015/transformingourworld/publication

United Nations (2018). Quality education: Why it matters? Retrieved from https://www.un.org/sustainabledevelopment/wp-content/uploads/2018/09/Goal-4.pdf

Gender Equality and Youth Development
With regard to SDG 5

Brown, B.D., & Ruwanpura, K. N. (2019).SDG 8: Decent work and economic growth–A gendered analysis. *World Development, 113*, 368-380.

Dave A. 2015. *Women Survivors of Violence: Genesis and Growth of a State Support System*, Mumbai: TISS and Orient Blackswan.

Gothoskar S. 2013. The Plight of Domestic Workers –Confluence of Gender, Class and Caste Hierarchies, Mumbai: *Economic and Political Weekly*, XLVIII (22), June 1, 63-75.

Hiraway I. 2009. Understanding Poverty: Insights Emerging from the Time Use of the Poor. In Antonopoulos, R. and Hiraway, I. (Eds.), *Unpaid Work and the Economy: Gender, Time Use and Poverty in the Global South*, UK.: Palgrave Publishers.

Jaswal S and Joseph J, 2008. Psychos Psycho-social Support and Mental Health Services in Disasters, Mumbai: Jamsetji Tata Centre for Disaster Management, Tata Institute of Social Sciences.

Jha M. and Kumar P. 2016. Homeless Migrants in Mumbai: Life and Labour in Urban Space, Mumbai, *Economic And Political Weekly*, LI (26 & 27), June, 69-77.

Kelkar-Khambete A. 2017. Why we do not talk about women farmers? https://yourstory.com/2017/07/women-farmers-gender-agriculture-labour/ accessed on 20-1-2018.

Patel V. 2007. Global Partnership for Development. In Patel, V and Karne M, (Eds.) *The Macro Economic Policies and the Millennium Development Goals*, Delhi: Gyan Publications, 313-324.

Patel V. 2015. Safe T Cities and Gender Budgeting, Jaipur: *Journal of Development Management and Communication*, II (3), July-September, pp. 285-291.

Patel V (Ed.). 2007. Gender Budgets in India.http://gender-financing.unwomen.org/en/resources/g/e/n/gender-budgeting-in-india-by-dr-vibhuti-patel, UN WOMEN, accessed on 20-1-2018.

Rajaram I. 2007. Women in the Eleventh Plan. Delhi: National Institute of Public Finance and Policy.

Shukla, S and Sawargaonkar, P.2010. Adolescent Girls in India. In Patel, Vibhuti (Ed.) *Girls and girlhoods at the Threshold of Youth and Gender*, Delhi: The Women Press, 1-34.

Siva Raju (Ed.). 2011 *Voices of Elderly in India*, Delhi: B R Publications.

Violence Against Women and Girls

A Barricade to Youth Development and SDGs.

AALI, n.d. Baseline Report: Rights of Women in Relation to Marriage in India, http://aalilegal.org/wp-content/uploads/2016/01/Publications_BaselineReport-RightsofWomen.pdf accessed on November 20, 2018.

AALI, 2010. Facing Reality: A Journey on the path of choice, http://aalilegal.org/wp-content/uploads/2016/01/Publications_FacingReality.pdf accessed on November 20, 2018.

Ambedkar, BR 1917. Castes in India: their Mechanism, Genesis and Development, http://www.columbia.edu/itc/mealac pritchett/00ambedkar/txt_ambedkar_castes.html accessed on November 20, 2018.

Amnesty USA, no date. The devastating impact of child marriage on girls around the world, https://www.amnestyusa.org/the-devastating-impact-of-child-marriage-on-girls-around-the-world/ accessed on November 20, 2018.

Armstrong, Gregory and Vijayakumar Lakshmi, 2018. 'Suicide in India: a complex public health tragedy in need of a plan', *The Lancet*, Volume 3, Issue 10. DOI: https://doi.org/10.1016/S2468-2667 (18)30142-7

Bajoria Jayshree, 2017. 'Everyone Blames Me: Barriers to Justice and Support Services for Sexual Assault Survivors in India', Human Rights Watch, https://www.hrw.org/report/2017/11/08/everyone-blames-me/barriers-justice-and-support-services-sexual-assault-survivors accessed on November 20, 2018.

Basu Moni, 2013. The girl whose rape changed a country. CNN, http://www.cnn.com/interactive/2013/11/world/india-rape/ accessed on November 20, 2018.

Centre for Child and the Law, National Law School of India University, Implementation of the POCSO Act, 2012 by Special Courts: Challenges and Issues.

Based on CCL-NLSIU's Studies on the Working of Special Courts in Five States 2018.

Centre for Enquiry into Health and Allied Themes (2018), Understanding Dynamics of Sexual Violence: Study of case records, CEHAT and MCGM, Mumbai, India.

Chakravarti Uma, 1993. Conceptualising Brahmanical Patriarchy in Early India: Gender, Caste, Class and State. *Economic and Political Weekly*. Vol. 28, No. 14.

Dave A & Solanki G (2001). *Journey from violence to crime: A study of domestic violence in the city of Mumbai.* Mumbai: Department of Family and Child Welfare, Tata Institute of Social Sciences.

Dave A, Pradhan Y andSriraman T, 2015. *Changing forms of violence: Violence within non- cohabiting, non-marital relationships- A study of the experiences of intervention at the Special Cells in Mumbai.*

Dhamija Gaurav and RoychowdhuryPunarjit, 2018. 'How women's age at marriage impacts domestic violence', *Ideas for India*, http://www.ideasforindia.in/topics/social-identity/how-women-s-age-at-marriage-impacts-domestic-violence.html accessed on November 20, 2018.

Dhingra Sanya 2017. Sex crimes against SCs/STs rising since 2014, experts say its power play, https://theprint.in/report/rape-sc-st-women-often-power-crime-statistics-show/24739/ accessed on November 20, 2018.

FE Online, 2017. With an average age of 29, India will be the world's youngest country by 2020', https://www.financialexpress.com/india-news/with-an-average-age-of-29-india-will-be-the-worlds-youngest-country-by-2020/603435/ accessed on November 20, 2018.

Business World, 2020. The economic impact of Covid-19 on India's younger generation and the way out, http://www.businessworld.in/article/Economic-Impact-Of-Covid-19-On-India-s-Younger-Generation-And-The-Way-Out/10-06-2020-194663/

Jhaveri Panchal (2017). Men, Intimate Partner Violence and Change: A study of Special Cell for Women (PhD Thesis)

Jhaveri Panchal &Ajgaonkar, 2019. *Multi Agency Response to Violence against Women: Feminist Social Work within the Police System.* New Delhi: Vitasta.

Kabeer, Naila, 2014. Violence against Women as 'Relational' Vulnerability: Engendering the Sustainable Human Development Agenda. UNDP.

Ministry of Statistics and Programme Implementation, 2017. Youth in India, http://mospi.nic.in/sites/default/files/publication_reports/Youth_in_India-2017.pdf accessed on November 20, 2018.

Ministry of Women and Child Development, 2017. NFHS-4 shows decreasing trend in under age marriages, http://pib.nic.in/newsite/PrintRelease.aspx?relid=168730 accessed on November 20, 2018.

Ministry of Youth Affairs and Sports, 2014. National Youth Policy.

National Criminal Records Bureau, 2016. Crime in India, http://ncrb.gov.in/StatPublications/CII/CII2016/pdfs/NEWPDFs/Crime%20in%20India%20-%202016%20Complete%20PDF%20291117.pdf accessed on November 20, 2018.

Nussbaum, Martha C., 2005. "Women's Bodies: Violence, Security, Capabilities" *Journal of Human Development*, 6:2,167-183, DOI: 10.1080/14649880500120509

Panchal, T. &Ajgaonkar, V, 2015. *Let them fly: A multi-agency response to child marriages in Haryana.* DWCD Govt. of Haryana & Tata Institute of Social Sciences.

S., Rukmini, 2018. Urban Indians still get married the way their grandparents did, Live Mint, https://www.livemint.com/Politics/mnVzCfIEbqvzEu01LTxqLM/Urban-Indians-still-get-married-the-way-their-grandparents-d.html accessed on November 20, 2018

Sakhrani, Monica and Panchal, Trupti Jhaveri, 2014. *Quest for Justice: A Study of the Implementation of the Protection of Women from Domestic Violence Act,* 2005. Mumbai: Tata Institute of Social Sciences.

SNEHA, 2018. Child marriages & impact on mental health, http://snehamumbai.org/2018/01/05/child-marriages-impact-on-mental-health/ accessed on November 20, 2018.

Special Cell for Women and Children, 2001. *Because the personal is political: A documentation of the work of the Special Cell for Women and Children (1984-1994).* Mumbai: Tata Institute of Social Sciences.

Special Cell for Women and Children, 2004. *Mission Statement and the Monitoring Indicators for Special Cell for Women and Children.* Mumbai: Tata Institute of Social Sciences.

Times of India, 2018. Honour killings: More than 300 cases in last three years, https://timesofindia.indiatimes.com/india/honour-killings-more-than-300-cases-in-last-three-years/articleshow/65908947.cms accessed on November 20, 2018.

TISS, PLD and CEHAT, 2017. National Consultation on Adolescent Sexuality, Health and the Law. https://www.academia.edu/36941131/National_Consultation_on_Adolescent_Sexuality_Health_and_the_Law_Mapping_Interventions accessed on November 20, 2018.

UN Women. SDG 5: Achieve gender equality and empower all women and girls, http://www.unwomen.org/en/news/in-focus/women-and-the-sdgs/sdg-5-gender-equality accessed on November 20, 2018.

UNESCO, no date. What do we mean by "youth"? http://www.unesco.org/new/en/social-and-human-sciences/themes/youth/youth-definition/ accessed on November 20, 2018.

UNICEF India, no date. Child Marriage, http://unicef.in/Whatwedo/30/Child-Marriage accessed on November 20, 2018.

United Nations in India, no date. SDG 4: Quality Education, http://in.one.un.org/page/sustainable-development-goals/sdg-4/ accessed on November 20, 2018.

UNODC,2018.Press Release, https://www.unodc.org/unodc/en/press/releases/2018/November/home—the-most-dangerous-place-for-women—with-majority-of-female-homicide-victims-worldwide-killed-by-partners-or-family—unodc-study-says.html accessed on November 20, 2018.

World Health Organization, 2017. Violence against Women, https://www.who.int/news-room/fact-sheets/detail/violence-against-women accessed on November 20, 2018.

United Nations, 2015. Population Facts, http://www.un.org/en/development/desa/population/publications/pdf/popfacts/PopFacts_2015-1.pdf accessed on November 20, 2018.

United Nations, 2016. The economic costs of violence against women, http://www.unwomen.org/en/news/stories/2016/9/speech-by-lakshmi-puri-on-economic-costs-of-violence-against-women accessed on November 20, 2018.

United Nations, 2017. *2017 Revision* of *World Population Prospects,* https://population.un.org/wpp/ accessed on November 2017.

From Recipients to Change Agents

Participation in Enhancing Health & Sanitation in Marginalised Urban Geographies

Aiyar S and ModyA, 2012 The Demographic Dividend: Evidence from the Indian States Available: http://www.ncaer.org/popuppages/EventDetails/IPF_2012/ShekharAiyarandAshokaMody.pdf

Apnalaya, 2017. *Annual Report 2016-17*. Mumbai http://www.apnalaya.org/annual-reports.php

Asker S and Gero A, 2012. *The Role of Child and Youth Participation in Development Effectiveness: A Literature Review*. Child Fund Australia https://www.unicef.org/adolescence/cypguide/files/Role_of_Child_and_Youth_Participation_in_Development_Effectiveness.pdf

Bartlett S, 2005. Water, sanitation and urban children: the need to go beyond 'improved' provision in Children, Youth and Environments. 15(1): 115-137 *Environmental Health, and Other Papers.*

Belur J, Parikh P, Daruwalla N, Joshi R and Fernandes R, 2017. Perceptions of gender-based violence around public toilets in Mumbai slums, *International Journal of Comparative and Applied Criminal Justice*, 41(1-2): 63-78. DOI: 10.1080/01924036.2016.1240094 http://dx.doi.org/10.1080/01924036.2016.1240094

Daruwalla N, Mishra T, Karandikar N, Pantvaidya S and Osrin D, 2017. Good girls and boys: findings from a cross-sectional survey on adolescent rights, relationships, and sexuality in an urban informal settlement in India. *International Journal of Adolescence and Youth.* DOI: 10.1080/02673843.2017.1371613

Desai K A, Moitra M and Dave B, 2017 Assessment of Operational Efficiency and Service Utilization of Adolescent Reproductive and Sexual Health Clinic in an Urban Health Center of Surat City. *Indian Journal of Youth and Adolescent Health*4(1): 5-10.

DFID-CSO Youth Working Group 2010. *Youth Participation in Development: A Guide for Development Agencies and Policy Makers.* SPW/ DFID-CSO Youth Working Group, London. http://www.restlessassets.org/wl/?id=umaETRcmVyn2VEpSrxu7JWWkHom5RYli

Harper C and Jones N, 2009. Child Rights and Aid: Mutually Exclusive? In*Background Note.* November 2009. Overseas Development Institute (ODI): 1-8 https://www.files.ethz.ch/isn/109624/2009_11_Child-rights.pdf

Hoopes A J , Agarwal P, Bull S and Chandra-Mouli V, 2016. Measuring adolescent friendly health services in India: A scoping review of evaluations. *Reproductive Health.* 2016. 13: 137 https://reproductive-health-journal.biomedcentral.com/articles/10.1186/s12978-016-0251-8

Hwang S and Kim J, 2017. *UN and SDGs: A Handbook for Youth.* United Nations ESCAP East and North-East Asia Office, Korea. http://www.unescap.org/sites/default/files/UN%20and%20SDGs_A%20Handbook%20For%20Youth.pdf

InayatullahSohail, 2016. Youth Bulge: Democratic Dividend, Time Bomb and Other Futures. *Journal of Futures Studies.* December 2016. 21(2): 21–34. https://jfsdigital.org/wp-content/uploads/2017/01/21-2-2.pdf

International Institute for Population Sciences (IIPS) and Population Council 2010. *Youth in India: Situation and Needs 2006–2007.* Mumbai: IIPS.

Ismail S, Shajahan A, Sathyanarayana Adolescent sex education in India: Current perspectives. *Indian Journal of Psychiatry.* 2015. 57:333-7

Rao T S and Wylie K. No date http://www.indianjpsychiatry.org/article.asp?issn=00195545;year=2015;volume=57;issue=4;spage=333;epage=337;aulast=Ismail

Lloyd Cynthia B (ed.), 2005. *Growing up Global: The Changing Transitions to Adulthood in Developing Countries.* The National Academies Press, Washington DC.

Ministry of Rural Development, Department of Drinking Water and Sanitation, Ministry of Urban Development, Government of India 2011. Enhanced Quality of Life through Sustained Sanitation: India Country Paper. *SACOSAN – IV (The IV South Asia Conference on Sanitation)* 4th-7th April 2011, Colombo, Sri Lanka.

Ministry of Youth Affairs and Sports, Government of India2012. *Exposure Draft National Youth Policy 2012.* NYP 2012. Available at: http://planipolis.iiep.unesco.org/upload/Youth/India/India_draft_National_youth_policy_2012.pdf

National Statistical Organisation, National Sample Survey Office, Ministry of Statistics and Programme Implementation, Government of India 2011. : *Key Indicators of Employment and Unemployment in India, 2009-10,* NSS 66th round, July 2009-June 2010.

National Research Council and Institute of Medicine 2005. Growing Up Global: The Changing Transitions to Adulthood in Developing Countries. In Cynthia B Lloyd (ed.) *Panel on Transitions to Adulthood in Developing Countries., ed. Committee on Population and Board on Children, Youth, and Families.* Division of Behavioral and Social Sciences and Education. Washington, DC: The National Academies Press.

Nussbaum M and Dixon R,2012 'Children's Rights and a Capabilities Approach: The Question of Special Priority' *University of Chicago Public Law & Legal Theory Working Paper 384.*

Office of the Registrar General and Census Commissioner 2011. Size, growth rate and distribution of population. Chapter 3. *Provisional Population Totals Paper 1 of 2011 India Series 1.* Office of the Registrar General and Census Commissioner, India.

Office of the Registrar General and Census Commissioner 2011. Size, growth rate and distribution of child population. Chapter 4. *Provisional Population Totals Paper 1 of 2011 India Series 1.* Office of the Registrar General and Census Commissioner, India.

Office of the Registrar General and Census Commissioner 2011. Size, growth rate and distribution of child population. Chapter 8. *Provisional Population Totals Paper 1 of 2011 India Series 1.* Office of the Registrar General and Census Commissioner, India.

Office of the Registrar General and Census Commissioner[c]2011. Size, growth rate and distribution of child population. Chapter 4. *Provisional Population Totals Paper 1 of 2011 India Series 1.* Office of the Registrar General and Census Commissioner, India.

Parasuraman S, Kishor S, Singh S K and Vaidehi Y, 2009 A Profile of Youth in India. *National Family Health Survey (NFHS-3), India, 2005-06.* Mumbai: International Institute for Population Sciences; Calverton, Maryland, USA: ICF Macro.

Planning Commission (Labour, Employment & Manpower Division) Government of India, 2008. Report of the Working Group on Labour Force & Employment Projections constituted for the Eleventh Five Year Plan (2007 – 2012).

Rajiv Gandhi National Institute of Youth Development (RGNIYD), Ministry of Youth Affairs and Sports, Government of India,2017. *India Youth Development Index and Report 2017.* Tamil Nadu.

Santhya KG, Prakash R, Jejeebhoy S and Singh SK, 2014. *Accessing Adolescent Friendly Health Clinics in India: The Perspectives of Adolescents and Youth.* New Delhi: Population Council. http://www.popcouncil.org/uploads/pdfs/2014PGY_AFHC-IndiaReport.pdf

Sen A, 1985. *Commodities and Capabilities.* North-Holland, Amsterdam.

Shaikh Z, 2016. Forgetting Strife to Build a Communal Bridge. *The Indian Express*. 5 January, Mumbai. http://indianexpress.com/article/cities/mumbai/forgetting-strife-to-build-a-communal-bridge/

Sivagurunathan C, Umadevi R., Rama R and Gopalakrishnan S, 2015. Adolescent Health: Present Status and Its Related Programmes in India. Are We in the Right Direction? in *Journal of Clinical and Diagnostic Research*. Published Online 2015 March. https://www.ncbi.nlm.nih.gov/pmc/articles/PMC4413087/

SNEHA (Society for Nutrition Education and Health Action) 2017 Unpublished Programme data from EHSAS (Empowerment Health and Sexuality of Adolescents) programme. Mumbai.

UNDP-World Bank Group 2016 *Transitioning from the MDGs to the SDGs*. UN System Chief Executives Board for Coordination (CEB) http://www.undp.org/content/undp/en/home/librarypage/sustainable-development-goals/transitioning-from-the-mdgs-to-the-sdgs.html

UNHABITAT 2012 Youth in the Prosperity of Cities, Overview and Summary of Findings, *State of the Urban Youth Report 2012/2013*, UNHABITAT, Nairobi.

United Nations 2009 : *Youth and the United Nations*. Accessed at www.un.org/youth

United Nations 2011 *World Population Prospects: The 2010 Revision*, Volume I: Comprehensive Tables. Department of Economic and Social Affairs, Population Division, United Nations, New York.

UNICEF2012 *Water, Sanitation and Hygiene (WASH) in Schools*. A companion to the Child Friendly Schools Manual. UNICEF, New York.

Wight Susannah (ed.) 2016. *Global Youth Development Index and Report 2016*. Commonwealth Secretariat, London.

Beyond Skilling

Alternative Praxis of Livelihood for Urban Poor Youth

Okada A (2012). Skills Development for Youth in India: Challenges and Opportunities. *Journal of International Cooperation in Education, Vol.15* (No.2), 169-193. Retrieved August 1st, 2018, from https://home.hiroshima-u.ac.jp/cice/wp-content/uploads publications/15-2/15-2-10.pdf.

Commonwealth Secretariat. (2017). *Youth Mainstreaming in Development Planning.* London: Commonwealth Secretariat.

ECOSOC Youth Forum (2016). *Concept Note, Breakout session: Poverty, Inequality and Youth Empowerment in Urban areas.* New York: ECOSOC Youth Forum.

European Commission (2015). *The contribution of youth work to address the challenges young people are facing, in particular the transition from education to employment.* Brussels: European Commission.

GOI(n.d.).*Maharashtra Minimum wages.* Retrieved January 30, 2018, from https://mahakamgar.maharashtra.gov.in/Images/pdf/minimum-wages.pdf

ILO (2017). *Global Employment Trends For Youth 2017.* Geneva: International Labour Organisation.

Kirk R (n.d.). *Youth Worker Voice Matters: A case and framework for developing autonomous youth workers.* Retrieved January 28, 2018, from http://web.augsburg.edu/sabo/YouthWorkerVoiceMattersKirk.pdf

MalikB K (2015). Retrieved January 25, 2018, from https://www.ncbi.nlm.nih.gov/pmc/articles/PMC4628033/

Matthew Desmond's *Evicted* Close-Up. (n.d.). Retrieved February 01, 2018, from https://inequality.org/great-divide/read-evicted-matthey-desmond/

Ministry of Skill Development and Entrepreneurship, Government of India (n.d.). *Annual Report 2016-2017.* Retrieved January 30, 2018, from http://www.skilldevelopment.gov.in/assets/images/annual%2 report/Annual%20Report%202016-2017%20-%20English.pdf

MOSPI, GOI (2017). *Youth in India.* New Delhi: Ministry of Statistics and Programme Implementation, Government of India.

Murphy D, Duggan M & Joseph S (2013). Relationship-Based Social Work and Its Compatibility with the Person-Centred Approach: Principled versus Instrumental Perspectives. *The British Journal of Social Work, Volume 43, Issue 4*, 703–719.

National Institute of Urban Affairs. (2016). *Status Of Children In Urban India, Baseline Study, 2016.* Delhi: National Institute Of Urban Affairs.

GOI: https://cfsc.niua.org/sites/default/files/Status_of_children_in_urban_India-Baseline_study_2016.pdf

National Skill Development Corporation (NSDC). (n.d.). Retrieved February 1, 2018, from https://www.nsdcindia.org/

National Youth Policy, NYP (2014) Ministry of Youth Affairs and Sports, Government of India.

Nuggehali R K (2017). *Let principles drive practice: Reclaiming youth work in India.* Mumbai: Sage Handbook.

Oxfam (2016). *Youth And Inequality, Time to support youth as agents of their own future.* OXFAM.

Pande S (2015, April 12). *You need a banking law to create a bank for the poor.* Retrieved February 03, 2018, from http://www.businesstoday.in/magazine/features/muhammad-yunus-interview-on-microfinance-sector-initiatives/story/217155.html

Richmond M E (1917). *Social diagnosis.* New York: Russell Sage Foundation. doi:https://www.historyofsocialwork.org/PDFs/1917,%20 Richmond,%20Social%20Diagnosis%20OCR%20C.pdf

The Commonwealth (2016). *Global Youth Development Index and Report.* London: Commonwealth Secretariat.

Times, A. P. (2017, July 21). *81% of money meant for malnourished children remains unused in Maharashtra.* Retrieved February 01, 2018, from https://www.hindustantimes.com/mumbai-news/81-of-money-meant-for-malnourished-children-remains-unused-in-maharashtra/story-VvNf26aGjIwE18xkl9SY8L.html

UN India (n.d.).*Gender Equality and Youth Development.* Retrieved January 29, 2018, from http://in.one.un.org/gender-equality-and-youth-development/

UN-Habitat and IRIS Knowledge Foundation (2012) 'State of the Urban Youth, India 2012:

Employment, Livelihoods, Skills', India.

Vyas M (2018, January 08). India's jobless growth is not a myth. Retrieved fromhttps://www.livemint.com/Opinion oIfsn1Djr4KpR1mNNe1zDN/Indias-jobless-growth-is-not-a-myth.html

Wheebox (2017). *India Skills report.2017.* Retrieved from https://wheebox.com/static/wheebox_pdf/india-skills-report-2017.pdf

YUVA (2017). *Unequal realities: Identity, Housing and Basic services in Four Indian Cities.* Navi Mumbai: YUVA.

Creating Level Playing Field

Participatory Action Research for Gender Equality and Youth Development

Appadurai A (1996) 'Right to Research' Globalization, Societies and Education, Vol. 4 No. pp 167 – 177

Freire, Paulo. (1970) Pedagogy ofthe Oppressed, New York: Seabury Press Municipal Corporation of Greater Mumbai (2010) Human Development Report 2009. New Delhi: Oxford University Press

Patil - Deshmukh A., Gangavane S. & Pinto M., with Chavan S., (2017) Partner for Urban Knowledge Action and Research (PUKAR): Barefoot Researchers for Better Communities, India. in Knowledge and Engagement: Building Capacity of the Next Generation of Community Based Researchers, PRIA. pp 197 - 207

Tata Institute of Social Sciences (2015) Socio Economic Conditions and Vulnerabilities.

Creating Spaces for Lifelong Learning Skills

Intervention to Generate Sustainable Workforce of the Future

Field J (2000).*Lifelong Learning and the New Educational Order.* Stoke on Trent, Trentham Books.

Government of India, Ministry of Statistics and Programme Implementation (2017), Youth in India.

HeriberT H, Schmit, H (Editor) (2016). Agenda 2030 – Education and Lifelong Learning in the Sustainable Development Goals, International Perspectives in Adult Education.

ILO (2015): Global Employment Trends for Youth 2015, p.6.

Redecker C, Leis M, Leendertse M, Punie Y, Gijsbers G, Kirschner P, Stoyanov S &Hoogveld B (2011): The Future of Learning: Preparing for Change, Luxembourg: Publications Office of the European Union.

Redecker C, Punie Y (2013): The Future of Learning 2025: Developing a vision for change, 3-17.

Marjan Laal et al. / Procedia - Social and Behavioral Sciences 116 (2014) 4052 – 4056.

Ministry of Education, Government of India (1964-66), Report of the Indian Education Commission.

Parasuraman S, Ahmed K, Afroz S, Chitturu S (2010): An Evaluation Study of National Service Scheme in India, *IJSW*, 71(3), 417-431.

Tyson S (2006).*Essentials of Human Resource Management.* 5th ed. Oxford: Butterworth Heinemann.

Shah SY (2018): Lifelong Learning in India: A Policy Perspective, ASEM Education and Research Hub for Lifelong Learning, http://asemlllhub.org/policy-briefs/lifelong-learning-in-india-a-policy-perspective/

Shukla R (2010): Indian Youth, Demographics and Readership, Results from the National Youth Readership Survey.

State of the Urban Youth, India (2012): Employment, Livelihoods, Skills,' a report published by IRIS Knowledge Foundation in collaboration with UN-HABITAT.

Online Sources

www.un.org/millenniumgoals/pdf/Think Pieces/4_education.pdf

http://www.thehindu.com/opinion/op-ed/the-nuts-and-bolts-of-skill development/article7020970.ece

http://www.un.org/sustainabledevelopment/news/communications-material/

https://www.unicef.org/lifeskills/index_7308.html

https://www.skillsyouneed.com/learn/lifelong-learning.html

http://archive.indiaspend.com/viznomics/indias-demographic-dividend-64-4-youth-27-3-children-in-2015-2015.

(http://blogs.worldbank.org/developmenttalk/youth-bulge-a-demographic-dividend-or-a-demographic-bomb-in-developing-countries).

https://www.linkedin.com/pulse/soft-skills-increasingly-crucial-getting-your-dream-guy-berger-ph-d-/?published=thttp://goo.gl/QphyAv].

(http://uil.unesco.org/fileadmin/keydocuments/LifelongLearning/en/india-2009-abstract-lll-strategy.pdf).

https://www.ilo.org/skills/pubs/WCMS_743485/lang—en/index.htm accessed on 20th June, 2020.

Brief Profiles of Authors

Dr Veerendra Mishra is the Ex- Director, National Service Scheme (NSS) and Executive Director, Nehru Yuva Kendra Sangathan (NYKS), Ministry of Youth and Sports, Government of India. Currently he is serving as Director, National Institute of Social Defence, New Delhi. He has served the country in three United Nations Missions. He has earlier worked as CEO/Secretary in CARA and as Assistant Inspector General of Police, Police Headquarters, Bhopal, and Madhya Pradesh.

Mr Mathew Mattham is the Secretary of Centre for Youth Development and Activities Pune, Chairperson Youth Aid Foundation, Pune; Chairperson, Youth Aid Global Pvt Ltd, Pune; Chairperson, Youth Aid Nidhi Ltd Pune. He has 30 years of experience in non-profit sector and 10 years of experience in WASH sector and in Entrepreneurship programmes in India.

Dr Shamim Suryavanshi is an educationist with solid grounding in classroom teaching, education management and research. In her 22 years of professional experience, she has interacted with hundreds of teachers in mainstream as well as NGO sector across the country. Having lived, taught and studied in different countries further adds to her understanding of societies and education.

Dr Vibhuti Patel is a Professor, Advanced Centre for Women's Studies, School of Development Studies, Tata Institute of Social Sciences, Mumbai. She retired as Professor and Head of Economics Department of SNDT Women's University, Mumbai. Her areas of specialisation have been Gender Economics, Women's Studies, Human Rights, Social Movements and Gender Budgeting.

Dr Trupti Panchal is an Assistant Professor & Chairperson, Centre for Women Centered Social Work, School of Social Work, Tata Institute of Social Sciences. She is also Project Director of two Field Action Projects viz. Resource Centre for Interventions on Violence Against Women (RCI-VAW) & Special Cells for Women & Children (Maharashtra) units located in police systems which give socio-legal services and a multi-agency coordinated response to the issue of violence against women.

Nolina S Minj is a researcher and writer, with a focus on gender and Adivasi issues.She has an Erasmus Mundus master's in Comparative Literature and Cultural Studies. She was working as a research officer in the Resource Centre on Interventions on Violence against women at TISS at the time of writing of this chapter during 2018-19.

Dr Rama Shyam is the Programme Director, Empowerment, Health & Sexuality of Adolescents (EHSAS) at SNEHA, Mumbai.

Dr Anuja Jayaraman is Director, Research at SNEHA, Mumbai.

Vinita Ajgaonkar is working in a leadership capacity at SNEHA, Mumbai.

Neeta Karandikar *is* Associate Programme Director, Empowerment, Health and Sexuality of Adolescents (EHSAS) at SNEHA, Mumbai.

Alicia Tauro is a Project Coordinator at Youth for Unity and Voluntary Action (YUVA), India that empowers marginalised people and communities to access their rights. Prior to this, she did her Masters in Social Work in the Centre for Equity and Justice for Children and Families from the Tata Institute of Social Sciences (TISS).

Sachin Nachnekar is a Youth Development Coordinator at Youth for Unity and Voluntary Action (YUVA). Having over 15 years of experience of working with young people as a mentor, counsellor and guide, he has successfully built many youth networks and collectives across the city of Mumbai.

Dr Anita Patil Deshmukh is the executive Director of PUKAR, Mumbai. A trained Neonatologist by profession, Anita received her Master's in Public Health from Harvard University and worked as a faculty Neonatologist at a teaching institution in Chicago for 20 years. She relocated to India in 2005 to contribute to the developmental sector.

Mr Sunil Gangawane is a trained facilitator and has used PRA for gender quality and youth development. During his decade-long career at PUKAR, he has facilitated participatory research studies, focusing largely on issues related to gender, sexuality and expression of identities. He has masters in psychology from University of Mumbai and diploma in development education from Mynooth University, Ireland and South Africa.

Payal Tiwari has worked as Research Associate in PUKAR, Mumbai.

Dr Saigita Chitturu is working as Assistant Professor at Tata Institute of Social Sciences. She has over 20 years of experience in Teaching, Training, Research, Curriculum Development and Liasoning work. She has been bestowed with the 'Bharat Vikas Award' by Institute of Reliance, Bhuvaneshwar for her contribution to the field of Youth Leadership. She is **Faculty, Centre for Lifelong Learning, TISS.**

Acknowledgement

The editor of this book would like to thank the following people without whom the writing and publication journey would not have been possible:

Firstly I express gratitude to my Institution, the Tata Institute of Social Sciences and to the Centre for Lifelong Learning. This workspace has constantly motivated and inspired me to work on this project.

Secondly to Prof Nasreen Rustomfram, Chairperson of the Centre for Lifelong Learning, for trusting me, for having supported me in all my endeavours and for writing a foreword in this book.

Thirdly I am indebted to my family – my Father, Mother, Brother, Sister, Cavya and my loving daughter Ishinavya, and my husband who have been the backbone of every task that I undertook in my career.

I am grateful to my friends' circle – Personal as well as Professional – for having been there whenever I needed them.

Further, I owe my special thanks to the authors for their contribution to this book without which, this book would have been a dream only.

My heartfelt thanks to every youth, every youth organisation and to the field of Social Development which has nurtured me throughout to grow.

Lastly to the Publisher, Vitasta, Renu Kaul Verma, for accepting this piece of writing and putting it up in the public domain.

India Volunteering Conclave 2019 organised by UNV/UNDP, Ministry of Youth Affairs & Tata Institute of Social Sciences on 8th -9th August, 2019, New Delhi.

Training of Trainers on 'Certificate in Youth Leadership and Social Change' for teachers and Volunteers of CSIBER Institute, Kolhapur held on 20th & 21st July, 2019.

Training of Trainers of District Youth Coordinators & Youth Organisers, MoYAS organisd and conducted by Centre for Lifelong Learning Tata Institute of Social Sciences, Mumbai on 28th & 29th August, 2019.

Facilitation Skills Training Programme organised by CLL, TISS & OAM on 7th March, 2020 at TISS.

Panel Discussion on National Youth Policy, 2019 organised and facilitated by CLL, TISS on 18th January, 2020 at TISS.

A session on 'Leadership Skills' for Mid Career Training Programme for Madhya Pradesh Police Officers organised by Centre for Law & Society, TISS from 28th October to 2nd November, 2019.